Trust, Realization, and the Self in Sōtō Zen Practice

Contemporary Issues in Buddhist Studies

Series Editor, Richard K. Payne

Trust, Realization, and the Self in Sōtō Zen Practice

Daijaku Kinst

Institute of Buddhist Studies
and BDK America, Inc.
2015

First Printing, 2015
ISBN: 978-1-886439-59-7
Library of Congress Catalog Card Number: 2015940110

Published by
BDK America, Inc.
1675 School Street
Moraga, California 94556

Printed in the United States of America

Contents

Foreword

Richard K. Payne

A well-known assertion regarding training in Sōtō Zen is Dōgen's claim that to "To study the Buddha Way is to study the self. To study the self is to forget the self. To forget the self is to be authenticated by the myriad things." While many students of the buddhadharma today desire to "forget the self," it seems as if they often attempt to leap over the step of studying the self. It sounds to me that what Dōgen is saying is that studying the self is a necessary step, not one that can be avoided.

The temptation to leap to forgetting the self is one of the difficulties for present-day practitioners. When being "spiritual" becomes a way to avoid the messy and uncomfortable and unpleasant aspects of our own being in the world, this is one manifestation of trying to leap over the step of studying the self. Dōgen's understanding of "the self" is, of course, quite different from the specifically psychological understanding that our own society focuses attention on today. Dōgen's understanding is informed by the full range of Buddhist thought on the emptiness and impermanence of the self. These conceptions of the self are all too often misunderstood to mean that the self does not exist, an interpretation either embraced as necessary to the eradication of the self, or rejected as obviously wrong, bad, and scary. Dōgen's understanding of these characteristics of the self grow out of the history of Buddhist thought as transmitted from India to China and Japan. To study the self in this sense includes bravely looking at how we, others, and the world interact in ways that harm us, harm others, and harm the world and, at the same time, studying the emptiness and impermanence of the self, which are the keys to liberation and change.

The desire for short-cuts, for quick fixes and immediate gratification is an often remarked-upon characteristic of late capitalist society. To the extent that we individually do want to experience the promised delights of awakening—the end of suffering at least, if not more positive promises of "true happiness"—then the temptation to try to eradicate the self immediately becomes a temptation. Indeed, much of the popular religious culture, informed as it is by Romantic notions of merging one's identity with something larger, something more meaningful than the daily drudgery of mundane life, tells us that the self is the problem. Slogans regarding living in the present moment—without judgments, without plans, without regrets—appeal to this understanding of the self with its habitual evaluations and calculations as the problem, and a problem that is solved by simply staying in the moment and thus "forgetting the self." Despite the appeal of this kind of sloganeering, despite the apparent ease and speed that is put on offer, Dōgen tells us that it is first necessary to study the self, to understand it, to watch what it does, to become its intimate, close friend—but not ally.

Practice in Sōtō Zen supports the self in such a fashion as to allow the practitioner to enter fully into the process of self-transformation. Supporting the self in this way is not antithetical to the teaching of emptiness and impermanence; rather it is necessary in order to enable the practitioner to have trust in the transformative process.

We are pleased to be able to publish Daijaku Kinst's *Trust, Realization, and the Self* as part of the Contemporary Issues in Buddhist Studies series. Thanks to the author for her perseverance in revising her work and her patience through all the steps of editing and production. Marianne Dresser performed the tasks of copyediting and layout with her usual expertise and good humor. Thanks also to Arlene Kato for the cover design, and to Naomi Linzer for indexing. As always, our deep appreciation to Brian Nagata, BDK America, and Bukkyō Dendō Kyōkai for their support. And a very deep *gasshō* to the members of the Buddhist Churches of America, and particularly to the Fraternal Benefit Association, for their generous support not only of this project but for all the work of the Institute of Buddhist Studies.

Acknowledgments

Daijaku Kinst

My gratitude goes to the many people who have made this possible.

First, my thanks to the Institute of Buddhist Studies—to the colleagues with whom it is my privilege to work, to the students who inspire and teach me, and to the wider IBS community, past and present, whose generosity has created a remarkable place of learning. Particular thanks to Richard Payne, Dean of the Institute of Buddhist Studies, for his insightful comments and patient persistence. Thanks also to Marianne Dresser for her skillful editing.

I would also like to extend my gratitude to BDK America and the Numata Foundation for their generous support of Buddhist scholarship. Our access to Buddhist texts and teachings, and our understanding of them, would be far more limited without their sustained support.

This work began as a doctoral dissertation at the California Institute of Integral Studies, completed in 2003 under the guidance of professors Carole Whitfield and Brendan Collins, and Zen priest Zoketsu Norman Fischer. Their dedication to creative and disciplined scholarship continues to guide my work.

My deepest thanks to Rev. Shinshu Roberts for her unflagging support and encouragement.

Finally to the Buddhas and ancestors, to Eihei Dōgen Zenji, to my teacher Sōjun Weitsman Rōshi, and to all who endeavor to realize the Buddha's Way in its many forms, I bow in deep gratitude.

Trust, Realization, and the Self in Sōtō Zen Practice

Chapter 1

Introduction

This study is based in an exploration of the simple question "What works?" What works to support the practitioner of Sōtō Zen Buddhism? How can she be encouraged and challenged in her efforts to fully engage in and embody the teachings? What understandings can we bring to the nature of this encounter that will be helpful? These questions have been constant companions as I have encountered the practice of Sōtō Zen in the depths of my own experience and in my work with others. They are questions that draw us into real conversations about actual people and the difficulties they face. They ask us to find what works and put it to use.

Sōtō Zen practice is rooted in Buddhist teachings that challenge the very foundation of our usual, lived, experience: the self. It asks the practitioner to enter each moment wholeheartedly, let go of the self as it has been habitually experienced, and allow a different subjective experience to emerge. This is not an abstract, disembodied process but one that is lived out in detail day by day and reverberates throughout every dimension of the practitioner's experience. From the perspective of Sōtō Zen, releasing the hold on the self is a necessary and radical event that is liberating. It is also a process that leads the practitioner to the edge of the known and beyond. The practice requires a willingness to allow everything on which one has relied and most intimately known—that is, the self and one's notions about the nature of reality—to shift and change.

If we look closely at this process, we find that the ability to allow it to unfold is intimately linked with the practitioner's capacity to trust, and requires an encounter with the many aspects of trust. It is built on the fundamental human experience that it is possible to open oneself to experience and not be threatened by it. This requires deep trust, not only in the practice and the teachings but also in one's capacity to realize them. Ultimately, it requires an abiding trust in life itself. An exploration of the two intertwined experiences of trust and the self, their relationship, evolution, and transformation in the context of Sōtō Zen practice, forms the core of my inquiry. Returning to the questions posed above, we ask how we can understand the process by which the experience of self and the reality of trust are transformed in Sōtō Zen Buddhist practice so that we can better support this transformative process.

This is where the investigation of human experience that has taken place in what is generally termed Western psychology can be of service. Many possibilities present themselves in response to the question of "what works" in this context. One could turn to practices within other Buddhist traditions, which I will discuss briefly further on in this study. One could bring in somatic practices such as yoga that engage with the body as a means of shifting experience. I have chosen to focus on the study of self-experience found in modern psychoanalytic theory. This reflects not only my personal interests but also the belief that psychoanalytic theory has developed a description of the self and self-experience that can be successfully used within a Buddhist context to explore the experience of individual practitioners. It is important to note that the self in this context is regarded as a form, an aspect of reality that, like all other forms, is to be treated with care and respect. While this attitude of care and respect does not extend to a belief in the permanence or supremacy of the self, nonetheless there is respectful attention to its lived reality.

Specifically, then, psychoanalytic theory can provide an articulatation of the development and experience of the self and the development and experience of trust that can serve us as we take up the question of what works. These, then, are the two interrelated threads I set out to follow, develop, and extend as I explore the question of how we can understand the human experience of Sōtō Zen practice so that it might be more fully lived and realized.

Though I focus on the Sōtō Zen tradition, I do not mean to imply that bridges cannot or should not be built to other Buddhist traditions or to non-Buddhist faiths. The very specificity of this inquiry is intended as an invitation to fruitful dialogue. By offering this exploration of the lived experience of Sōtō Zen and bringing in the language and concepts of psychoanalytic theorists in such a way that the experience of individual practitioners can be more deeply understood, I aim to present one aspect of a much wider field of study.

Context for Study

Contemplative psychology addresses the personal psychological dimension of contemplative development within a tradition and is oriented toward deepening our understanding of how to support that development. Han de Wit describes contemplative psychology as the study of "what happens psychologically to people in their thoughts, words, and deeds when they walk the contemplative path."[1] Situating this inquiry in the larger field of contemplative psychology provides both context and perspective. The term "psychology" here is not synonymous with Western psychology but rather implies the broader meaning, as given in *Webster's Dictionary,* of the study of mental life and its relationship to behavior. (In order to explicitly include the affective realm in this description, I am expanding this understanding to include not only mental but emotional life, and not only outward behavior but also mental behavior, i.e., what we do with our thoughts and emotions.)

A contemplative psychological study is carried out taking the tradition itself, not a Western psychological interpretation of it, as its base. This is important to note, since it places any introduction of Western psychological theory squarely in the service of the tradition, avoiding reductionist errors while allowing a significant contribution to be made to an understanding of contemplative life and development. Western psychological theory, in this context, is one of many means that can be used to explore the ways in which contemplative development can be supported. It is a tool that specifically addresses certain aspects of the human experience and provides a well thought out language in which to discuss them. From this perspective, one can assiduously mine Western psychological theory for insights into aspects of psychological experience that can support or hinder contemplative development, while leaving intact the mystery of a life dedicated to realizing the Buddha Way.

Contemplative psychology allows for a sustained focus on praxis as opposed to theory. Its goal, as de Wit points out, is "to make the [contemplative] way concretely viable." He goes on to emphasize the practical orientation of contemplative psychology by noting that the primary concern of contemplatives of any given tradition, because of their responsibility for others committed to a path of practice, is the efficacy of methods. This concern determines the use of theories and language in a contemplative tradition. In keeping with this, I will maintain a focus not on theory or philosophical debates but on the lived practical experience. In regard to this orientation, de Wit writes:

> In this sense contemplative psychologies are somewhat disappointing disciplines, perhaps. They do not tell us much about God, the Divine, or enlightenment. . . . But they do tell us a lot about ourselves, about the contemplative function of our attitude towards life, our longings, our hope and fear . . .

> [and provide us with] a profound exploration into the practitioner's development of spiritual insight and loving care.[2]

This perspective provides the context for an emphasis on praxis and attention to the experience, rather than on the philosophical aspect, of a tradition. Adopting this viewpoint allows us to include the language and concepts of psychoanalytic theory within a Sōtō Zen context without confusion.

Within the overall context of contemplative psychology, this study takes place at the intersection of three distinct but overlapping areas: Buddhist studies, psychoanalytic theory, and feminist critique, and the nature of this intersection reflects the aim of this work. In keeping with the contemplative psychological perspective, this is not an effort to combine or integrate Buddhism and psychoanalytic psychology. I intend a conversation between perspectives, not a dialectic aimed at synthesis.

The process is akin to the questioning of psychoanalytic theory by Sōtō Zen in order to understand a particular dimension of the experience of practice. It can be seen as analogous to going to an experienced yoga teacher for help with developing a stable physical posture in zazen. It is a respectful process that acknowledges the wisdom, insight, and expertise of the other, but it is aimed at including what the other has to offer in a preexisting context. The tradition remains the base. Though it may be influenced by and adapt to new information, its fundamental orientation or purpose, in this case the realization of the teachings of Sōtō Zen, does not change.

For many years, Buddhism has been cheerfully raided, sometimes respectfully and with clarity and at other times with apparent abandon, by those who have a limited understanding of its complexities. I therefore want to be very clear about my intent in this work: I am importing into a Buddhist context concepts and ideas from psychoanalytic theory that I believe will be helpful in articulating aspects of the experience of Sōtō Zen practice. It is important to state my intention in order to clarify the orientation of this study, distinguish it from efforts that have been made to synthesize Buddhism and psychology, and avoid possible confusion about its aim.

While I include a discussion of central principles of Sōtō Zen, my approach to the first area, Buddhist studies, is marked by an emphasis on the practice as carried out in the lives of present-day practitioners, and by my choice to limit my discussion to Sōtō Zen. I have chosen to limit this study in this way for several reasons: it reflects my experience, it supports in-depth discussion, and it reduces the confusion that has sometimes occurred about the nature of Buddhist practice(s) due to overgeneralization and a lack of specificity in the use of terms. Because my own life of practice has occurred within the Sōtō Zen Buddhist tradition, and because my aim is to shed light on the experience of that practice, my discussion is centered in this tradition. In my experience, the embodiment of a tradition is the work of a lifetime. It is also my experience that enriching dialogues and the fruitful inclusion of other perspectives comes when this view of practice is acknowledged, even celebrated.

For this project to succeed, it is essential to establish a sound understanding of Sōtō Zen thought and practice, and accomplishing this necessitates presenting the core teachings that underlie the practice, as well as various dimensions of the practice itself. Although these descriptions cannot contain the reality of the practice or the tradition, nor convey the subtlety of experience that comes with a direct encounter, they can provide the basis for deep and meaningful discussion.

Buddhism is an enormously rich and multifaceted tradition.[3] Included under the mantle of the term is a vast and complex philosophical and religious field with myriad practices. There are central elements shared by all forms of Buddhism, but there are also real differences in philosophy and praxis. Glossing over those differences, particularly in the realm of practice, and subsuming all of Buddhism under one general label serves only to deny this complexity and erase its richness. In the same way, identifying Buddhism as a whole with one particular tradition or practice misrepresents both Buddhism and the particular tradition, and can mislead and confuse the reader. To avoid this pitfall and bring clarity and depth to the teachings introduced, it is important to state where, exactly, one is situated in the field and develop a good understanding of the fundamentals of practice and the teachings behind them.

As stated above, although this study focuses exclusively on the practice of Sōtō Zen this does not preclude its potential relevance for those who follow another tradition, no specific tradition, or no tradition at all. On the contrary, in my experience one of the beautiful aspects of grounding oneself in one's own experience and practice, as one respectfully encounters another, is that it becomes apparent that difference does not mean irrelevance. The richness available to us when we genuinely open to all the possibilities of human experience can be truly inspiring. Recognizing difference without creating divisions that refute another's truth may open up possibilities that would otherwise remain invisible.

In this spirit, it is my hope that the very particularity of this work indicates a welcoming and respectful attitude toward other ways. This study is meant not just for those who have taken up the practice of Sōtō Zen, though this tradition is the focus of my attention, but for anyone who wishes to investigate the ways in which we humans enter deeply into our lives.

Psychoanalytic theory, specifically the writings of contemporary self psychology and intersubjective theorists on the self and selfobject relationships, Eric Erickson's discussion of basic trust, and D. W. Winnicott's understanding of transitional space, offer a vital and in-depth exploration of human experience, which can fruitfully be included in a discussion of the human experience of Sōtō Zen practice. The use of psychoanalytic understandings of self-experience may also be of particular relevance to Western Buddhist practitioners, as these understandings emerged from and reflect the cultural assumptions on which the Western psyche is formed. By incorporating the work of those who have carefully studied self-experience from this perspective, we can gain access to insights that can help in understanding the process by which we encounter and express the practice of Sōtō Zen, particularly subjectivity and the experience of trust.

It is also important to note the areas of study within Western psychology I have not included in this inquiry. The applicability of Buddhist insights to the practice of psychotherapy and psychological theory, though interesting and relevant to many practitioners, is not the focus of this work. Theories that propose explanations of Buddhist practice in terms of Western psychology offer a fundamentally different perspective than the one I follow here.

The field of transpersonal psychology, which aims to develop an overarching theory of psychospiritual development, also has a fundamentally different perspective and goal than my own in this work. It is my belief that one can only understand a tradition and a practice from the inside. Interreligious dialogue is a vital and invigorating endeavor that benefits the participants. However, such dialogues are based on mutual respect and recognition, not the erasure of difference. I may be enriched and find inspiration in reading Christian texts, but I read them from a Buddhist perspective. I therefore cannot presume to know what such texts may mean to a Christian, and I may miss some very important insights if I limit the dialogue by assuming some sort of fundamental sameness between my Buddhist beliefs and those of Christianity. In this way, I adopt a position that prizes diversity and does not aim for unity.

My experience of reading transpersonal literature is that, in general, the level of understanding of Buddhism and the Buddhist path in these materials is limited. I can only presume that practitioners of other traditions would find this equally true of their own paths. For these reasons, and because this work does not make these kinds of connections to other traditions, the transpersonal perspective is not applicable. As stated above, the nature of the intersection of these fields of study is not one of synthesis.

Feminist theory or critique informs and shapes not only the content but also the approach to this inquiry. Gender (as well as other characteristics) can influence the way the practice is perceived, experienced, and expressed. A discussion of this aspect of the practice experience, in any depth, would entail a study all its own. My aim here is simply to not ignore the relevance of gender, and throughout the work I will return to this perspective.

Chapter Outline

The content and arrangement of the chapters reflect the aim of this study. A brief outline of each chapter and the main points it covers follows. From a foundation in Sōtō Zen and a description of the psychoanalytic terms used, the discussion turns to the relationship of trust and the self, as they are experienced and impact the practice of Sōtō Zen; an examination of the environment in which this occurs; and finally, the nature of maturity.

The focus of Chapter Two is the development of a sound, useful, and nuanced understanding of the philosophical and practice aspects of Sōtō Zen Buddhism, including an appreciation for the mystery and silence at its core. My intention is to create a context for subsequent chapters that includes not only a substantive intellectual understanding of the teachings but also a sense of the paradox and ambiguity that pervades Sōtō Zen practice. In the first section I present the central teachings of emptiness, dependent co-arising, and no-self as well as the bodhisattva ideal. I also introduce the interpretations brought to these core teachings by Eihei Dōgen, the founder of Sōtō Zen. In addition, I discuss such characteristic Sōtō teachings as the identity of practice and realization and of buddha-nature and all beings. I then describe the central aspects of the practice that make up the day-to-day experience of the Sōtō Zen practitioner: zazen, work practice, and relational life. Included is a discussion of the self, the body, and gender as understood in Sōtō Zen.

Finally, I discuss the importance of faith in Dōgen's teaching. My aim is the creation of a context within which we can build an understanding of the shift in subjective experience and the evolution of trust that together lie at the heart of the practice.

In Chapter Three I introduce selected psychoanalytic concepts and relate them to the overall discussion of Sōtō Zen practice. The first section describes how we can legitimately include the work of Erik Erikson, D. W. Winnicott, and self-psychology and intersubjective theories within a Buddhist context. I then take up how specific concepts, such as the relational nature of the self, self-structure, and selfobjects in self psychology and intersubjective theory, Winnicott's discussion of transitional space, and Erikson's formulation of basic trust, contribute to our understanding of self-experience in way that can be fruitfully applied to aspects of the Sōtō Zen practitioner's experience.

Chapter Four is, in a sense, the heart of this inquiry. I follow the two interrelated aspects of self-experience and trust using the language and context developed in the previous chapters. The first section of this chapter deals with elements that contribute to the ability to simply attend to one's experience. Specifically, drawing from the language of psychoanalysis, I discuss the role of basic trust and self-cohesion as well as the effect that fragility and the absence of basic trust can have on the capacity for openhearted awareness.

The second section explores a realm that is closer to the core of the practice and which approaches the limits of descriptive language. In this section I discuss the practitioner's encounter with the teachings of emptiness, the difficulties and confusion to which this encounter may give rise, and how the teachings can be understood. The chapter concludes with an exploration of the nature of trust and its transformation (from trust in the self and reliable selfobject relationships to trust in life itself). I introduce the notion of absolute trust and discuss its relationship to faith, and relate this to the transformation of subjective experience (from a sense of self as a separate entity to a subjective experience of itself as dependent co-arising).

In Chapter Five I explore dimensions of the practice environment as they relate to the evolution of self-experience and trust, and the maturation of the practice. The importance of relationships that function to support the maturation of the known self, as well those that function to transform subjective experience, are discussed. Key relationships that occur within the sangha (one's fellow practitioners) and with a teacher are an area of particular focus. I conclude with an exploration of maturity as it is understood in Sōtō Zen, and how it relates to the topics of trust and the self previously discussed. Maturity in this sense does not posit a simple or grandiose vision but is grounded in human complexity and is respectful of our continued effort to follow the bodhisattva way. Finally, Chapter Six presents a summary and conclusion.

Methodology: A Buddhist Inquiry

As Anne Klein writes, "Buddhist theorizing is in principle aimed at practical benefits for real people."[4] According to Buddhist teachings, all things arise from causes and conditions. That is, all phenomena are interdependent and embody the context from which they emerge. This work is no different—it too is a result of causes and conditions. Yet we often do not see all that goes into a written work, particularly the author's biases and assumptions. In discussing methodology, I aim not only to delineate the methods on which I have relied, but also to illuminate some of the factors that inform and shape, as well as inspire, this work.

My life as a Sōtō Zen practitioner, priest, and teacher is the foundation for this work. Sōtō Zen is a tradition that rests on and in the process of deep inquiry, questions that can only be asked and responded to with one's whole body, heart, and mind. This tradition not only encourages inquiry but requires it as a living, breathing, embodied practice. If there is one methodological thread that runs through this work, it is this attitude of questioning and deep inquiry. This study is not an objective investigation, if such a thing were even possible; it is grounded in and reflective of my embeddedness in the tradition and practice of Sōtō Zen. It also reflects the study of psychology and psychoanalytic theory, as well as training and practice in both of these areas, which grew out of my life of practice. There is no separate point from which this field of inquiry is examined. I am in its midst and have set about making provisional understandings based on my own unique perspective and priorities.

A part of the methodological basis for these provisional understandings is an acknowledgement of the conditions that contribute to their creation. Many people have noted that Zen Buddhism, as practiced in Europe and North America, continues to be predominantly white and middle class. I believe this to be true. My own white, middle-class background, and that of most of the people with whom I have practiced, contributes to a cultural limitation in my writing. So often members of minority groups and women are marginalized, their wisdom lost or recorded only in fragments, their concerns left unaddressed. Those of us committed to some form of contemplative, religious, or spiritual path must take responsibility for changing this. Each of us, both within our own traditions and across traditions, needs to reclaim this wisdom, address these unmet needs, and find ways to encourage one another to speak. We must learn to recognize the power and beauty of each person's unique gifts and cultivate in ourselves and in others the ability to learn, teach, and lead with confidence and humility. Again, as with a feminist perspective, this orientation is not in the forefront of this work but nonetheless structures the nature of the entire project. By asking what works and how to understand the nature of trust and the self, I am asking, I hope, questions that will support each person's practice.

From this background, we can turn to three ways of understanding the methodology of this work: Buddhist hermeneutics, contemplative methodology, and feminist methodology. Although distinct, these fields inform one another. Each has contributed to the overall shape of this work and to my investigation of the questions at its root.

Buddhist Hermeneutics

In his book *Buddhist Hermeneutics* Donald Lopez broadly defines hermeneutics as "concerned with establishing principles for the retrieval of meaning especially from a text."[5] A fundamental teaching in all forms of Buddhism is that one should not take the Buddha's words on his authority alone but must investigate them in one's own experience. In this way, a dialogue develops between one's own experience and the Buddha's teachings. Lopez also writes that in Mahāyāna Buddhism at least, the ability to apprehend the teachings can only be accomplished with the enlightened mind/heart. It is the enlightened capacity—that is, Buddha—that understands the Buddha's teaching, and it is assumed that this is a realizable goal.

The effort of Buddhist scriptural study can be thought of as the effort of Buddha meeting Buddha in the context of the sūtras.[6] Lopez describes this as a "symbiotic process along a Moebius strip," in which the scholar and the sūtra mutually inform each other, and each meaning is an expression of the Buddha's skillful means. Lopez reminds us that in this process "the interpreter becomes the arbiter of meaning, the interpreter becomes the author as the author sits in silence."[7] In this way meaning, which is fluid and provisional, and silence become a unitary whole.

Leaving aside for the moment how the image presented below can limit our understanding of the life of a practitioner—that is, that the Buddha is, in fact, very much alive in the form of the teacher, the sangha, and all things—we can nonetheless appreciate Lopez's descriptions of the process:

> The Buddhist exegete suffers from a displacement, an absence; he did not sit in the circle at the feet of the Buddha and hear the doctrine that was intended especially for him. Now, the Buddha is gone, the audience is gone; now the teachings must be the teacher. The exegete is constantly in search of his place in the absent circle, and hermeneutics provides the compass.[8]

The Buddhist exegete, then, is searching for a way to settle within the awakening that lies in her own heart.

In regard to this thesis we can ask, what does this have to do with a study that is clearly focused on practice? Two replies are possible. First, this work uses Buddhist texts to build a basis for an understanding of the practice. Second, the sūtras that form the foundation of the Buddha's teaching are regarded, in the Mahāyāna, as not different from the very body of the Buddha, and in Sōtō Zen as not different—not separate—from our lives. In the *Perfection of Wisdom Sūtra in Eight Thousand Lines* (Skt. *Aṣṭasāhasrikā Prajñāpāramitā-sūtra*), the Buddha tells his disciple Ānanda:

> Therefore, Ānanda, do I entrust to and transmit to you this perfection of wisdom so that it might not disappear. . . . You should attend to this perfection of wisdom. . . . For as the dharma-body of the past, future, and present Tathāgatas [i.e., buddhas] is this dharma-text authoritative.[9]

Eihei Dōgen, the founder of Sōtō Zen Buddhism, commenting on a portion of the *Lotus Sūtra* in his fascicle *Nyorai zenshin* ("The Whole Body of the Tathāgata"), writes:

> The volumes of the Sutra are the bones of the Tathāgata. Because this is so, bones may be this Sutra. Even if we know that volumes of the Sutra are the bones, if we do not know that bones are volumes of the Sutra, that is not yet the Buddha's truth. . . . The human world, the heavens above, the ocean, space, this land, and other realms are all real forms, are volumes of the Sutra, and are bones. Receiving, retaining, reading, reciting, interpreting, and copying bones we should disclose realization. . . .[10]

We can understand, then, the study of our Buddhist practice, of our lives, as a study of the sūtras, an interpretation of our experience as an interpretation of the sūtras, and this study as an example of Buddhist hermeneutics.

Feminist Methodology

Shulamit Reinharz writes that the way to most accurately and inclusively describe feminist methodology and research is to describe what feminists are doing.[11] Without delving into the debates that have occurred in feminist circles regarding the question of what a feminist is, my position is simply that sex and gender matter. In many instances women's experience can be different from men's, those who have a complex sex/gender identity can also have significantly different experiences, and these differences can be and often are dismissed, ignored, or unarticulated. Simply taking this into account is to adopt a feminist stance. Even when, as with this study, the experience of women or a discussion of the effect of gender is not at the forefront of the work, one's position on such matters is still inextricably linked to the questions that are asked and the perspective from which the inquiry arises. A clear statement of my own relationship to the study, as well as an openness to the question of whether and how gender affects the experience of Sōtō Zen practice, situate this work within feminist research.

The effort to exhibit sensitivity to difference and the experience of those who have been defined out of the dominant culture also marks feminist inquiry, and extends it beyond the characteristic of gender. By this I mean that feminist research does not turn away from the experience of anyone who does not fit into dominant cultural assumptions. This can include the impact of a wide range of factors, including ethnicity, race, class, physical ability, mental or emotional difficulties, or cultural factors. Again, this perspective is not at the forefront of this work, but I am holding myself responsible and asking others to hold me responsible for continuing to bring awareness to these areas by stating that this work is feminist research.

Feminist research is also marked by an inclusion of the writer's personal experience and assumptions, a stance I have explicitly stated from the outset. Finally, a key aspect of feminist research is, as Reinharz writes, "finding one's voice."[12] To write with honesty is to find and use one's voice. Thus, this study is an exercise in feminist research because of my approach to the material and because of the writing itself.

Contemplative Psychology and Methodology

Han de Wit outlines a contemplative methodological perspective that is relevant to this work. He defines methodology in general as referring to "a set of actions that are conducive to the acquisition of valid and trustworthy empirical knowledge." He goes on to point out that while contemplative traditions have always contained such methodologies, their intent is not merely, or even primarily, the acquisition of knowledge but the clarification of confusion and the dispersion of ignorance, with the ultimate aim of "the transformation of the entire individual." As he writes, "Contemplative traditions are not primarily interested in . . . having knowledge but in being wise."[13]

De Wit identifies two ways in which confusion and ignorance are reduced in contemplative life. First, in the realm of the intellect, a conceptual framework is established for the practitioner, using what he calls "conceptual strategies." These are then tested out by the practitioner in her own experience by using the second methodology, "awareness strategies."[14] These include methods of prayer, meditation, or other practices. In this context, the methodology of this thesis can be described as the development of a conceptual strategy with which to reduce confusion about the experience of Sōtō Zen practitioners in order to better meet their needs.

Perhaps the best overall way to understand the methodology of this work is that described by Tibetan Buddhist scholar Anne Klein at the beginning of this section: Buddhist theorizing. This implies the construction of language and concepts aimed at deepening our understanding of the practice of Sōtō Zen with the aim of supporting individual practitioners. Another term for describing this methodological perspective is skillful means (Skt. *upāya*). Skillful means is the activity of carefully meeting each situation in the most beneficial way. In this case, skillful means could be understood as paying careful attention to the means by which I build this thesis so that it has validity and relevance and contributes to a better understanding of the factors that support the practice of Sōtō Zen. Each of the elements I have described above, as well as the overall context, support this goal, but its root is honest and open inquiry aimed at reducing suffering, which is an expression of Sōtō Zen practice itself.

In this spirit, I present this work as an offering—an offering to those who have committed themselves in some way to the mystery of uncovering our true human life and its compassionate expression, what I understand as following Buddha's Way. The basic premise of this work is one of exploration, not explanation of what is "true." It is an effort to articulate an aspect of the experience of Sōtō Zen practice in the hope of contributing to the support of those who take up the Way.

A study is, inescapably, made up of words. This may be an obvious point, but before we delve into the fundamental mystery of Sōtō Zen practice, it is important to simply note the fact that the entire edifice of scholarly inquiry is built of language. As Zen teacher Dainin Katagiri asserts, "You have to say something."[15] One must respond to the world. To simply remain silent is an insufficient or less than full expression of the Way. Silence may be a more accurate representation of the nature of reality, and certainly it can be a more accurate representation of the practice of Sōtō Zen, but it is not enough. From this perspective and from a desire to contribute what I can to the flourishing of this ancient way, I venture into the world of words and concepts. I do so in the hope that I do not add to confusion but instead encourage a deeper investigation of the nature of our human life.

Chapter 2

Fundamental Teachings of Sōtō Zen and Sōtō Zen Practice

To develop an understanding of Sōtō Zen practice it is necessary to gain familiarity with the teachings that underlie and inform it. It is also important to know something of the multiple dimensions and spirit of the practice itself. An introduction of the philosophical underpinnings of Sōtō Zen helps build the necessary conceptual basis for exploration of the practice. From this foundation, it is possible to effectively discuss the forms the practice takes in the lives of practitioners.

An image often used in Buddhist teachings to portray the interdependent nature of reality is that of a jeweled net, each jewel reflecting, and reflected by, all the others. When we enter the world of Sōtō Zen teachings and practice, we are entering just such a multifaceted interconnected web of jewels. In our studies we move from one jewel to the next, and it gradually becomes clear to us that we are on an endless journey of ever-deepening richness. Anyone taking up this study must be willing to tolerate complexity and the experience of ambiguity and paradox. For the Sōtō Zen practitioner the willingess to abide with complexity, ambiguity, and paradox is essential, as is an understanding that what is most important is not achieving complete or perfect understanding but deeply engaging with the practice based on the teachings. Only through embodying the teachings in this sort of engaged practice can the true fruit of study be realized.

Two central elements create the context of Sōtō Zen practice: the teachings inevitably encountered by practitioners, and the forms of practice that express them. The central teachings of Sōtō Zen pervade a practitioner's life—whether or not he or she is explicitly aware of it. Building a solid foundational understanding of these teachings allows us to form a clearer understanding of the lived experience of the practice. Because all the teachings relate, reflect, and depend on one another, some patience is required in this effort. The teachings begin to take shape, but of course they then shift and blend into one another (and hopefully our lives); this is the nature of a living teaching.

The first, and perhaps most fundamental, teaching we will consider is the Madhyamaka ("Middle Way") teaching of emptiness (Skt. *śūnyatā*) and its relationship to dependent co-arising (*pratītyasamutpāda*), impermanence (*anitya*), no-self (*anātman*), and the middle path. Also essential is an understanding of buddha-nature, as taught by Eihei Dōgen, the founder of Sōtō Zen, its antecedents, its relationship to the teachings of emptiness, and its expression in the term "thusness." Dōgen's teachings on the nature and interrelationship of time, practice, and realization are also key to the practice of Sōtō Zen.

A consideration of influential Yogācāra teachings on the nature of consciousness highlights a process through which the transformation of the self is understood to occur. Finally, no understanding of Sōtō Zen practice would be complete without a discussion of the centrality of the bodhisattva ideal, the bodhisattva path, and the bodhisattva vow, as well as the very important relationship of wisdom and compassion.

An understanding of the essential dimensions of daily Sōtō Zen practice illuminates its basic intention and spirit. Zazen, work practice, rituals, study, relational life (for example, practicing with fellow practitioners and teachers, and participating in the life of the wider community), as well as how the bodhisattva precepts are understood and practiced, are all central to the life of a Zen practitioner. Equally important is an understanding of the nature of the self in Sōtō Zen teachings and practice, and the key element of faith.

It is important to note that Zen is sometimes mistakenly thought to be somehow divorced from its Buddhist roots. Dōgen fiercely refuted this point in his fascicle *Bukkyō* ("Buddhist Sūtras").[1] Such a notion does not accurately portray the Zen lineage. Zen is firmly embedded within the Buddhist tradition, and in order to develop an understanding of Zen it must be situated within the context of the overall development of Buddhism. To address this I will include a (necessarily limited) historical background as I present the basic teachings that should be understood in order to appreciate Sōtō Zen practice.

As has been noted, Buddhism is an enormously diverse religion, one that has developed in a variety of cultures over two millennia. As Paul Williams writes, it is a religion that has

> no . . . popes, no creeds, and although there were councils in the early years, no attempts to impose uniformity of doctrine over the entire monastic, let

> alone lay, establishment. Buddhism spread widely across Central, South, South-East, and East Asia . . . [and] interacted with indigenous civilization, modifying its doctrine and behavior in the process.[2]

Williams also notes that Buddhism, particularly the later development of Mahāyāna Buddhism of which Zen is a part, incorporates a counter to any tendency toward a fixed, immutable creed:

> Buddhist philosophy from its inception embodied a sustained criticism of [any] essentialist fallacy. As far back as we can trace the teaching of the Buddha we find a penetrating analysis by which unities are dissolved into their constituent parts and true diversity is revealed. . . . [This] was always an integral part of Buddhist philosophy and spiritual practice.[3]

The presence of multiple traditions, teachings, or visions of the Buddhist Way imparts a richness and complexity to the study of the buddhadharma that some might find daunting. For example, early Buddhism, commonly referred to as the Theravāda tradition, posits a soteriological vision of the path that seems at odds with later Mahāyāna teachings. Indeed, it is not difficult to find in the history of Buddhism, as in most major religions, heated debates between adherents of different schools, sometimes over the most arcane minutiae of various philosophical positions. In this study I bring in only those aspects of the diversity of Buddhist teaching that are relevant to the goals of this inquiry. I leave it to the reader to further explore the enormously rich resource of Buddhist teachings.

Core Teachings

The teaching of emptiness (*śūnyatā*) is fundamental to Sōtō Zen. It is essential to gain a proper understanding of this teaching in order to understand the Sōtō Zen way. Eminent practitioners and scholars have written volumes about this concept and any aspect of it could easily be the subject of an entire treatise. In keeping with the aim of this work, my discussion seeks to illuminate how these teachings affect the everyday practice of the Sōtō Zen practitioner.

The translation of the Sanskrit term *śūnyatā* as emptiness is, perhaps, one of the most misleading pieces of translation ever done in the effort to bring Buddhism to the West. *Śūnyatā* has a very specific meaning with profound implications for the way we view and experience the world. Unfortunately, the English word "emptiness" has many connotations, particularly for a native speaker, that directly oppose the meaning of *śūnyatā* and have resulted in considerable confusion.

A brief overview of the roots of the term will help put it in context. One of the Buddha's first teachings was dependent co-arising (*pratītya-samutpāda*). Fundamental to all forms of Buddhism, this core concept is found in the earliest Buddhists texts, such as the *Nidāna Saṃyutta* or the *Mahānidāna Sutta*,[4] and is central to the later teachings of the Mahāyāna. The *Saṃyutta Nikāya* states:

> When this exists, that comes to be; with the arising of this, that arises.
> When this does not exist, that does not come to be; with the cessation of this, that ceases.[5]

All phenomena arise and pass away in concert with all other phenomena. They are dependent for their existence upon each other. This interdependence has implications for the very nature of the phenomena themselves, implications that the Buddha included even in his earliest teachings. All things are mutually influenced, and everything is in a state of perpetual change and is impermanent (*anitya*). It is easy to see change in our world: we are born, we grow old, and we die; all of the things, people, and animals we see around us change and pass away. The teaching of impermanence tells us that change is the constant.

It is also not difficult to notice that all things affect one another, and that they are in fact so deeply influenced by one another that they cannot be said to be truly separate. This is the teaching of no-self (*anātman*). There is no fixed, eternal essence that can be found in an entity. I will take up the implications of this teaching in detail later; at this point it is essential to understand that the teaching of no-self does not imply the nonexistence of phenomena, only that they exist in constantly changing patterns with no fixed, inherent identity or selfhood. The early teachings give many examples to demonstrate this, for example, a chariot. We say we know what a chariot is, but as we dismantle it we can ask about each of its parts: Is the wheel the chariot? The axle? The spokes of the wheel? At what point does the thing we call a chariot come into being or cease to be a chariot?

The structure of a stone arch also demonstrates the interdependent nature of phenomena. The arch is made up of stones, each of which is crucial to its formation. If any one piece is removed, the arch collapses. Yet we cannot say of any particular stone that it is the arch. Rather, the arch is formed by mutually dependent factors. This illustrates another aspect of the early teachings: phenomena are made up of elements of existence. To continue with the example of the arch, the phenomenon "arch" does not exist without the component stones, yet neither can the stones be called the "arch." If we remove the stones, there is no arch. So too is it with dharmas, the discrete elements of existence. Various opinions were held in early Buddhism about the number, kind, and makeup of these elements.[6] The key factor in this context, however, is that all things are co-constituted.

The teaching of impermanence and no-self posit, then, that change is constant and that mutually effecting movement is the nature of reality. Because of this, phenomena cannot be said to be stable, nor can they be said to have an essence that remains unaffected by this movement. The term "empty" (*śūnya*) is thus used to describe the fluid nature of phenomena—that is, they are empty of a fixed, solid nature.

The Buddha taught that this empty nature is also true of the self. In the *Anattalakkhaṇa Sutta*, the Buddha states that because of the pervasiveness of impermanence and the fact that the self cannot be said to be separate or unaffected by it, thinking "This is mine, this I am, this is my self"[7] is neither appropriate or useful. The Buddha went on to say that thinking in this way only increases the experience of suffering or unsatisfactoriness (Skt. *duḥkha;* Pāli *dukkha*).

The self, it was taught, is made up of five *skandha*s ("aggregates"): form/matter (*rūpa*), sensations (*vedanā*), perceptions (*samjñā*), mental formations (*samskāra*), and consciousness (*vijñāna*). In the same way that the chariot or the stone arch is made up of constituent elements, none of which can be identified separately as the thing itself, so the self is made up of constantly changing, fluid aspects (the *skandha*s). Our false belief that what is impermanent is permanent, and that we exist as a separate independent entity, leads us to attempt to create and to cling to necessarily temporary experiences of stability and satisfaction. This causes suffering.

It is interesting to note that the Buddha continually focused on what would encourage people to follow the path and bring suffering to an end. Often likened to a physician, the Buddha returns again and again to a practical orientation when interacting with followers.[8] Indeed, he refused to answer certain questions, or remained silent when asked purely speculative questions. He advised those who posed such questions as "Was I in the past? Was I not in the past? What was I in the past? . . . Shall I be in the future . . . Am I? Am I not? What am I? How am I? Where has this being come from? Where will it go?" to neither focus on the past or future nor be overly skeptical about the present. Instead, he said, it would be wiser to try to understand things as they have come to be.[9]

This is an important point and it sets the tone for all later philosophical developments within Buddhism. The practitioner and the teacher are encouraged to focus on the cessation of suffering, not on merely building a conceptual framework for a particular apprehension of the truth. Such frameworks were, and are, helpful only so long as they support and encourage the practice of the Way. In addition, the practitioner is enjoined to investigate the teaching for him- or herself and base his or her faith in the teachings on actual experience. The experience of reality itself is the ultimate teacher.

Various Buddhist philosophical schools developed over time, interacting and critiquing one another. The early Buddhist schools (often referred to as the Theravāda, "Way of the Elders," though only one of the schools present at the time) developed highly sophisticated schemas and maps of consciousness and the nature of human experience. Part of the contemporary philosophical debate was whether or not there were any irreducible elements present in consciousness.

Early in the first millennium, a movement that later came to be known as the Mahāyāna ("Great Vehicle") developed. Among other things, it critiqued earlier teachings and placed emphasis on extending the teaching of no-self to all phenomena, beginning the teaching of "emptiness" (*śūnyatā*) as we know it.[10] The Perfection of Wisdom (Prajñāpāramitā) literature formed the basis of the Mahāyāna and the foundation for the great Buddhist philosopher Nāgārjuna's treatise, the *Mūlamadhyamakakārikā.*[11] Briefly, we can say that Nāgārjuna logically refutes any position that would lead one to conceive of phenomena as having constituent elements (a position taken, for example, by the Sarvāstivāda school), and presents a radical formulation of no-self that explicitly negates any possible way of conceiving of a substantive independent entity.[12] This teaching, *śūnyatā,* was rendered into English as "emptiness."

Regarding the teachings of no-self and *śūnyatā,* I take the position put forth by Sue Hamilton in her book *Early Buddhism: A New Approach,*[13] that the difference between early Buddhist teachings on the nature of the self and the later Mahāyāna understanding may be more apparent than real. She maintains that the shift in the teaching regarding the nature of self and phenomena that emerged with the Mahāyāna represented a shift of emphasis rather than an entirely new interpretation of the Buddha's original teachings.

Returning to the example of the stone arch, the Mahāyāna teaching of emptiness emphasizes the fact that, according to these teachings, not only is the arch a conceptual construct, dependent on the configuration of its constituent elements, the stones; but so too are the stones. All phenomena are without "own-being" (*svabhāva*).

The word "emptiness," then, when used as a translation for the term *śūnyatā,* represents a shortened version of the phrase "empty of inherent existence or own-being." This means there is no entity or phenomenon, including the self (or the factors that can be said to constitute a self) that has an independent, permanent, solid essence or existence. For example, when we see a cloud we usually do not think of it in terms of all the factors that go into its formation. We see the phenomena and call it a cloud. We understand that clouds function in certain ways. But a cloud is not separate from the earth, or water, or wind. It is made possible by many factors and it is not separate from those factors. "Cloud" is a construct, a division of reality.

In addition, the construct "cloud" cannot be separated from the eyes that see it or the mind that names it. For "cloud" to exist, all these things, including the perceiving mind, must be present and work together. This is another important point: according to the teachings of emptiness, reality does not exist in some absolute way separate from the perceiver. There is no essence of cloud that appears and is perceived by an equally separate and solid entity called a person. All of the causes and conditions must be present to make up the moment of cloud/person. Saying this, however, does not in any way negate the cloud or ourselves—we see the cloud, we recognize it, and it rains.

Jay Garfield writes:

> When a [Madhyamaka] philosopher says of a table that it is empty, that assertion by itself is incomplete. It invites the question, Empty of what? And the answer is, Empty of inherent existence, or in more Western terms, essence. Now, to say that the table is empty is hence to say that it lacks essence and importantly not to say that it is completely nonexistent. To say that it lacks essence . . . is to say . . . that its existence as the object that it is—as a table—depends not on it, nor on any purely nonrelational characteristics, but depends on us as well. That is, if our culture had not evolved this manner of furniture, what appears to us as a unitary object might instead be correctly described as five objects: four quite useful sticks absurdly surmounted by a pointless slab of stick-wood waiting to be carved. Or we would have no reason to indicate this temporary arrangement of this matter as an object at all, as opposed to a brief intersection of the histories of some trees. It is also said that the table depends for its existence on its parts, on its causes, on its material, and so forth. Apart from these there is no table.[14]

So how do we regard our experience of the cloud and the fact of getting wet in the rain, or our idea of a table and bumping into the table? When we speak of something existing or not existing, what do we mean?

When we say a cloud or table exists, are we implying that it has an essential nature that is fixed and permanent? This is exactly what Nāgārjuna refutes and, if we believe the Madhyamaka version of Buddha's teaching, this misapprehension is the basis of delusion and suffering. If we do not mean that there is an independent thing in itself, how then can we understand the term "exist"? Another essential Mahāyāna concept, the doctrine of the two truths, conventional truth (*saṃvṛti-satya*) and ultimate or absolute truth (*paramārtha-satya*), becomes helpful here. Garfield writes:

> There is a conventional world of dependently arisen objects with properties. . . . And in that world there is a conventional truth: Snow is white. Grass is green. Individual humans are distinct from one another and from material possessions. But there is also an ultimate truth about this world: It is empty (of inherent existence). None of these persons or objects exists from its own side (independent of convention). From the ultimate point of view there are no individual objects or relations between them.[15]

While the introduction of the two truths is important, like many philosophical concepts it can raise more problems than it solves. It is possible to reify emptiness, to make it into a thing with its own, perhaps exalted, inherent existence, and to denigrate the conventional. Nāgārjuna solves the potential problem of reifying emptiness with the teaching that "emptiness is itself empty"[16]—that is, since there is no inherently existing entity that can be found, there can be no eternal state called "emptiness." This is the completion, in a sense, of the emptiness teachings and counters any tendency toward nihilism that may arise, since the opposite of the reification of emptiness, a position of materialism, is the nihilistic stance that nothing, in fact, exists. The "middle path" is said to exist between these two pitfalls of essentialism and nihilism, and it is consonant with the identity of emptiness and dependent origination.

Nāgārjuna writes:

> Whatever is dependently co-arisen
> That is explained to be emptiness
> That, being a dependent designation,
> Is itself the middle way.
>
> Something that is not dependently arisen,
> Such a thing does not exist.
> Therefore a nonempty thing
> Does not exist.

Garfield comments:

> The extreme of reification of the phenomenal world depends upon viewing emptiness nihilistically; the extreme of reification of emptiness requires us to be nihilistic about the phenomenal world. A middle path must reify neither and hence must regard emptiness, as well as all empty phenomena as empty. Both extremes presuppose that to exist is to exist inherently. They only disagree about whether this inherent existence is properly ascribed to conventional phenomena or to their ultimate nature. Nāgārjuna will deny exactly that supposition, arguing that to exist is to exist conventionally and that both conventional phenomena and their ultimate nature exist in exactly that way. . . . Nāgārjuna is asserting that the dependently arisen is emptiness. Emptiness and the phenomenal world are not two distinct things. They are rather, two characteristics of the same thing. To say of something that it is dependently co-arisen is to say that is empty. To say of something that it is empty is another way of saying that it arises dependently.[17]

Thus, phenomena are both real and empty of a fixed, essential nature. The world we inhabit is fluid and constantly changing, and this change is not the shifting of substantive units of reality or permanent building blocks of life. The Madhyamaka teachings refute the idea of *svabhāva,* "own-being." There is nothing that is not a relational entity dependent on other phenomena for its very existence. Recognizing this does not lead to a nihilist view but to a recognition of the vibrancy of dependent origination. That this also includes the self presents us with a special challenge and an opportunity for liberation. As Anne Klein writes, "The importance of emptiness to the Buddhist tradition is not just that emptiness is considered true, but that understanding it changes the subject in desirable ways."[18]

This brings us back to the question of how one lives with and realizes this truth. And that is the role of practice and the heart of the Sōtō Zen Way.

Eihei Dōgen

At this point it is helpful to introduce the founder of Sōtō Zen, Eihei Dōgen, one of the foremost religious leaders of medieval Japan.[19] Dōgen was born into an aristocratic family in 1200, and it is generally thought that he lost his father at the age of two and that his mother died five years later. He is said to have deeply experienced impermanence as he watched the incense smoke at his mother's funeral. We are also told that before she died, his mother expressed the wish that he become a Buddhist monastic. He was raised and educated to become a member of the ruling elite, but he turned away from this life and became a monk at age twelve. He trained as a Tendai Buddhist monk at Mt. Hiei but left the mountain following the need to answer for himself the question, "If we are already enlightened, why engage in spiritual practice?"[20] After studying with other non-Tendai Japanese teachers, Dōgen ultimately traveled to China where he met and practiced with the teacher Rujing, and resolved, as he says in the fascicle *Bendōwa* ("On the Endeavor of the Way") in the *Shōbōgenzō,* "the great matter of my entire life."[21]

In his many writings, Dōgen expressed a profound religious and philosophical vision that grew out of, and evolved from, the resolution of this fundamental question, his experience of the relationship between practice and realization and the nature of reality itself. Engaging with Dōgen's writings can be difficult but also very rewarding, as the depth and subtlety of his teachings become clear. Hee-Jin Kim has done a masterful job of explicating Dōgen's creative and poetic use of language, as well as the way Dōgen shifts our understanding of Buddhist teachings, through an examination of subtle alternative meanings of words and phrases. For example, regarding the teachings of emptiness, Kim points out that Dōgen expressed a "radical reinterpretation—alternately referred to as intentional misinterpretation—based on various aspects of this principle [i.e., emptiness]."[22]

Dōgen's writings are rich, deep, complex, and challenging. We will focus on some key elements and representative sections from his work necessary for understanding Sōtō Zen practice. In fact, this constitutes a type of a practice itself—reading, reflecting on, and studying the works of Dōgen (or other Buddhist texts) are part of the life of a Sōtō Zen practitioner.

Buddha-nature

The term "buddha-nature" is commonly used in Sōtō Zen teaching, and commonly misunderstood. Western ears often hear echoes of "soul" or essence, or a substantive center of spiritual faculties. Buddha-nature is none of these. Instead, it is a way of speaking that attempts to bring us closer to a subtle truth that is not easily grasped, expressed, or embodied. Dōgen's teachings on buddha-nature tell us that we are each fully capable of realizing the Buddha Way—indeed, we already *are* the Buddha Way.

To understand buddha-nature as taught in Sōtō Zen, it is helpful to return to one of Dōgen's most famous statements in his teachings on buddha-nature. In *Busshō*[23] Dōgen reinterprets the meaning of a Chinese character and shifts a statement about buddha-nature in the *Mahāparinirvāṇa-sūtra* from the usual understanding that all beings have buddha-nature—that is, they possess the capacity to realize the Buddha Way—to all beings *are* buddha-nature.

Clearly, we must develop a further understanding of buddha-nature in order to enter into a dialogue with this statement. However, even without a deeper understanding we can appreciate the shift in meaning. To have something implies duality, a division of the object from its possessor: we have a job, or a house, or an experience. There is a separation between the object and ourselves, and we describe our relationship to the object as one of possession, of having. But if we say that we *are* something, that duality evaporates and our understanding of both aspects—ourselves and the object—is transformed.

We encounter this shift in perspective directly when we ask, what is buddha-nature? This is a legitimate question but one that pushes us into dualistic categories of is/is not, and toward the tendency to envision buddha-nature as an "it," a describable object. As we will see below, this is a mistaken notion that undercuts the very basis of Sōtō Zen Buddhist practice, the teaching of emptiness and no-self. Therefore, in order to understand the concept of buddha-nature, we must venture into a relationship with it that requires statements and definitions, while at the same time building an understanding that prevents, as much as possible, objectification. Approaching this topic from many, sometimes contradictory perspectives, as does Dōgen, allows us to build a rich relationship to it and at the same time hold loosely any particular conceptualization.

The concept of buddha-nature is associated with the Tathāgatagarbha teachings that posit the existence of the buddha potential (*tathāgata* is an epithet for a buddha) and the "womb" (*garbha*) or capacity through which it comes to realization. Despite the contemporary tendency to set Yogācāra and Madhyamaka in opposition to one another, as this teaching developed it was not conceived of as opposing Madhyamaka emptiness teachings but rather of completing them. This is a key point, for the language of buddha-nature is a positive language, which can be easily interpreted to mean that there is an existent essential nature.

Discussing the *Buddha Nature Treatise* (a text sometimes attributed to the great Buddhist philosopher Vasubandhu, of which only a Chinese translation exists), Sallie B. King writes that the author of the treatise "begins with the straightforward statement that Buddha nature really, truly exists."[24] She goes on to point out that such language does not imply a fixed, essential entity that resides in a person. Instead, such statements reflect a different, more positive (kataphatic) use of language. As with the teachings of emptiness, these statements are essentially soteriological in nature and aim to break down our usual catagories of existence and nonexistence, not reinforce them. Quoting from the *Buddha Nature Treatise:*

> Emptiness is not merely a matter of negation; supreme truth does not merely negate worldly truth. The contents of emptiness or supreme truth cannot be so limited as to be exhausted by functioning in a destructive manner; there also must be a positive revelation in emptiness. Therefore (implicitly) because emptiness is not exclusively negative, it need not conflict with a Buddha nature that, though not an own-nature, is affirmed as existing aboriginally.

King comments:

> When the two extremes of existence and non existence (or being and non being) are negated . . . the laws of language based on those principles likewise are no longer to be assumed. At such a point, we are wide open to the new use of language. Nāgārjuna stepped into this language void and filled it with *śūnya* language. The *Buddha Nature Treatise*'s author stepped into the same void and filled it with a very different kind of language and could speak positively of such things as Buddha Nature. . . .[25]

King discusses this use of language and its implication for our understanding of buddha-nature, its relationship to the teaching of emptiness and the term "thusness" (Skt. *tathatā;* sometimes translated as "suchness") in an examination of the *Treatise*'s statement, "Buddha Nature is the Thusness revealed by the dual emptiness of persons and things." She writes:

> The word for Thusness, in Chinese *ru,* means "like as." "[*Ru*], 'like as much as,' comparing qualities and actions rather than things, is related to [*ran*], 'thus' (like this, as much as this). . . ." Although it does have an ontological quality, Thusness refers to how something is, rather than what it is; it speaks of an adjectival quality of things rather then a nominative thingness as such. All it means is that things are "as they are. . . ." As the *Awakening of Faith in the Mahāyāna* says, the word Thusness is not a term that has the qualities or attributes of being "this" or "that"; it is a word by which words are undone, a word that points at our language and indicates what it will not do. Yet the term Thusness does not have the negative connotations of *śūnya,* a term that functions in a similar way to "undo" language. Hence, to equate the Buddha nature with Thusness is to indicate that there is something positive about it—one says it is "real," it "exists"—but the use of the term Thusness

> serves to remind us that the direction in which our minds begin to move upon hearing the terms *real* and *exists* will not be a totally appropriate one.[26]

Buddha-nature, then, both makes a clear statement that something is, and at the same time requires us to keep as provisional, as incomplete, any view of what that something is. In keeping with its essentially soteriological nature, it reminds us that it is meant solely to encourage the direct engagement with reality on which Zen practice is based. This understanding must form the background to any discussion of buddha-nature in Dōgen's writing (and how it functions in Sōtō Zen practice) in order to avoid confusion and a distorted essentialist position.

Dōgen, commenting on his shift from the teaching that all sentient beings possess buddha-nature to the idea that all of existence (i.e., all sentient beings) is buddha–nature, writes:

> What is the point of the World-honored One's words that "All living beings totally exist as the Buddha-nature?". . . Those called "living beings," or called "the sentient," or called "all forms of life," or called "all creatures," are living beings and are all forms of Existence. In short, "Total Existence" is the Buddha-nature, and the perfect totality of Total Existence is called "living beings." At just this moment, the inside and outside of living beings are the Total Existence of the Buddha-nature. . . . Remember, the Existence [described] now . . . is beyond the "existence" of existence and non-existence.[27]

As Kim points out, by making this shift in meaning Dōgen accomplishes (at least) two points. First, he removes any tendency toward the reification of buddha-nature. Second, he shifts our understanding of "all beings" from individual entities to all existence. Kim also writes that Dōgen denied an "anthropomorphic or biocentric" understanding of buddha-nature, and instead "declares the absolute inclusiveness of Buddha-nature within which sentient as well as insentient beings are equally subsumed."[28]

Dōgen states in *Busshō:*

> Note the following: Existence completely embraced now by Buddha-nature is not that being which is in opposition to nonbeing. All existence is the words of the Buddhas, their tongues, the eyeballs of the Buddhas and ancestors, and the monastics' nostrils. It goes without saying that the word "all existence" . . . cannot be labeled by such words as subject or object, noumenon or phenomenon . . . in the entire universe there is not even a single object alien to Buddha-nature, nor is there any second existence other than this universe here and now.[29]

In addition, Dōgen asserts that this "all existence" is not different from emptiness:

> You must surely know emptiness is a perfect grass. This emptiness is bound to bloom, like hundreds of grasses blooming. . . . Seeing a dazzling variation of the flowers of emptiness, we surmise an infinity of the fruits of emptiness (*kuka*). We observe the bloom and the fall of the flowers of emptiness and learn the spring and the fall of them.[30]

When we read this we recognize a shift in the definition of buddha-nature from a potential to be cultivated ("all beings have buddha-nature") to a reality to be expressed, embodied ("all beings are buddha-nature"). Dōgen puts it another way:

> We do not say "all beings are Buddha-nature" (*issai-shujo soku bussho*) [for even the word "are" smacks of dualistic thinking] but instead "all-beings-Buddha-nature-of existence" (*issai-shujo-u-bussho*). This should be considered carefully.[31]

Dōgen's emphasis on the immediacy of all that is, in the teachings on buddha-nature, also points us back to thusness and to the teaching of emptiness. Dōgen clearly points to the emptiness of buddha-nature, that it has no separate inherent existence. He reminds us, in *Busshō,* that "Impermanence is in itself Buddha-nature" and that "Because the Buddha-nature is empty it is said to be no-thing."[32] Kim uses a story, referred to by Dōgen, to illustrate his teachings on emptiness:

> One day [Shigong Huizang] asked [Xitang Zhizang,] "Can you grasp emptiness?" [Xitang] replied "Yes I think I can." [Shigong] continued "How would you grasp emptiness?" Using his hand, [Xitang] then grasped at empty space. [Shigong] replied "You don't understand how to hold emptiness." "How would you grasp it then?" asked [Xitang. Shigong] seized [Xitang's] nose and pulled it. [Xitang] exclaimed "Ouch! Ouch! You are going to pull off my nose!" [Shigong] said "You can grasp emptiness only in this way."

Kim points out:

> Commenting on this koan . . . Dōgen observed that that which grasps and that which is grasped are, after all, one and the same emptiness—emptiness grasps emptiness.[33]

Returning to the statement in the *Buddha Nature Treatise,* "Buddha nature is the Thusness revealed by the dual emptiness of persons and things,"[34] we could say that this exchange was buddha-nature grasping buddha-nature.

But this does not convey the same spirit of the statement, would not challenge our minds in the same way. It could easily be misunderstood to mean that there was (or is) some core inner nature that grasps another core inner nature. We could also say that this was thusness grasping thusness, or perhaps more accurately that the thusness of the moment was made abundantly clear in the "ouch" emitted by Xitang. This comes closer to the spirit of the story—in that moment of "ouch" something is revealed, experienced, realized in a direct way.

Examining this story using these three formulations of the teachings (emptiness, thusness, buddha-nature), we get a feel for their interconnectedness and the way they call attention to or express different aspects of our human experience. We can also see that emptiness and buddha-nature are not simply abstract principles to be reflected upon but actualities as concrete and pointed as the pain of a pinched nose. These three interrelated ways of expressing the nature of things also point us back to an understanding of ourselves that undercuts limited notions and helps us let go of them.

Returning to thusness, Dōgen says, "I too am thusness and you are thusness also."[35] Thusness is our true nature and it is empty of any fixed essence.

Shohaku Okumura illustrates this in his discussion of Dōgen's reinterpretation of the term *nyo* in the fascicle *Tsuki:*

> The common meaning of the word *nyo* (如) is "to be like," "such as," "as if," or "to be equal to." In Chinese, the final sentence from [the *Konkōmyōkyō* (*Sūtra of the Golden Radiance*)], "The true Body of the Buddha . . . responding to things . . . manifests forms. It is like the moon and water." 如水中月 can be read as "It is like the moon in the water." This is an accurate translation, but Dogen reads the *nyo* (如) in this sentence as the *nyo* of *shinnyo* (真如). *Shinnyo* is a Chinese translation of the Sanskrit word *tathata* which is translated into English as "thusness," "suchness," "as-it-is-ness," or simply "true reality."
>
> "The thusness of the 'like the moon in water' is the moon-water. . . . 'Thus' does not mean 'to be like.' Thusness is thisness."[36]

As Kim writes:

> [B]oth mind and its essence are invariably the expression, or more precisely the self-expression (*jidoshu*) of Buddha-nature. In short, there is no expression that is not Buddha-nature.[37]

Buddha-nature, thusness, emptiness, then, is not a potential that can be located and engendered, something outside our ordinary world, or something we carry inside of us. Buddha-nature is no different from all existence, and all existence is impermanent and empty of inherent existence. Buddha-nature, thusness, emptiness—this is a living, present reality to be realized, and it is no different from the effort to realize it because this realization does not entail transforming into something else.[38]

Following from this, it becomes clear that there is one more important aspect of this topic to take up, if briefly, in order to build an adequate foundation for understanding the relationship between Sōtō Zen practice and buddha-nature. This is the topic of time as presented in Dōgen's teaching. This may seem abstract at first and perhaps too obscure for consideration but, in fact, it is key to understanding the teachings that underlie Sōtō Zen practice.

Dōgen's teachings on time are subtle and sometimes difficult to penetrate. What is essential for us to understand is that Dōgen challenges our usual experience of linear time and the sense that we are a creature separate from time that observes its passing. Dōgen teaches that we are, in fact, in no way separate from time, and that time itself is not what we may think it is. Time is not a passing parade of events and stories; it is not linear. While Dogen does not negate the ordinary experience of the passage of time, he points to another experience of time, one that is based on the identity of being and time.

Kim quotes Dōgen's fascicle *Uji* ("Being-Time") or, as Kim translates it, "Existence-Time":

> You should examine the fact that all things and events of this entire universe are temporal particularities (*jiji*). . . . All existence and all worlds are contained in a temporal particularity. Just meditate for a moment: Is any existence or any world excluded from this present moment?[39]

There is no difference between this moment and all of the phenomena existent at this moment. Dōgen uses the term *nikon,* "the immediate present of being time."[40] Time is not independent of being, nor is being independent of time; there is only time-being. The experience of this moment includes all existence. That is the interconnected reality of our lives. Our world is not filled with separate discrete entities changing "over time," but is instead the dynamic reality of the present. Past and future collapse into the present, from this perspective. As Peter Harvey notes, the Perfection of Wisdom literature states that thusness, the as-it-isness of phenomena (which, as we have seen, is not different from buddha-nature), "belongs to nowhere, is neither past, present nor future, and the same thusness is found in all dharmas (phenomena)."[41] As we will see when we take up the topic of practice realization, with this understanding it becomes impossible to sustain the idea of a self transforming into something else, for example, a deluded human becoming an enlightened entity.

Again, it is important to remember that Dōgen is not denying our usual experience of time. Rather, he is pointing to a full experience of being and time that requires us to loosen our grip on who and what we perceive ourselves to be. The notion of linear time cannot be separated from the sense of a separate observer. If a rock is in the middle of a river, we can say that the river flows by—but the sense of the river's movement, its flow, is described only in relation to something that is unmoving, the rock. But this is not the complete story. If we identify not with the rock but with the river—in other words, if we do not posit an immobile object outside of movement of the river—how then can we speak of flow?

The dynamic working of this moment is impermanent if viewed from the position of an observer; letting go of the position of observer and identifying with all existence, time as we usually know it is not relevant. This may be referred to as eternal, not in the sense of lasting forever in linear time, but as being outside of time in its usual sense. In this way, time and liberation are intimately linked.

Returning to the topic of buddha-nature, Dōgen quotes the sixth Zen ancestor Huineng: "Impermanence is Buddha-nature."[42] This impermanence, buddha-nature, thusness, is both the vital reality of this moment and the potential to realize it. Nothing can be separated out, nothing is not buddha-nature. Realizing this, being liberated from our usual notions of this and that, self and other, transforms our world not into something else but into what is. As Kim writes, "Buddha-nature was not to be enfolded in, but to unfold through, human activities and expressions."[43]

Practice Relization

The teaching of the identity of practice and realization (*shushō itto*) is central not only to Dōgen's teaching but also to the daily life of a Zen student. The fundamental spirit of zazen and all Sōtō Zen practice is contained within it. It is important, therefore, in coming to know Sōtō Zen practice, to have an understanding of what Dōgen means when he says in *Bendōwa:*

> In buddha dharma, practice and enlightenment are one and the same. Because it is the practice of enlightenment, a beginner's wholehearted practice

> of the Way is exactly the totality of original enlightenment. For this reason, in conveying the essential attitude for practice, it is taught not to wait for enlightenment outside practice. This must be so because [this practice] is the directly indicated original enlightenment. Since it is already the enlightenment of practice, enlightenment is endless; since it is the practice of enlightenment, practice is beginningless.[44]

Kim provides a slightly different translation of the same section that can help us to understand practice enlightenment:

> The view that practice and enlightenment are not one is heretical. In the Buddha-dharma they are one. Inasmuch as practice is based on enlightenment (*shojo no shu*), the practice of a beginner is entirely that of original enlightenment. Therefore, in giving the instruction for practice, a Zen teacher advises his/her disciples not to seek enlightenment beyond practice, for practice itself is original enlightenment. Because it is already enlightenment of practice there is no end to enlightenment; because it is already practice of enlightenment, there is no beginning to practice.[45]

In a sense this teaching is quite simple—this moment of practice is the complete manifestation of Buddha's Way—but its implications are subtle and profound. Many questions naturally arise: How could the zazen of a person who has just stepped into the meditation hall for the first time be the same as the realization of all the buddhas and ancestors? Are there no steps toward enlightenment? What is practice? What is enlightenment? These are some of the questions with which a student of Zen must wrestle in order to make the teachings a living reality.

To start with, perhaps it is useful to bring some clarity to the terms "enlightenment" and "practice." As with all the terms we are using, a nuanced understanding will evolve as we progress. But to prevent misunderstanding I suggest a basis: fundamentally, we can understand practice as the activity a person takes up that allows her to deepen her understanding, realization, and expression of Buddha's teaching, thereby reducing suffering for herself and others.

Enlightenment (Skt. *bodhi*), a basic Buddhist term, could serve as the subject of a lengthy discussion, particularly with regard to how it has been understood and presented by the various schools and traditions that have evolved over millennia.[46] It is a term both used and turned away from in Sōtō Zen. Fundamentally, "enlightenment" or *bodhi* means "to see things as they are" (i.e., dependently arisen); *bodhi* literally means to be awake and carries with it the notion that by awakening, delusion and its consequent suffering cease.

It is also a term that, perhaps more than any other, bears the projections and hopes of Buddhist practitioners. Each person comes to practice with his or her own version of what enlightenment means. Usually these notions, often unconsciously held, arise from the self's desire for comfort, safety, and ultimate ease. This is not the understanding of enlightenment present in Sōtō Zen—or in any other form of Buddhism, for that matter. The idea of attaining ultimate ease for the self contradicts the basic notion that clinging to the self is the root of suffering. So what is this state? What does the term "enlightenment" point toward?

The term enlightenment or *bodhi,* along with its correlates, for example nirvana (more often used in Theravādin Buddhism), are indicators, not definitions. Walpola Rahula, in his classic text on the Buddha's early teaching, writes:

> Now, what is Absolute Truth? According to Buddhism, the Absolute Truth is there is nothing absolute in the world, that everything is relative, conditioned and impermanent, and that there is no unchanging, everlasting, absolute substance like Self, Soul, or Atman within or without. This is the Absolute Truth. . . . The realization of this Truth, i.e. to see things as they are (*yathabhutam*) without illusion or ignorance (*avijja*), is the extinction of craving 'thirst' (*Tanhakkaya*), and the cessation (*Nirodha*) of *dukkha* [suffering, dissatisfaction], which is Nirvana. . . . It is incorrect to think that Nirvana is the result of the extinction of craving. Nirvana is not the result of anything. . . . Nirvana is neither cause nor effect. It is beyond cause and effect. Truth is not a result or an effect. It is not produced like a mystic, spiritual state.[47]

Nirvana, truth, is not the result of anything, nor is it produced. However, our experience of truth, our realization of nirvana, is seeing things "as they are," without illusion or ignorance. From an individual's perspective, enlightenment can be understood (for the time being) as the state in which the immediate moment is experienced in its fullness, clinging to the illusory self is released, and the suffering that arises from a false belief in self and other ceases. Enlightenment can also be understood as the fact that things are the way they are—that is, an interdependent dynamic whole.

Practice, then, is the way in which enlightenment is realized. Francis Cook describes early Buddhist presentations of practice and enlightenment as including an emphasis on the purification of defiling elements, for example, the "three poisons" of greed, hatred, and delusion (see, for example, the *Visuddhi-magga, The Path of Purification*) and the belief that this purification will take many lifetimes to be completed.[48] Thus, enlightenment was conceived of, in the ordinary practical terms of the practitioner, as something that occurred only at the end of a long and strenuous path.

With the emergence of the Mahāyāna, the belief in this lengthy path did not change. In Chinese Buddhism, however, we see a clear emphasis on the notion that "seeing things as they are" is possible in this very life. Cook contends that this may have been due to the more fluid nature of Chinese society and the fact that

> [The Chinese] had their own [Daoist] models of spiritual perfection antedating the appearance of Buddhism in China and these models established a different criteria for perfection [that] . . . affirm[ed] ordinary persons as capable of awakening to their essential nature.[49]

Returning to Dōgen's teaching about enlightenment and practice from the *Bendōwa,* we find the term "original enlightenment." A brief review of some of the historical background of this term and how it informed Dōgen's teaching helps illuminate his writings on the nature of the path and its relationship to realization and enlightenment. It also serves as an example of the organic, evolving nature of Buddhist philosophy and adds depth to our discussion of these basic tenets.

As previously noted, Dōgen's early years were spent as a Tendai monk at Mt. Hiei, where he was steeped in the Tendai teaching of original enlightenment (*hongaku*).[50] Jacqueline Stone writes:

> In this medieval Tendai context, "original enlightenment thought" denotes an array of doctrines and concepts associated with the proposition that all beings are enlightened inherently. Not only human beings, but ants and crickets, mountains and rivers, grasses and trees are innately Buddhas.[51]

Stone's work gives a detailed explication of the philosophical threads that came together to form the basis for the teachings of original enlightenment in China that were later carried to Japan. She writes that the text that most deeply influenced the development of the teaching of original enlightenment was the *Dacheng qixin lun* (*Awakening of Faith in the Mahāyāna*).[52] In this text, Tathāgatagarbha teachings of the inherent buddha-potential and Yogācāra teachings that detail different aspects and functions of the mind are brought together.

A slight detour into the Yogācāra system of Buddhist philosophy may be helpful at this juncture for our understanding of the underpinnings of Sōtō Zen practice. The Yogācāra school, which developed in the third century in India, is a sophisticated and complex philosophy about the nature of reality, the nature of human consciousness, and the nature of delusion. It presents a description of the functioning of human consciousness and posits a model of eight consciousnesses. The first six are the five sense consciousnesses (sight, sound, smell, taste, and touch) and the mind consciousness (*manovijñāna*), which is the basic capacity to differentiate "this" from "that." There is no real conception, as we usually think of it, in the process to this point; the objects of sensory input are simply distinguished one from the other.

Yogācāra posits that it is the seventh consciousness (*manas*) that organizes experience into categories. *Manas* is the meaning-maker and is the basis for both judgments and actions. It is also the site of a separate sense of "I." The eighth consciousness (*ālayavijñāna*), or "storehouse" consciousness, is called the basis and forms the foundation for the others. It is not volitional and does not exist in the realm of subject and object. The *ālayavijñāna* is said to contain the seeds (*bīja*s) that are the result of past actions. These seeds "ripen" with causes and conditions and form the world of phenomena that we experience. This, in turn, leads to further attitudes and actions, which result in more seeds being formed, and the process continues.

For our purposes in this discussion, it is important to understand the relationship between *manas* and *ālayavijñāna,* because, according to this system, this is where the potential for awakening or delusion occurs. According to the Yogācāra, *manas* perceives itself to be different from *ālayavijñāna* and acts according to this misperception. From this view, the basic mistake of *manas,* taking itself for an object, leads to a sense of separateness and a subsequent desire to protect and defend that perceived-as-separate entity.

This entire dynamic depends on the *ālayavijñāna* and is not separate from the seeds it contains. The function of practice, according to this model, is to bring awareness to each moment, each phenomena, and to respond with insight and compassion, thereby eliminating the unwholesome seeds that lead to delusion, and laying down wholesome seeds that will ripen into phenomena and perceptions that support a deepening wisdom. The *manas* is the key in this long transformative process, since it is the volitional site that can act to bring clarity and harmony to the entire process.[53]

What arose from the cross-fertilization of the Tathāgatagarbha and Yogācāra teachings was a description of consciousness that entailed, according to Stone,

> two inseparable aspects of one mind: the mind as suchness or the mind in terms of the absolute, and the mind as arising and perishing (that is, the

> [Yogācāra] *ālayavijñāna*). These two aspects correspond respectively to the ultimate truth (*paramārtha-satya*) and conventional truth (*saṃvṛti-satya*) in Madhyamaka thought. Because the mind as arising and perishing is grounded in the mind as suchness . . . it is said to possess the aspect of "original enlightenment."[54]

Therefore, Stone points out, there are two aspects of enlightenment according to this teaching: original enlightenment and "actualized" enlightenment. Original enlightenment, or suchness, is never absent, even in the midst of deluded thinking. Recognizing this is actualized enlightenment.

Later, in China, the Huayan and Tiantai systems and their dialogue were also formative in the development of the original enlightenment teaching. Both of these schools posit a dynamic world of mutually constituted and interpenetrating phenomena. Central to Huayan philosophy is the teaching of the one mind, which is both pure and unchanging and responsively dynamic (phenomena).[55] In the Huayan system, which had as a central text the *Awakening of Faith in the Mahāyāna,* we first find the metaphor of the ocean and the waves so often used in Sōtō Zen teachings. In this description of the nature of the reality, the ocean is identified as "true suchness,"[56] and the waves (phenomena) as the responsive condition of the water. Phenomena, the felt experience of our ordinary lives, are essentially identical with the one mind that is pure suchness. This understanding of delusion as fundamentally not different from enlightenment leads to an understanding and experience of practice that deeply influenced Sōtō Zen. As Stone writes:

> The teaching of origination from suchness in effect grounds the arising of phenomena in the one pure mind and this obliterates any ontological distinction between them. . . . Liberation lies in discerning that the differentiated phenomena of the samsaric world [the ordinary world of suffering] are, in their essence, no different from the one mind and thus originally pure.[57]

The Tiantai school, which takes the *Lotus Sūtra* as a central text, emphasizes the Madhyamaka perspective and, from the point of view of the emptiness teachings, provides a corrective for any essentialist tendencies attributed to the Huayan. According to the Tiantai, there cannot be said to be any basis from which phenomena arise. Stone quotes the great Tiantai teacher Zhiyi:

> One may say neither that the one mind is prior and all dharmas posterior nor that all dharmas are prior and the mind posterior. . . . All one can say is

> that the mind is all dharmas and all dharmas are the mind. Therefore the relationship is neither vertical nor horizontal, neither the same nor different.[58]

In fact, as with all the unfoldings of Buddhist thought and practice, both the Huayan and Tiantai schools borrowed from and influenced one another.

In this, we can see the ongoing tension between the teachings of emptiness—that all things are fluid and interdependent—and what can be thought of as a tendency of the human mind to lean toward the conception of an essence or basis. Always cautioning against the twin dangers of nihilism and essentialism, Buddhism has threaded its way between these two positions for millennia. To state that nothing exists (in a conventional sense) is incorrect and leads to nihilism. To state that something does exist as a solid separate entity is, according to Buddhist teachings, to fall into essentialism and travel further down the road of suffering.

All of this comes into play in Dōgen's teaching of practice realization. Dōgen consistently states, as in the quote above from *Bendōwa,* that enlightenment cannot be regarded as a discernable goal at the end of a long practice journey. It is, in fact, simply things as they are.

Cook writes that Dōgen, in his use of language, emphasizes this point:

> The term he uses very often and which he seems to prefer . . . is not *satori* [the Sino-Japanese translation for *bodhi,* awakening] . . . but rather *sho* and its verbal form, *sho suru,* "proof," "evidence," "a certificate" . . . "to prove, to guarantee." [F]undamental to just about everything we mean when we speak of "Dōgen's Zen" is his central teaching that everything, including ourselves, is already a Buddha right from the beginning, and consequently what we call "awakening" or "enlightenment" can only be a process of proving to ourselves this fact.[59]

Practice, then—the process of "authentication," to use Cook's translation—is not separate from that which is authenticated. It is in fact the activity of that which is authenticated, buddha-nature. Kim states that Dōgen rejected the term *kenshō* (seeing into one's own nature) because of an implied dualism. He goes on to say that for Dōgen, "the activity of seeing was itself one's own nature."[60]

Cook also points out that Dōgen's teachings clearly emphasize that realization is not transcendence or liberation *from* the conditions of the world but rather liberation *to* the conditions of the world.[61]

As Kim writes:

> The crucially important thing to note . . . is that in Dōgen, opposites or dualities are not obliterated or even blurred; they are not so much transcended

> as realized. The absolute freedom in question here is that freedom which realizes itself in duality not apart from it. . . . In Dōgen's view . . . the dualistic world remains real, not dissolved. Therefore the unity [of practice and realization] in question does not replace distinction but is unobstructed by it.[62]

He says further:

> Whether he speaks of humans or nature, Dōgen inevitably (and quite consistently) returns to the nondualistic metaphysics of Buddha-nature, radically conceived with the logic of realization, rather than the logic of transcendence. Humans and nature, myriad configurations and forms, share their destinies, while coming into existence and perishing, as flowers of emptiness, characterized in Dōgen's favorite expression as "the whole body of emptiness leaping out of itself" (*konshin-choshutsu*).[63]

Realization, then, of this "whole body leaping," is the key, and this is the realm of daily practice. I will discuss the details of Sōtō Zen practice more thoroughly below, but it is important to note that the word "practice" can take on many shapes and shades of meaning. Practice in a Sōtō Zen Buddhist context can mean the taking up of specific activities but, more fundamentally, it is the repeated shift from the perspective or perception of oneself as a discrete, separate entity to the perspective or orientation of taking this moment and the activity of all beings as center, which is no different from enlightenment. As Shohaku Okumura has said, "The subject of practice is not this person."[64] In fact, practice itself is letting go of a self-centered orientation.

This does not mean that one becomes passive or simply reflexively responsive to surrounding conditions—in fact, the aim of practice is freeing one's full responsiveness and aliveness. It is important to remember that the practitioner as a unique individual does not disappear. Each person is, in fact, a part of the ecology of reality. What is meant by this shift is the letting go of habitual self-centered notions and opening into the reality of the moment.

Discussing Dōgen's *Sansuigyō* (*Mountains and Rivers Sūtra*), Okumura says:

> It is Buddha studying Buddha's way through our practice. And it is Dharma (the way all beings are) studying Dharma through our study. When we sit it is not us sitting zazen but zazen sitting zazen. . . . Our practice is Buddha's life, it is the manifestation of Buddha.[65]

The practice spoken of by Dōgen in *Bendōwa,* quoted above, is the activity of shifting habitual identification with this illusory, limited separate self to identification with the reality of this moment, to all beings. If, as Dōgen states, all beings are buddha-nature, then making this shift is realizing buddha-nature. The practitioner's reference point becomes not the "small self" but the living reality of the moment—everything is included. It is not, then, that the practitioner moves toward realization each time they shift their center to this moment, but that this shift is the arising of awakening, is enlightenment. And each person is not other than this—when all is included, how can we be "other"?

Thus, practice is the practice of enlightenment, the activity of the way things are, and is based on the teaching that there is nothing other than this dynamic functioning of emptiness, thusness. There is no other reality, no buddha-nature separate from this. As Dōgen says in the fascicle *Genjō kōan* ("Actualizing the Fundamental Point"), "the appearing is absolute reality,"[66] and in *Tenzo kyōkun,* his instructions to the monastic cook, he quotes the elderly *tenzo* of Ayuwang as reminding him that "nothing is hidden."[67]

If we take seriously the identity of buddha-nature and the living reality of the moment, and Dōgen's teaching on the nature of time and being, we cannot set up a linear timeline that allows us to understand practice as proceeding from the (presumably deluded) past to the (hopefully enlightened) future.

This is the spirit of Sōtō Zen practice and the fundamental paradox at its heart. Enlightenment is not a goal to be reached after long practice, it is the foundation on which practice is built, and it is this very moment of practice and reality. It is also the foundation and source of the actions of the practitioner, and the life of the bodhisattva.

Bodhisattva Path

The next aspect of Buddhist teaching that is important to consider in building a foundation for an understanding of Sōtō Zen practice is the concept of the bodhisattva. The bodhisattva ideal is central to the teachings of the Mahāyāna and Sōtō Zen. Indeed, the bodhisattva path is the path to realization of the entire Mahāyāna, including Sōtō Zen.

We should first define the term "bodhisattva." *Bodhi,* as we have seen, means enlightenment or realization; *sattva* means sentient being.[68] So a bodhisattva is literally an "enlightenment being," one whose aim is supreme enlightenment or buddhahood. What is essential to remember about the bodhisattva ideal is that the intention is not just enlightenment for oneself but to bring all beings to enlightenment. Whatever realization the bodhisattva may attain in the course of practice is achieved in order to alleviate the suffering of all beings, not simply one's own.

In his dissertation on the early Mahāyāna, Gil Fronsdal points out other accepted meanings for the word *sattva:*

> The first is as a synonym for *citta* or mind. In this case a bodhisattva is "one whose mind, intentions, thoughts or wishes are fixed on *bodhi*. . . ." The second meaning takes *sattva* as a wrongly Sanskritized version of the Pāli *satta* which may have originally meant "to attach or cling to." The appropriate Sanskrit would be *bodhisakta* or "one who is devoted or attached to *bodhi*. . . ." An etymology for *sattva* . . . found explicitly in the Tibetan word for bodhisattva is "strength, energy, vigor, power, courage." In this case the bodhisattva means "one whose energy and power is directed toward *bodhi*. . . ." [This] translation choice conveys well the philosophy of heroism which was integral to the early bodhisattva ideal.[69]

This "heroic" attitude of living one's life for the benefit of all beings, described by Fronsdal in the early bodhisattva ideal, forms the foundation for all Mahāyāna practices.

Although interesting, it is beyond the scope of this writing to delve into the historical development of the bodhisattva.[70] What is essential for our purposes is the understanding that the bodhisattva ideal evolved as the Mahāyāna evolved and is rooted in the Perfection of Wisdom (Prajñāparāmitā) teachings. When we remember this, we return again to the teachings of emptiness and how they inform our understanding of what a bodhisattva is and what a bodhisattva does. From this perspective, we can understand how the bodhisattva path provides a means for the embodiment of the Mahāyāna teachings.

It is important to note, as Kim writes, that

> The bodhisattva can be considered in two different contexts: one as the person of the bodhisattva as the object of faith and devotion; the other, the way of the bodhisattva as the model for the believer's life.[71]

The most widely known example of a bodhisattva as an object of faith is Avalokiteśvara (Ch. Guanyin; Jpn. Kannon; Tib. Chenrezi). This bodhisattva, who appears in both male and female forms, embodies fully the quality of compassion. An object of devotion in many parts of the Buddhist world, Avalokiteśvara is also present as the protagonist, so to speak, in the *Heart Sūtra,* a distillation of the Perfection of Wisdom literature and a text central to all forms of Mahāyāna teachings. As the "Hearer of the Cries of the World," Avalokiteśvara is also the subject of Zen teaching stories and the expression of living compassion.

Perhaps the clearest way of understanding the bodhisattva as the model for a practitioner's life, the bodhisattva ideal, is through an examination of the bodhisattva vow recited by Mahāyāna practitioners:

> Beings are numberless, I vow to save them.
> Delusions are inexhaustable, I vow to end them.
> Dharma gates are endless, I vow to enter them.
> Buddha's way is unsurpassable, I vow to become it.[72]

There are various translations of this vow, some with different emphases. For example, in the first line "beings" is often understood as sentient or living beings and "save" has also been translated as "free," in the sense of to liberate. In the last line, "become" is sometimes translated as "realize" or "attain." All of these modifications and differences simply reflect subtleties in the basic message: the bodhisattva takes on the inconceivable task of bringing realization and freedom from suffering to all. All beings everywhere, throughout time and space, are to be freed from suffering. All delusions are to be ended. All dharma gates, that is, every way through which one may encounter the teachings and become awakened (which is the same as every moment and activity of our day), are to be fully and consciously entered, taken up. Buddha's Way, the reality of this moment as lived and experienced in awakening, is to be fully embodied and expressed. These vows are the day-to-day activity of a bodhisattva.

To our ordinary way of thinking, this seems like a Herculean, indeed impossible, task. If the practitioner thinks of herself as an individual among countless individuals, saving all beings sounds like an endless process of running from one being to the next attempting to help. Dharma gates and delusions stretch endlessly into the future, and embodying something unsurpassable seems impossible. In order to make these vows a means by which suffering may be alleviated and not increased, something must shift.

The shift occurs when we return to the basic teachings of the Mahāyāna. The beings that are numberless are also the beings that are the expressions of dependent co-arising—that is, the interconnected reality of this moment—and so is the bodhisattva who is making the vow. In taking this vow, the practitioner is pushed to confront the paradox of the two truths. Beings exist and suffer and bleed, and the compassion that arises as the practitioner wakes up to the interconnectedness of all beings requires that she respond. The *Perfection of Wisdom Sūtra* (Skt. *Prajñāpāramitā-sūtra*) says of the bodhisattva, "Great compassion . . . takes hold of him."[73] At the same time, there is the recognition that all beings, including oneself, are empty of inherent existence—in fact, there are no beings to save. The paradox inherent in the vow demands selfless action and the acknowledgment of suffering, as well as cultivation of the wisdom that clearly sees the nature of reality.

The *Diamond Sūtra* (Skt. *Vajracchedikā-prajñāpāramitā-sūtra*) says:

> As many beings as there are in the universe of beings . . . all these I must lead to Nirvana. . . . And yet, although innumerable beings have thus been led to Nirvana, no being at all has been led to Nirvana. . . . If in a Bodhisattva the notion of a "being" should take place, he could not be called a "Bodhi-being."[74]

In Buddhist teachings, wisdom and compassion are thought to arise together and are expressed as skillful means, the third inseparable element of practice. Wisdom sees the nature of all things, compassion is its natural outcome, and skillful means are its natural expression. In this way, the practitioner is directly connected to Mahāyāna ideals. Regarding the relationship of wisdom, compassion, and the experience of the Sōtō Zen practitioner, Kim writes:

> The essence of the bodhisattva ideal is great compassion (Skt. *mahākaruṇā;* Jpn. *daihi*). It is essentially the reconciliation of the dualistic opposites of self and nonself, sentient and insentient, Buddhas and sentient beings, man and woman, and so forth. As Dōgen writes "The way of the bodhisattva is 'I am thusness; you are thusness.'" The identity of "I" and "you" in thusness rather than identity in substance, status, or the like, is the fundamental metaphysical and religious ground of great compassion.[75]

Great compassion, then, is compassion grounded in and expressive of the interconnected nature of reality—"thusness." Kim writes that these teachings

> point up the same truth—the mystery of Avalokiteśvara's—all bodhisattvas' and humans' for that matter—compassion in its dynamic operation throughout the universe, in which infinite compassion, myriad arms and eyes, and body mind are one indivisible thusness. Avalokiteśvara in this view is not an object of faith the ordinary individual believes in, but the way of bodhisattvahood which every one can exemplify by and for oneself. In brief, Avalokiteśvara is not the object but the subject of faith. The object of faith and the model of living in question are not two discreet concerns, but one and the same in the nonduality of infinite compassion and of the thousand arms and thousand eyes of Avalokiteśvara.[76]

It is from this perspective that the practitioner takes up Dōgen's injunction to serve others:

> Working for the welfare of all beings means that you contrive ways to benefit all sentient beings, high and low. In other words, you carefully investigate others' distant and near futures, and think of the various means which will be the most congenial to their well-being. Commiserate with a turtle in trouble, and take care of a sparrow suffering from injury. When you see the distressed turtle or watch the sick sparrow, you do not expect repayment for your favor, but you are moved entirely by your desire to help others.
>
> Fools may think that if another's benefit is given priority, their own good must be lost. This is not the case. The practice of benefiting others is the total truth (*ippo*), hence, it serves both self and others far and wide. . . . Therefore, serve enemies and friends equally, and assist self and others without discrimination. If you grasp this truth, [you will see that] this is the reason that even grass and trees, the wind and water are all naturally engaged in the activity of profiting others, and your understanding will certainly serve others' benefit.[77]

The great seventh-century Indian Buddhist philosopher and teacher Śāntideva, in the *Bodhicharyāvatāra* (*Guide to the Bodhisattva's Way of Life*), beautifully states the spirit of the bodhisattva's life:

> May I be a protector for those without one,
> A guide for all travellers on the way;
> May I be a bridge, a boat and a ship
> For all those who wish to cross [the water].
>
> May I be an island for those who seek one,
> And a lamp for those desiring light,
> May I be a bed for those who wish to rest. . . .
>
> Just like space
> And all the great elements such as earth,
> May I always support the lives . . .
> For all the realms of the varied beings
> That reach unto the ends of space.[78]

Śāntideva goes on to state that this vow, itself, is the path to realization. It is the "supreme ambrosia," the "supreme medicine," the "tree that shelters all beings," and the "universal bridge."[79] He says:

> For all those guests travelling on the path of conditioned existence
> Who wish to experience the bounties of happiness,
> This will satisfy them with joy
> And actually place them in supreme bliss.

Śāntideva is telling us that the vow itself, not a hypothetical future where all beings are "saved," is the place of happiness and joy. Returning to the relationship of wisdom and great compassion, we can understand that the bodhisattva undertaking this vow not only cultivates compassion and a life lived for the benefit of others, but also dissolves attitudes and actions based on a belief in a separate self. The practitioner begins to realize that, according to the Mahāyāna, as Kim puts it, "individual liberation is a contradiction in terms."[80] Wisdom and compassion, alleviating the suffering of others and liberating oneself from suffering, all become part of the same process.

The practitioner realizes that "the true fruit of the religious life is an unbounded nondiscriminatory compassion rooted in enlightened understanding" and aims his or her life at the "dynamic expression" of this truth. This (ideal) expression or "action" is

> pure spontaneity, without any question of weighing the consequences for oneself. For this reason, compassion is a very simple matter; one forgets the self and does what is needed.[81]

This is, fundamentally, the life of the bodhisattva and the life of the Zen student.

Practice

Like any religious discipline or activity, Sōtō Zen practice can only be fully understood from the inside. I present here the shape, color, and texture of the practice, a representation that provides a means for understanding the beauty and difficulties encountered on the way. There are many ways that Sōtō Zen practice can be approached. I begin by returning to the fundamental spirit of the practice, then describe the actual elements and activities of Sōtō Zen life, and, finally, take up important dimensions of the practice that run through these activities.

It is important to note that practitioners vary greatly in the degree to which they participate in various aspects of practice, and the form their participation takes also varies. For example, a person may sit zazen at home, spend some time studying the dharma, perhaps attend an occasional dharma talk, meet with a teacher, and be involved in the relational aspects of practice within his or her family. Another person may regularly attend extended sittings, see a teacher frequently, and volunteer time at a dharma center. Still another may take up residential practice and spend time in extended retreat or monastic life. Each of them can have a deep and vital practice. It is less the circumstances than the devotion that determines the depth of engagement with the Sōtō Way.

As noted above, Sōtō Zen is a part of the greater Buddhist world, and Sōtō Zen practice is an expression of Buddhist teaching. Peter Harvey points out that

> The name of the [Chan], or "Meditation" school (Jap. Zen) is an abbreviated translation of the Sanskrit *dhyāna,* referring to the state of deep meditation (Pāli *jhana*).[82]

Sōtō Zen practice emphasizes the identity of practice and realization (*shushō itto*) and what Kim describes as a nondualistic way of existence.[83] Practice, in whatever form, is not a means to an end. One does not sit zazen to become enlightened, nor does one work in order to sit zazen. We can say, as I have previously, that practice is the activities the practitioner takes up that allow her to deepen her understanding, realization, and expression of Buddha's teaching, thereby reducing suffering in herself and others—but we must remember that in Dōgen's teaching the practitioner does not become anything other than what he or she already is.

The very first movement toward practice, the first step on the bodhisattva way, what is called the "thought of enlightenment" (Skt. *bodhicitta*), is the manifestation of enlightenment, according to Dōgen. This thought of enlightenment is, fundamentally, an intention to take up the bodhisattva path, to realize awakening in order to alleviate the suffering of all beings. This constitutes a shift away from self-experience, based in the belief that one is simply a separate, discrete entity, toward a perspective that takes all beings as the center of one's existence. Again, it must be remembered that this does not mean that the unique individual is lost, rather that the individual flourishes in the context of the whole of reality.

With regard to the identity of this movement with enlightenment, Dōgen writes:

> As for the Buddha way, when one first arouses the thought [of enlightenment,] it is enlightenment. . . . First, last, and in between are all enlightenment . . . when one musters one's entire mind and body and practices the Buddha Way, this is the entirety of the Buddha Way.[84]

Practice, then, means letting go of the aim to attain constructed notions of enlightenment and returning again and again to this moment with the faith that this moment is Buddha, and that the practices one takes up are the natural manifestation of Buddha. With this emphasis, all activities can be included in the term "practice." There is no division of life into realms of practice and not practice. Zazen, work, relationships—all are included. Dōgen writes in *Bendōwa:*

> Those who regard worldly affairs as a hindrance to buddha-dharma only think that there is no buddha-dharma in the secular world, and do not understand that there is no secular world in buddha-dharma.[85]

Having said that, the practice of zazen is essential to Sōtō Zen. It is the center of the practice mandala and Dōgen is very clear about the importance of dedicated effort in the practice of zazen. Forming an understanding of zazen allows for a fuller appreciation of other dimensions and activities of practice.

Zazen Practice

The word *zen* (Ch. *chan*) comes from the Sanskrit word *dhyāna,* which is usually translated as "meditation." Zen, therefore, can be understood as the school whose main focus is meditation. In Sōtō Zen, this meditation is called *shikantaza,* "just sitting" (*shikan,* "just, only"; *taza,* "sitting"). "Just" has the meaning, as Sawaki Kōdō has said, of "just doing something wholeheartedly."[86] *Shikantaza* forms the heart of Sōtō Zen practice. Meditation is often thought of as the process of meditating "on" something in order to calm the mind or to produce a desired effect or transformation. In Dōgen's teaching of practice realization, however, this understanding does not apply. Dōgen tells us in *Bendōwa,* "Each moment of zazen is equally wholeness of practice, equally wholeness of realization."[87] He discusses this specifically in the fascicle *Fukanzazengi* ("General Recommendations for Doing Zazen"), written just after his return from China:

> The zazen I speak of is not learning meditation. It is the dharma-gate of repose and bliss. The practice realization of totally culminated enlightenment. It is the manifestation of ultimate reality.[88]

This is not to say that there is no effort to be made in practicing zazen. Dōgen writes:

> You should know that in order not to defile realization, which is inseparable from practice, buddha ancestors always caution you not to be slack in your practice. If you release the inconceivable practice, the original realization fills your hands; if you become free from the original realization, the inconceivable practice is upheld with your whole body.[89]

Dōgen is very clear on this point. Practice requires wholehearted, energetic engagement. According to Dōgen, this very moment is the manifestation of ultimate reality; but he also taught that realization and practice arise together, therefore practice is paramount. Realization requires practice to be manifest. Kim expresses the essential nature of practice this way: "Dōgen's whole works—written or otherwise—are simply footnotes to zazen-only."[90]

Dōgen describes in detail the actual practice of zazen. In *Zazengi* ("Rules for Zazen") he tells us that it is best to sit zazen in a moderately lit, quiet room with loosened robes on a round cushion. He advises us to "[s]et aside all involvements and let the myriad things rest," to "not desire to become a buddha" yet "engage yourself in zazen as though saving your head from fire."[91] He details the upright posture one should adopt, with specific instructions for the position of the hands, feet, head, and even tongue.

He also tells the practitioner to "think non-thinking."[92] This does not mean that one is not supposed to think, but rather to cultivate a new relationship to one's thoughts and emotions. This relationship is based on an understanding and realization that conceptual, relative reality is just that—conceptual—and that our thoughts and judgments are simply thoughts and judgments, not something to be gotten rid of or suppressed, but rather to be seen for what they are. Dōgen writes in *Genjō kōan* that just as a fish swims in water or a bird flies in the air, so we swim in delusion, the Buddha swims in this reality. To attempt to take Buddha from our ordinary reality, to remove ourselves from the ordinary reality of our lives, is akin to removing a fish from the water or a bird from the air.[93] The point, then, is not to extricate oneself from one's reality, nor to suppress thoughts in order to arrive at a peaceful serene state, but rather to enter fully into reality and realize it completely. This is true wisdom and is not related to special experiences, though these may arise as one frees oneself from habitual identifications.

In this regard Kim writes:

> The function of non-thinking is not just to transcend both thinking and not-thinking, but to realize both in the absolute and singular act of immovable sitting itself . . . [it] is not the elimination of intelligence but the realization of it. Furthermore, what intelligence does in zazen is to unfold rather than circumscribe the mysteries of existence. . . . [Zazen] is that psycho-metaphysical activity, undefiled by and unattached to dualistic categories, events and things, that our perception and intellect creates, while living with them and using dualities. For the dualistic world remains real, not dissolved. Therefore, the unity in question does not replace distinction but is unobstructed by it.[94]

What this means for the individual practitioner of zazen is complete engagement of the body, heart, and mind in this moment without judgment and without seeking anything else. Seated in zazen, with the back erect, shoulders relaxed, chin slightly tucked, hands resting with the left palm in the right, the thumb tips lightly touching, the eyes softly open and unfocused, she gently attends to each passing moment, posture, breath, thoughts and emotions, knowing, at least to some extent, that just this moment is the complete manifestation of enlightenment. Letting go of concepts, opinions, and ideas, letting go of clinging to self-centered notions, the practice emerges.

Key to this emerging practice is faith, and at least a glimmer of understanding that, as Shunryu Suzuki is quoted as saying, "Zazen sits zazen." Or, as Okumura Sensei put it in a lecture at the San Francisco Zen Center, "The subject of this practice is not this person."[95] With this understanding, notions of reality, in which habitual self-reference and self-clinging take center stage, can be released and a different experience of moment-by-moment reality can be experienced. Dōgen writes in *Genjō kōan:*

> Do not suppose that what you realize becomes your knowledge and is grasped by your consciousness. Although actualized immediately, the inconceivable may not be apparent. Its appearance is beyond your knowledge.

In the same fascicle, he writes:

> When buddhas are truly buddhas they do not necessarily notice that they are buddhas. However they are actualized buddhas, who go on actualizing buddhas.[96]

These statements challenge our ordinary notions of knowledge and realization and bring up the relationship of the individual to realization. In zazen, and other forms of practice, there is the request and the opportunity to dissolve one's notions of self and knowing. There is the possibility for a transformation of what it means to know, along with the question of who is it that knows. This does not deny realization but instead strips away conceptualizations of what it entails. Shohaku Okumura, in a discussion of the term *fue,* "not knowing," says that Dōgen asks the practitioner to actively drop conceptualizations and "not know" in order to be present for reality itself.[97] The individual, then, comes to be understood and experienced not as a locus of knowing but as an expression of realization. This is a crucial point in understanding Sōtō Zen. The question of whether or not "I" have come to some realization becomes, to some extent, irrelevant—for the "I" that is implied is dissolved in the living of moment-by-moment practice.

This implies a shift in understanding of what it means to take up a religious discipline. The goal becomes not one's deliverance to a state of ease but the dissolution, in a sense, of the person who started the journey, the movement of the center of one's life from "this one" or "I, myself" to all beings. As stated previously, this does not imply a loss of personal identity or personality, but rather a full flowering of uniqueness and humanity. The shift in perspective can be understood as the difference between gaining experiences that reduce one's own suffering exclusively and the freedom of entering life without restriction. This is the vow of the bodhisattva and the life of Buddha, which may or may not, at any given moment, include the pleasure or even the "knowing" we usually associate with realization. The heart of this transformation occurs in the practice of *shikantaza.*

A willingness to simply allow this moment, moment by moment, in the faith that this is actually the complete manifestation of Buddha's way, is an essential aspect of the practice and supports the emergence of zazen as zazen. The practitioner of *shikantaza,* then, sits upright, attending to each moment, in the faith that she is (already) Buddha. What may objectively appear to be a form of meditation aimed at attaining a state of calmness and insight (and the instructions for which may even reify this idea), is, in fact, based on a completely different premise. "No special state of mind" is an expression heard often in a Sōtō Zen temple. "No gaining idea." "Just this is it." All of these convey an essential flavor of Sōtō Zen practice both on and off the cushion.

While zazen is the center of the practice mandala, the realms of work practice, relationships, and studying or listening to the dharma are taught to be equally important.

Work Practice

One of the hallmarks of Sōtō Zen is its understanding of and teaching about the nature of work and work practice. If each moment is a complete manifestation of Buddha's way, it follows that all activities are a field of practice. Taking care of the ordinary objects and activities of daily life is considered an integral part Sōtō Zen practice.

For example, in the Sōtō Zen monastic tradition, the position of *tenzo,* head cook, is a respected senior position. In the fascicle *Tenzo kyōkun* Dōgen writes that the *tenzo* should "See the pot as your own head; see the water as your life blood" and that "The Way-seeking mind of the *tenzo* is actualized by rolling up your sleeves." He goes on to instruct the cook to "[h]andle even a single leaf of green in such a way that it manifests the body of the Buddha. This in turn allows the Buddha to manifest through the leaf."[98]

Dōgen also warns against discriminating between ingredients as superior or inferior, and instructs the *tenzo* to simply accept whatever comes, caring for it wholeheartedly. In this way, the "one taste" of "the world itself as it is" is realized.

> Likewise, understand that a simple green has the power to become the practice of the Buddha, quite adequately nurturing the desire to live out the Way. Never feel aversion toward plain ingredients. As a teacher of [people] and heavenly beings, make the most of whatever greens you have.[99]

Dōgen's instructions for the cook can be understood as teachings in how to live one's life in such a way that practice is lived out in every situation. With the understanding that each "green" that comes the practitioner's way is the very "body of the Buddha" and has "the power to become the practice of the Buddha," the ordinary things of life, whatever they may be, become, like the *tenzo*'s pot, not separate from but aspects of oneself, to be treated with the utmost respect and reverence.

This is the beauty of work practice in the Sōtō tradition. It breaks up any attachment to zazen and undermines feelings of being somehow special, or perhaps superior, to others because one is doing a "spiritual" activity. It also teaches that experience and reality are transitory, as one moves from the zendo (meditation hall) to the compost heap, the garden, or the kitchen. Perhaps most centrally, it teaches the practitioner that by caring for things with respect she has an opportunity to directly experience interconnectedness, practice compassion, and come to know that engagement in and careful attention to ordinary activity is itself the realization of the Buddha's way. There are no special experiences or miraculous powers to be gained. Ordinary activities are the miraculous powers of life as it is. Dōgen quotes the "outstanding disciple" Layman Hō Unko: "Miraculous power! Marvelous activity! Drawing water and carrying firewood."[100]

Relating to the world in this way transforms not only one's experience of the world but also one's experience of oneself. Each act is done for its own sake, not for an end result; no act is more important than another; all are done wholeheartedly. To hear the sound of the broom, see the beam of light as it glances across a clean window, and enter into that experience fully is to loosen one's attachment to self and become free from preferences and clinging. This is practice grounded in Dōgen's teaching in the *Genjō kōan*. Francis Cook states that the term *genjō kōan* should be understood to mean that "the appearing is absolute reality."[101] Dōgen writes:

> When you find your place where you are, practice occurs, actualizing the fundamental point. When you find your way in this moment, practice occurs, actualizing the fundamental point. . . . Accordingly, in the practice-enlightenment of the buddha way, meeting one thing is mastering it—doing one practice is practicing completely.[102]

Dōgen writes about this dimension of practice in a slightly different way in his teaching of the "total exertion of a single thing" (*ippo gujin*) or the "total experience of a single thing" (*ippotsu*):

> The total experience of a single thing does not deprive a thing of its own unique particularity. It places a thing neither against others nor against none. To place a thing against none is another form of dualistic obstruction. When total experience is realized unobstructedly (*tsu o shite tsu no ge nakarashimuruni*), the total experience of a single thing is the same as the total experience of all things. . . . The total experience of a single thing is one with that of all things.[103]

Just as one "thing" is not placed against another, so one practice moment is not placed against another. Again, it is important to remember that entering into the moment is not done in order to find an essence or have a special experience. In Sōtō Zen, this moment is itself the fullness of realization.

Dōgen uses the painting of a rice cake, juxtaposed with an actual rice cake, to show us that we do not realize the Way by contrasting the painting with the "real" rice cake, but rather by fully entering into our experience of "painted rice cake." He writes in his fascicle *Gabyō* ("Painting of a Rice Cake"):

> [A] painted rice-cake, made of rice flour, is neither born nor unborn. Since this is so, it is the moment of realization of the way. . . . The paints for painting rice-cakes are the same as those used for painting mountains and waters. . . . Accordingly, "painted rice-cakes" spoken of here means that sesame rice-cakes, herb rice-cakes, toasted rice-cakes, millet rice-cakes, and the like are all actualized in the painting. Thus, you should understand that a painting is all-inclusive, a rice cake is all-inclusive, the dharma is all-inclusive. In this way, all rice-cakes actualized right now are nothing but a painted rice-cake. If you look for some other kind of painted rice-cake, you will never find it, you will never grasp it.[104]

The practice, then, takes place not in a rarified realm of special experiences and "real" rice cakes. Practice is active in whatever circumstances and activities in which one is currently engaged—cooking, sitting zazen, raising children, cleaning toilets, driving to work. Zen teacher Sojun Mel Weitsman notes that in each moment the practitioner "steps into the painting,"[105] in a sense penetrates the painting, knowing that the painting is not different from themselves and that this nondifference does not imply a loss of uniqueness or particularity. This is realizing the Way and it is possible in all activities.

Relational Practice

A third key element of Sōtō Zen life and practice occurs in the realm of relationship. This includes relationships to all beings, but I will focus on three primary dimensions: the sangha, or community of practitioners; the teacher; and, in a separate section, the precepts.

The foundation for entry into any Buddhist tradition is taking refuge in the Buddha, Dharma, and Sangha (Three Refuges or Three Treasures, Skt. *triratna*). What is meant by the term "refuge" varies, but essentially it means to return to, rely on, respect and commit to. The Buddha can be understood as the model, exemplified in the life of Śākyamuni Buddha. In Sōtō Zen the first refuge is often understood to be taking refuge in one's "true nature." The student commits to returning to one's identity with emptiness and dependent arising, that is, Buddha's Way. Dharma is generally understood to mean the teachings, or the way things are. Sangha is the community of practitioners. In some contexts, the term "sangha" is limited to ordained monastics. In Sōtō Zen practice, however, it is understood to include all those who are endeavoring to study the Way together (whether lay or ordained). In its broadest sense, sangha can also be understood as the relational web of all beings, all life.

Along with zazen and work, life in the sangha forms the basis of Sōtō Zen practice. Zen practice is a communal event. In traditional monastic life, practitioners undertake all monastic activities, for example zazen, ritual, work practice, and meals, as a group. Monastic life and relationships are regarded as opportunities for enacting and realizing the truth of Buddha's teachings. Harmony is deeply valued and the training of monastic life was (and is) highly structured.

Taigen Daniel Leighton and Shohaku Okumura, in their translation of Dōgen's *Eihei shingi,* return to a term he used for zazen—*jijuyu zammai,* "the *samādhi* [meditative state] of self joyousness"—to illuminate the relationship of the individual and the sangha in Sōtō Zen monastic life.

> The *ji* of *jijuyu* means self. The compound *juyu* means joyful or fulfilled, but separately the two characters mean to receive or accept one's function. . . . This self-realizing *samādhi* is itself simply the reality of life (and death), and is not limited to the sitting posture. The purpose of Zen training and community practice is not just to extend this zazen awareness into everyday life but to actually discover the deep satisfaction and joyfulness of *jijuyu samādhi* emerging in all of our daily activities and relationships.[106]

There is an emphasis on "selfless participation in communal activities":

> Such a communal life is likened to the blending of milk and water or to crossing the ocean aboard a single boat. Initially the members may enter into the community individually, but they gradually realize that they are born of the same common root of absolute emptiness; hence they are not an assemblage of isolated individuals but the children and flowers of emptiness. Monastic education is intended to help each of them realize this common root in emptiness.[107]

Sōtō Zen monasteries and practice centers focus on the way in which practitioners work together, even move together—as in walking meditation in the zendo. This focus, this communal movement, is aimed at reducing self-centered concern and allows for a loosening of self-clinging and self-centered preferences. As an expression of harmony, attentiveness to the needs of others and the entire situation at hand is highly valued. This attentiveness, however, does not take the form of intrusiveness. One is expected to take care of one's own responsibilities, allow others to tend to theirs, and work together effectively without "attachment to fame and gain." In this way, the practitioner is trained to shift focus from "this one" to the entire web of relationships and reality.

At the same time, the personal experience of the practitioner is transformed in the crucible of community. Suzuki Rōshi spoke in his lectures of "potato practice": the most efficient way to clean potatoes is not to wash them individually but to put them in a sack together, shake them up, and let them knock the dirt off one another. The sangha is the place where this happens. In the community, ideally, the individual is accepted and supported in his practice. Personal difficulties, struggles, and limitations emerge and are transformed in a joint effort with others who are also endeavoring to realize wisdom and compassion.

The Teacher

The teacher-student relationship is another essential dimension in Sōtō Zen practice. Han de Wit describes the teacher-student relationship as a "natural hierarchy."[108] In Sōtō Zen the teacher-student relationship is one of mutual respect and dedication to the dharma and the practice. In this way, each member of the relationship is equal to the other. The teacher does not occupy the position of an exalted guru but, because of her maturity, functions to express the teachings that the student seeks to realize. Dōgen writes in *Gakudō yōjinshū* ("Guidelines for Studying the Way"):

> The practice of Buddha's teaching is always done by receiving the essential instructions of a master, not by following your own ideas. In fact, Buddha's teaching cannot be attained by having ideas or not having ideas.[109]

The teacher is a guide, an examplar, and an embodiment of practice, and, when trust is sufficient, a means by which the student's habitual self-clinging can be effectively challenged. There is a strong element of disrupting ordinary expectations in the student-teacher relationship. The student is not, however, expected to unquestioningly follow the teacher. There is always a give and take. Ideally, what develops is a profound intimacy based on the shared intention of realizing the Buddha's teaching. This intimacy has less to do with personality than with what Buddhist teacher Yvonne Rand has called the "benthic layer" of relationship.[110] The benthic layer is the deepest layer of the ocean. It is not influenced by tidal patterns, much less by waves on the surface. In this context, the word reflects the deep, often unexplainable connection between teacher and student, and it is marked by gratitude. The relationship is a living one and changes as both student and teacher develop. The teacher-student relationship is the means by which the dharma is transmitted and lived out in concrete interpersonal reality.

It is important to note that many people function as teachers within the community and can hold different roles. Some relationships may be more friendly or casual, others more formal. Dōgen and his descendents stated clearly that every being, every situation, may serve as a teacher, nothing is despised. Still, there is a distinction made between teaching situations, more informal teachers, and the dharma teacher who is recognized in the lineage and by the community as having responsibility for and a commitment to this particular tradition. Dōgen describes this person as (ideally) "A right teacher . . . in whom living and understanding correspond to one another."[111]

Using language, silence, and gesture, the teacher aims at helping the student realize the nature of reality, his true nature. This can take place in a formal, private interview with the teacher (*dokusan*), in public question/response ceremonies (*shosan*), or in more casual encounters. The formal interview with a teacher holds a special place in Sōtō Zen and is illustrative of a key dimension of the student-teacher relationship. As Kim points out, the teacher and student engage in a "deeply personal dialogue (*mondo* or *shuryo*) in [the] search for the truth." This requires that the student approach the teacher with openness and honesty, and that the teacher is skilled at guiding and challenging the student effectively. With such encounters, the teachings take root in the soil of real experience, not fantasy, and genuine realization is supported.

The nature of the teacher-student relationship is, according to Dōgen, one of "responsive communion" (*kanno-doko*).[112] This communion does not necessarily entail verbal dialogue or any other form of direct communication in each encounter. A story about the Chinese Chan master Daowu and his disciple Longtan illustrates this point and imparts a sense of the overall feeling of the teacher-student relationship in Sōtō Zen practice:

> After some time [studying with Daowu, Longtan] said to the master, "Since I came, I have not received any essential instructions on the mind from you, Master." The master replied, "Ever since you came, I have not ceased for a moment to give you essential instructions about the mind." More mystified then ever, the disciple asked, "On what points have you instructed me?" The master replied, "Whenever you bring me the tea, I take it from your hands. Whenever you serve the meal, I accept it and eat it. Whenever you salute (greet) me, I lower my head in response. On what points have I failed to show you the essence of mind?"[113]

Simply working beside a teacher or being present with their embodied response to the world conveys the teaching. It is also important to note, however, that, though the teacher may impart specific teachings to the student, this is not a process of receiving something from outside, but rather of the student realizing her essential identity with Buddha.

Precepts

The cultivation of and adherence to fundamental ethical principles (Skt. *śīla*) is central to all forms of Buddhist practice. The path to liberation, as articulated in the Buddha's first teaching, is commonly described as containing three elements: ethics (*śīla*), meditation (*samādhi*), and the cultivation of wisdom (*prajñā*). The cultivation of wisdom (and compassion) and the practice of meditation are understood to be dependent upon the clarity of mind made possible by a firm foundation in the ethical principles of non-harming. According to tradition, in the Buddha's lifetime and after, as the monastic community grew and difficulties arose, a specific system of conduct (*vinaya*) evolved based on the experiences and needs of the individual practitioners and the monastic community as a whole.[114] Those wishing to enter the community were required to commit to this system of conduct, and all other practices were understood to rest on this foundation.

The core principles of not killing or harming beings, not stealing, not telling falsehoods, and not engaging in sexual misconduct or "unmindful states due to alcoholic drinks or drugs"[115] were understood as essential for all practitioners, including lay practitioners. Embarking on the Buddhist path, either as a lay or an ordained practitioner, entailed a commitment to follow various sets of precepts, the guiding ethical principles of the tradition. The advent of the Mahāyāna saw an increasing emphasis on the bodhisattva vow and a shift toward understanding the precepts as reflections of the awakened mind. In Sōtō Zen there are sixteen bodhisattva precepts that are taken by both lay and ordained practitioners.

As noted above, taking refuge in Buddha, Dharma, and Sangha is a central aspect of commitment to the Buddhist path and to following the principles that support it. Taking refuge, as Peter Harvey notes, means orienting oneself to "three guides to a better way of living." It does not refer to "a place to hide, but . . . something the thought of which purifies, uplifts, and strengthens the heart."[116] Taking refuge in the Buddha is often expressed as making a commitment to return to and trust the spacious compassionate reality of ourselves and all being. Taking refuge in the Dharma, the teachings, implies returning to the teachings for guidance, and taking refuge in the Sangha means engaging with the community of pracitioners as a source of support and transformation. These three form the basis for a life of practice.

The three pure precepts are the commitment to, first, avoid wrongdoing (the term "evil" is sometimes used, but this can have problematic associations with theistic traditions); second, to do good; and third, to live to benefit all beings. These three fundamental guidelines are further described in the ten grave precepts, which are presented as proscriptions: to not kill, to not take what is not given (at base, this means not stealing, but it also carries the meaning of being aware of the subtleties of taking from others), to not misuse sexuality (that is, not engaging in self-centered or aggressive sexual behavior), to not lie or use "false speech," to not intoxicate the mind and body of oneself or others, to not slander, to not praise oneself at the expense of others, to not be possesive of anything (not even the teaching), to not harbor ill will, and to not abuse (disparage, or cause harm to) the Three Treasures.

These precepts form a framework and support on which the practitioner builds his practice and conduct. As with any form of Buddhism, adhering to these guidelines is understood in Sōtō Zen as a way to calm the mind and allow for the growth of wisdom and compassion. They are not divinely revealed commandments, but are simply descriptions of what works, conduct that avoids creating suffering for oneself or others. They are also understood, in Sōtō Zen, to be descriptions of how an awakened mind expresses itself in the world. Some contemporary Zen teachers have paired each of the ten grave precepts with a positive statement to underscore this. For example, "not to kill" is paired with "to cherish life."[117]

The precepts thus function as a guide for behavior that supports practice. At the same time, they also describe the behavior and attitude present in realization. The point, for the practitioner, is not perfect adherence, which could lead to a kind of perfectionism that violates the spirit of compassion that is the foundation of all Mahāyāna teachings. Instead, the practice of the precepts is meant to lead the practitioner to an ever-deepening awareness of the ways in which realization is or is not supported and expressed in one's own thought and conduct. An acceptance of the practitioner's human frailty, as well as the priority placed on compassion and service, undercuts any tendency toward legalistic or rigid adherence, and supports efforts aimed at embodying the precepts.

The precepts are the expression of awakening in the world and, as we have seen, zazen is not different from realization. In this way, the precepts can be understood as being fully present in the practice of zazen. Dōgen writes, "Observing the precepts singlemindedly is none other than practicing *shikantaza* and following the activities of the ancient masters."[118] We can understand this to mean that when a person operates in the world based in the realization of dependent co-arising, he responds in harmony with the precepts—not in order to fulfill them, but because this ethical conduct is what naturally unfolds.

In the Sōtō Zen lineage, both lay and ordained practitioners take the precepts in a public ceremony. The lay practitioner forms a relationship with a teacher, requests to receive the precepts, and vows to do their best to live by these guidelines. A candidate for ordination undertakes and lives by the very same vows. For the priest there is the added dimension of "home-leaving," vowing before the community to take on a formal relationship to the tradition and to the needs of the community. It is significant that in the Sōtō Zen tradition this does not include a vow of celibacy.[119] It is also important to note that the usual career of a contemporary Sōtō Zen priest includes a period of monastic training followed by a return to the wider sangha and a life of service in the world.

Dōgen wrote of the availability of full realization to any sincere practitioner, lay or monastic, most clearly and forcefully early in his teaching. Later, for example in the fascicle *Shukke kudoku* ("The Merit of Leaving Family Life"), he spoke directly about the need for ordination as a monastic.[120] In both instances, however, the key element was devotion to the practice, including full engagement with the precepts. Whatever form adopted by the practitioner in expressing these precepts, the bodhisattva vow is always the foundation. Living out this vow in zazen, work, and relationships lies at the heart of the Sōtō Zen way.

Forms and Ritual

Ritual forms of practice are an obvious and essential part of Sōtō Zen practice. In the zendo, during a retreat, or in monastic situations there are established forms for most activities, from chanting to eating, greeting one another with a silent bow, or moving in the zendo. For example, in *Eihei shingi* Dōgen wrote in minute detail about the manner in which to carry out almost every conceivable activity. While this level of detail is not lived out in most practice centers or in most practitioners' ordinary lives, the impact of this attention to form continues.

Daily forms of practice can be thought of as serving three functions. First, they are easily understood as a means by which the practitioner can become aware of her bodily actions and speech, and thus engage in respectful interactions with the world of physical objects. Attending to the careful placement of one's chopsticks on a bowl during a formal zendo meal (*ōryōki*) requires awareness and deepens one's appreciation of the bowl, the utensils, and the food. Second, clearly delineated forms of practice promote harmonious interactions with others and support the ideal of the community blending together "like milk and water." For example, the fact that there are specific instructions on how to quietly enter, be seated, and get up from zazen means that confusion, noise, and extraneous interactions are kept to a minimum, and the calm and focused atmosphere of the zendo is preserved.

Third, and perhaps most important, the forms themselves are a means for transmitting the dharma. I will discuss this further below when I take up the subject of the body in Sōtō Zen, but we can say, for example, that experiencing a full bow, touching the head to the floor, brings the practitioner into contact with the teaching in a direct, physical way that may not yet be available to the intellect or expressible in language.

Ceremonies also play a key role in the life of the individual practitioner and the community. Each morning at a Zen temple there is an offering of incense to the Buddha, bows, and chanting. Key texts, such as the *Heart Sūtra,* are chanted, and often a recitation of the lineage (the names of the teachers who are regarded as having transmitted the teaching) is included. The merit of the chanting is then dedicated to the benefit of all beings. There are ceremonies in which practitioners receive the precepts, ordinations, and monthly ceremonies in which the community comes together to renew their bodhisattva vows. In addition, funeral services, celebrations of Buddhist holidays, such as the (purported) day of the Buddha's death, and Buddhist interpretations of more general holidays such as New Year's and Thanksgiving in North America, are conducted.

Outside of monastic or retreat settings, practitioners participate to the extent that they feel comfortable. There are many Zen practitioners who participate in scheduled periods of zazen and attend dharma talks but find the ritual aspects of the tradition personally meaningless or even repugnant. This, too, is part of the whole fabric of the community, and participation in rituals and ceremonies is generally not compulsory.

Study

The study of the dharma, the teachings of the Buddha in the form of sūtras and commentaries, has been an essential component in Buddhist practice from the beginning. The Buddha's lectures were carefully preserved, first through oral transmission and then in written form, and these discourses formed the foundation for all later developments in Buddhism. In addition, the writings and commentaries of later teachers are a basis for studying the dharma. As the Mahāyāna developed, great lengths were taken to establish the new teachings as legitimate even though they were not recorded as having been spoken by the Buddha.[121] In the Mahāyāna certain texts came to be regarded as the embodiment of the Buddha and his teaching. The *Saddharmapuṇḍarīka-sūtra* (*Scripture of the Lotus of the True Law,* more commonly known as the *Lotus Sūtra*) states: "If anyone can keep (i.e., read, copy, or recite) this sūtra, it will be as if the Buddha were present."[122] It is important to note, however, that in the Buddhist tradition, texts are not considered to be revelations from a divine source, as the Bible is considered to be within some Christian sects.

In the Zen tradition, tension developed between an emphasis on study of the sūtras and a desire to undercut tendencies toward mistaking a purely intellectual understanding of the teachings for transformative insight. The emphasis in Zen is on the practice of zazen, the direct encounter between teacher and student, and community life. Practice and realization are said to be "beyond words and letters," and this has led, at times, to a misconception that Zen does not value or include intellectual or textual study.

Dōgen fiercely defended the need to honor and study the sūtras in his fascicle *Bukkyō:*

> [C]ertain unreliable stinking skin-bags have said, "We must not keep in mind even the sayings of ancestral masters. Still less should we ever read or rely upon the teaching of the sutras. . . ."
>
> Words like these are stupid in the extreme; they are the talk of madmen. There is no mystery in the authentic transmission from the ancestral Master that differs from the Buddhist sutras, or even from a single word . . . therein.[123]

Dōgen places this pointed critique of teachers who advocate dispensing with study in a context that includes a reminder that we must be careful not to confuse abstract concepts with direct experience.[124] In addition, he adds a deeper meaning to our understanding of the nature of the sūtras. Commenting on a portion of the *Lotus Sūtra* in the fascicle *Nyorai zenshin*, he writes:

> The volumes of the Sutra are the bones of the [Tathāgata]. Because this is so, bones may be this Sutra. Even if we know that volumes of the Sutra are the bones, if we do not know that bones are volumes of the Sutra, that is not yet the Buddha's truth. . . . The human world, the heavens above, the ocean, space, this land, and other realms are all real form, are volumes of the Sutra, and are bones. Receiving, retaining, reading, reciting, interpreting, and copying bones we should disclose realization. . . .[125]

By equating the Buddha with the sūtras and the sūtras with human bones, the bones of the universe, Dōgen makes a final link between the Buddha, the sūtra, and the lives of individual practitioners. Just as the buddhas and the sūtras have a reciprocal relationship, so too do the sūtras, and therefore, the Buddha, have a reciprocal relationship with human experience. Studying the sūtras is studying life; studying life is studying the sūtras. This approach to textual study undercuts any tendency to get carried away with intellectual understanding alone. Textual study, from this perspective, is grounded in a living practice of the teachings. It is also balanced, as Okumura has pointed out, by what Dōgen termed *fue*, "not knowing."[126] Not knowing is the willingness to let go of conceptions about the nature of things; it is an active stance that keeps a purely intellectual understanding from being mistaken for embodied realization. Approached with this attitude, textual study comes alive and it can bring fresh insight to ordinary experience.

Other Central Aspects: The Body

Buddhist practice is often spoken of in terms of the activities of body, speech, and mind, and in order to understand Sōtō Zen practice it is important to have a basic understanding of how the body is regarded in the tradition. Perhaps the most important thing to understand is that the aim, in Sōtō Zen practice, is not to transcend the body and physical experience but to fully realize them. In *Bendōwa* Dōgen tells us, "[B]ecause the body necessarily fills the mind and the mind inevitably penetrates the body, we call this permeation body-mind." He continues with this theme in *Yuibutsu yobutsu* ("Only Buddha and Buddha"):

> You should see the truth that as all Buddhas of the past, present, and future are awakened and practice the Way, they do not leave out their bodies and minds. To doubt this is already to slander them. As we reflect quietly upon this matter, it seems quite reasonable that our bodies and minds enact the Way.[127]

The Sōtō tradition puts a distinct emphasis on body and mind as an indivisible unit, the vehicle of realization, and the embodiment of the Way. Dōgen writes in the *Shōbōgenzō* fascicle *Shinjin gakudō* ("Body-and-Mind Study of the Way"):

> To study the way with the body means to study the way with your own body. It is the study of the way using this lump of red flesh. The body comes forth from the study of the way. Everything which comes forth from the study of the way is the true human body. The entire world of the ten directions is nothing but the true human body. . . . The true human body is the bones and marrow of the realm beyond consciousness and unconsciousness.[128]

This emphasis is apparent in the shape of the practice; for example, the detailed instructions given by Dōgen on correct zazen posture or the attention paid to the physical realities of daily life, food, clothing, and temple or house cleaning. In the realm of ceremony, it is a part of the tradition that the ritual forms themselves express and transmit the teachings. When a practitioner puts his hands together palm-to-palm in *gasshō,* he is expressing directly the nature of the bow. Thus, the forms themselves are teachers of the tradition—and sometimes the teaching is more eloquently and precisely accomplished through ritual forms than through words. Through these forms, the body directly receives the wisdom of the teachings. And because mind and body form an indivisible unit, the mind also directly receives this wisdom as well. The practitioner returns to the core teaching that practice, in whatever form, is not merely a method that leads to a spiritual reality but *is* that reality.

Faith

Faith is an essential element in the practice of Sōtō Zen. Francis Cook asserts unequivocally:

> Dōgen's Zen is the Zen of faith. That is, it is a religion in which faith is the very mechanism whereby the goal is achieved, and in the absence of which the door to the truth remains closed. It is therefore not simply one important element among others; it is the indispensable prerequisite.[129]

Willingness to engage fully in each moment, with the understanding that the moment is not different from Buddha, is the basis for all practice activities. Faith is expressed and formed by a deep engagement with the teachings, the practice, and life as a whole. Trust in the veracity of the teachings and their embodiment in the teachers to which one relates is essential for this engagement to occur but, as Cook writes:

> Also, and most important of all, one must have faith in one's own intrinsic Buddha nature, for Zen teaches that all things are the Buddha. It is no exaggeration to say that this faith is the very door through which one enters the Dharma. . . . Thus, faith is the entry way to the Dharma, but at the same time, correct practice is based on the faith that one is already Buddha, for there is nothing that is not Buddha. "Grass, trees, all are [Buddha] mind and body," says Dōgen in *Hotsu mujō shin*. . . . Consequently, unless practice is undertaken in the faith that oneself is the Buddha, and that everything else, even a speck of dust, is also the Buddha and preaches the Dharma with a clear voice, realization of the fact will be impossible.[130]

In *Gakudō yojinshū* ("Guidelines for Studying the Way") Dōgen writes:

> It is imperative for those who practice the Way to believe in it. Those who have faith in the Way should know for certain that they are unfailingly in the Way from the very beginning. Believing in this manner and penetrating the Way thus, practice accordingly. Such is the fundamental to learning the Way.

He states further in the *Shōbōgenzō* fascicle *Sanjushichihon bodaibumpo* ("The Thirty-seven Virtues of Bodhisattvahood"):

> Faith is so called when the entire body becomes faith itself (*koshin-jishin*). Faith is one with the fruit of enlightenment; the fruit of enlightenment is one with faith. If it is not the fruit of enlightenment, faith is not realized. . . . [F]aith is the entrance to the ocean of Dharma. Indeed, where faith is attained, there is the realization of the Buddha and ancestors.[131]

The faith expressed in the practice is, in a sense, the practice itself—a willingness, an allowing of this moment, completely revealing dynamic, compassionate, empty reality. And faith is accompanied by its companion, doubt. Doubt, in this sense, is not skepticism about the teachings, although the Buddha consistently reminded practitioners that they should not believe something simply because it was handed down but should test the teachings in their own experience. The practitioner must have a basic trust in the teachings in order to engage with them. Nor are we speaking here of a corrosive doubt in one's ability or one's identity with the Way. Doubt, in this context, means putting one's whole body and mind into the deepest possible questioning of reality. Questioning in this way is often phrased as "What?" or "How?" There is no conventional answer to such questions; rather, it is the living of them that transforms the questioner. Doubt such as this is an essential part of Sōtō Zen practice. Faith, then, does not define or determine our experience but supports our ability to be open to this deep questioning.

Stephen Batchelor, a Buddhist scholar, teacher, and former monk, writes:

> The Zen tradition often speaks of three factors that need to be cultivated along the path: great faith, great doubt, and great courage. Thus, faith and doubt are brought together. Clearly, doubt in this context does not refer to the kind of wavering indecision in which we get stuck, preventing any positive movement. It means to keep alive the perplexity at the heart of our life . . . to question whatever arises within us. The acceptance of such doubt as basic to Buddhist practice qualifies the meaning of faith. Faith is not equivalent to mere belief. Faith is the condition of ultimate confidence that we have the capacity to follow the path of doubt to the end.[132]

Expressing this kind of faith is the realization of thusness, that is, the day-to-day practice of the student of Sōtō Zen, and it requires a profound letting go of the self.

Self/No-self

In Sōtō Zen the term "self" is widely used and can take on different meanings. This can cause confusion and lead to a notion that, contrary to the teaching of emptiness, some kind of essential, permanent self truly exists. The term no-self (Skt. *anātman*) can give rise to nihilistic notions that the person does not exist. A brief review of the teachings of emptiness and *anātman* makes it quite plain that neither of these two positions is valid.

In clarifying confusion about the meaning of these terms, it is important to note that the Buddha's teaching of *anātman* does not imply that a personality, an individual, does not exist in an ordinary, conventionally perceived way. Garma C. C. Chang, in his discussion of the doctrine of no-self, points out that this teaching aims at the liberation of the practitioner from a belief in an unchanging, indivisible, completely independent self that is held together by the "glue" of self-clinging and delusion and is the source of suffering. He writes:

> On the common sense level, however, Buddha never rejected the idea of self, for he himself used the first-person pronoun "I" all the time, nor did he deny the continuation of a changing self-series.[133]

Steven Collins, in his book *Selfless Persons: Imagery and Thought in Theravāda Buddhism,* explicates in detail the early Buddhist teaching of no-self. In one example of the language used by the Buddha to indicate persons and at the same time elucidate the teaching of *anātman,* he points out that the Pāli words *atta* (Skt. *ātman*) and *puggala* (Skt. *pudgala,* also *puruṣa*) "are used frequently in simple narrative contexts where the intention is simply to denote a particular person or persons."[134] The existence of a "particular person or persons" is not denied. What is denied is their status as permanent, discrete entities.

The point of the teachings of no-self is not the obliteration of the ordinary personality or center of conscious experience, nor the removal of the individual from relational reality. Instead, the aim is the liberation of the individual from the constricted states of suffering that are the result of clinging to the illusion that this self is a permanent, independent entity.

Anne Klein, a scholar of Tibetan Buddhism, in her brilliant work on the "art" of the self, notes that the practitioner comes to understand that the self, as it is usually conceived of, does not exist.

> However, one does not conclude from such reflection that no self whatsoever exists, only that the self one had previously assumed and is now looking for

> does not exist. The danger of confusing the negation of that self with the negation of the self in general is great.

She goes on to say that a person making such a mistake "would miss the central point that emptiness and selflessness are fully compatible with dynamic personal agency" and "an integrated sense of self worth."[135]

The West's encounters with Buddhism, particularly the early encounters, were sometimes marked with confusion on this point. Francis Cook writes:

> The understanding of Buddhist self-forgetting [*anātman*] has passed through several phases in the West, ranging from early reactions of shocked disbelief and horror to a more recent understanding of its nature and spiritual implications. However, usually still missing from discussions of this doctrine is the understanding that the process of self-forgetting involves a paradox which contains very interesting implications for human society: this is that the process of self-forgetting is simultaneously a process of encompassing more and more of experiences as "self," and that such a process in the individual promotes an enhanced humanness, not a diminished humanness.[136]

The "authentic self," as Cook describes it, is a subjective position embedded in moment-by-moment reality. This "self" is dynamic and relational because "such a self has no existence prior to or apart from the experience which in fact constitutes it."[137] Anne Klein describes this as "ontological non-dualism," a subjectivity that is based in the "co-extensiveness" and interdependence of the conventional and the ultimate, as well as "the assertion that one does not in any way contradict or cancel the other out." This is an understanding of self as an expression of dependent co-arising.[138]

In Dōgen's writings we find an understanding of self that is well grounded in the teachings of emptiness and dependent co-arising. He writes in *Zenki* ("Undivided Activity"):

> Life is, for example, like people sailing in a boat. Although we set sail, steer our course, and pole the boat along, the boat carries us and we do not exist apart from the boat. By sailing the boat, we make the boat what it is. Study assiduously this very time. At such a time, there is nothing but the world of the boat. The heavens, the water, and the shore—all become the boat's time (*fune no jisetsu*). . . . Hence, I make life what it is; life makes me what I am. In riding the boat one's body and mind, the self and the world are together the dynamic function of the boat (*fune no kikan*). The entire earth and the whole empty sky are in company with the boat's vigorous exertion. Such is the I that is life, and the life that is I.[139]

He writes in *Yuibutsu yobutsu:*

> What Buddha means by the self is precisely the entire universe (*jindaichi*). Thus, whether one is aware of it or not, there is no universe that is not this self.[140]

This does not mean that the self as we experience it loses its uniqueness. Kim writes:

> Quite obviously, [according to this teaching] my self is not merely the psychophysical ego but that self which is one with the world—both the self and the world being the expressions (*jidoshu*) of emptiness. Yet this self is my self with an individual's own unique doubts, fears, hopes, agonies, and aspirations. Hence, it is neither an abstract speculation about the self in relation to the world . . . nor a subjectivistic involvement with the empirical "I."[141]

Returning to the teachings of emptiness, we can account for the presence of this uniqueness: we are told in the *Heart Sūtra* that not only is form emptiness but emptiness is form.[142] The teachings of emptiness and the identity of the self with the whole world do not obliterate distinction and vibrant particularity.

From this perspective, we can understand more fully what is meant by the statement often heard in Zen teachings, "When you become you, Zen becomes Zen." That is, when you become the complete you of this moment, moment by moment, Zen, the expression of Buddha's teaching, is manifest. As Shohaku Okumura said in his teaching on Dōgen's *Sansuigyō:*

> Uniqueness is very important. In this uniqueness, Buddha is studying Buddha's way through our practice. The mountains, without altering their own body and mind, with their own mountain continence, have always been studying themselves in this way.[143]

Okumura said further that there is no self, no fixed thing that is a self, "yet each thing is one hundred percent itself at this time." Each individual is a real, complex, ever-changing, unique manifestation of reality, and each is none other than this moment. There is no other self outside of this. Put another way, the way in which the "the self encounters the self" is complete engagement in each particular moment.

Dōgen says in *Genjō kōan:* "To study the Buddha Way is to study the self. To study the self is to forget the self. To forget the self is to be authenticated by the myriad things."[144] This is the paradox of self and no-self, form and emptiness. It is the day-to-day activity of a Sōtō Zen practitioner.

Through the unfolding of experience in awareness and a willingness to dissolve dualistic notions of this and that, self and other, the practitioner makes an effort through what Dōgen calls "the total engagement in a single thing" (*ippotsu*).[145] That is, the practitioner engages completely with present reality, releases clinging, and lets go of notions defining reality. The fact that reality includes the unique constellation of characteristics that comprise what we commonly understand as the self only poses a difficulty when we mistakenly attribute a permanent status to them; each of these characteristics is empty of inherent existence. This aspect of the emptiness teachings greatly influences how specific characteristics of individuals are regarded, as I will discuss below in the section on gender.

The self is not an obstacle to be overcome, a problem to be solved, or an impediment to be obliterated. To think of it in this way is to set up another opposition that only reinforces dualistic thinking. At the same time, taking up Buddhist practice means making an effort to realize what Francis Cook calls the "authentic self"—the "self" that is the concrete manifestation of this moment. In his commentary on Dōgen's *Genjō kōan,* Cook writes that when the self

> is constituted solely of the experience, in the total absence of judgment and self-consciousness, when the experience is pure and lacking in self-referential and self-serving meaning, then the "true self" is nothing more than just this pure experience disclosed in its genuineness. Here, in this kind of direct, unmediated experience of bodily states, there is no prior-existing self to be the passive recipient of presumably external events, but rather the only self that exists in any true sense is merely this bare content of experience.[146]

Anne Klein describes a "visceral coherence" of the self that is based not in a narrative account or specific content but in the moment-by-moment experience of the body/mind. Fluidity and flexibility, as well as interconnectedness, are constituent elements of this self-experience. It is, as she puts it, "a self that is both contextually constructed and viable as an agent, a force to contend with, but not the center of the world."[147] This does not mean that one's personal narrative or history is irrelevant or false, only that it does not define one's subjective experience.

This brings up one more important connection to be made when speaking of the teachings of self and no-self: the place of compassion. Klein points out that the significance of compassion, as well as the importance of ethical conduct, is "a vitally important context that is often overlooked in Western discussions of 'selflessness.'"[148] As noted above in the discussion on emptiness, the degree to which a person experiences her complete embeddedness in the web of reality is the degree to which she experiences the lives and experiences of others as her "own." The subjective experience of interconnectedness is marked by mutuality with all beings. This carries the implication that what arises from this experience is compassion and compassionate action. As Shohaku Okumura has said, this is the "reality of love" that permeates all the teachings and both supports and sustains the bodhisattva vow.

Gender

It is important to address a final aspect of the topic of self and no-self: how specific characteristics of self are regarded.[149] The Mahāyāna teachings of emptiness make clear that phenomena, as well as any characteristics assigned to them, are fluid, mutable, and empty of inherent existence. There can be no essential qualities attributed to any sentient (or insentient) being. While this has important implications for all practitioners, it is of special significance for women.

If there is no essential nature that can be found, categories based on any proposed essential qualities cannot apply. Therefore, unless one takes away from women (or any category of person) human status, traditionally regarded as the state in which the realization of the Buddha's way is possible, regarding them as categorically barred from full realization is a contradiction of the teachings. While this view of women's inadmissibility to the ranks of those for whom full realization is possible exists and continues to hold sway in many parts of the Buddhist world, if one takes the teachings of emptiness as reflective of the way things truly are (a core Mahāyāna tenet), then it is clearly illogical to assign a lesser status to one category of human being.

A frequently cited explication of this aspect of the emptiness teachings is a section of the Mahāyāna *Vimalakīrtinirdeśa-sūtra.*[150] In this text a goddess presents the teachings of emptiness to Śāriputra as a response to his question as to why she does not change her gender, taking rebirth in a male body (a necessary prerequisite to continuing on the path toward enlightenment in some interpretations of Buddhist teachings). The goddess responds, "I have been here twelve years and have looked for the innate characteristics of the female sex and haven't been able to find them. How can I change them?" She then proceeds to change Śāriputra into a likeness of herself and transforms herself into a likeness of Śāriputra. She tells him:

> Just as you are not really a woman but appear to be female in form, all women also only appear to be female in form. . . . Therefore, the Buddha said all are not really men or women.

The goddess then returns Śāriputra to his original form and asks him, "Where are the female form and innate characteristics now?" Śāriputra replies, "The female form and innate characteristics neither exist nor do not exist."[151] The implication is that attributions of status based on conventional characteristics such as gender do not hold up when viewed from the ultimate perspective of emptiness.

We find this same point stated quite clearly and forcefully in Dōgen's fascicle *Raihai tokuzui* ("Paying Homage and Acquiring the Essence"). In this essay Dōgen discusses the importance of seeking out and revering teachers who can transmit the dharma. In discerning the worthiness of such teachers, Dōgen decries the use of any criterion other than realization. Age, gender, social status—all are irrelevant. He says that attending to such characteristics means turning one's back on the very teachings one is attempting to embody. Only "stupid people" would consider any of these characteristics as anything other than empty phenomena. He writes about the relative status of women and men:

> Why should men be higher? Space is space, the four elements are the four elements, the five aggregates are the five aggregates, and women are also like this. As regards attainment of the truth, both [men and women] attain the truth, and we should just profoundly revere every single person who has attained the Dharma. Do not discuss man and woman. This is one of Buddhism's finest Dharma-standards.

Regarding the association of women solely with sex and sexual desire, Dōgen says:

> Furthermore, nowadays extremely stupid people look at women without having corrected the prejudice that women are objects of sexual greed. Disciples of the Buddha must not be like this. If whatever may become the object of sexual greed is to be hated, do not all men deserve to be hated too?[152]

With the statement, "whatever may become the object of sexual greed is to be hated," Dōgen appears to be referring to the practice of developing repugnance for the female form in order to reduce sexual desire. In her study of female images in Indian Buddhist literature, Liz Wilson describes how consideration of the female body and "disgust-inspiring representations of women" were used in Indian Buddhism to reduce sexual desire in male monastics. She points out that the reverse was rarely true.[153] Setting aside the question of whether or not such practices constitute a "hatred" of women, Dōgen's point is that if one category of humans is to be regarded as repugnant, then that view must also pertain to any category of human beings.

Both of Dōgen's statements point back to the mutable, dependently arisen nature of all characteristics. Regarding characteristics in this way has implications both for women's access to the teachings and how their spiritual potential is evaluated. Dōgen is clear that not only are nuns (*bhikṣunīs*) and laywomen fully capable of realizing Buddha's Way, but also they should not be denied access to the teachings. He states in *Raihai tokuzui* that a practice place that refuses to admit women is a "particularly laughable institution" that does not accord with Buddha's teaching. To bar women from the teachings, he says, is "utterly deranged" and practiced only by "very stupid fools." He goes on to say that many nuns have great realization. In fact, the exclusion of women, when it is understood that they are capable of full realization, is nonsensical.

> When a woman has [thus] already become buddha, is there anything in all directions that she cannot perfectly realize? Who could aim to bar her from passing? She already has virtue that widely illuminates the ten directions; what meaning can a boundary have?[154]

This does not mean that Dōgen or any of his followers perfectly followed this teaching. This was a highly contested issue even in Dōgen's day. However, these statements clearly outline a perspective that uses the teachings to support the equality of women as human beings fully able to realize and express the Buddha Way. Cultural manifestations of sexism have been and remain commonplace, but there is also a strong thread of affirmation of women as practitioners and teachers. Emptiness teachings undercut any possibility of formulating or attributing inferior status to women. This has made it possible for women of deep realization to emerge throughout the history of Sōtō Zen, and it also offers encouragement to contemporary women practitioners.[155]

Neither does this deny that women and men differ, at times, in their experience or practice. The immense impact of culture on the construction of the self and the way it has been experienced is well documented.[156] This cultural influence is carried over into the way in which the Buddhist teachings are heard and engaged.

For example, Anne Klein writes that in her experience, women are "the ones most powerfully and adversely affected" by the misinterpretation of the teaching of no-self as meaning that either no self exists or, if it does, that it is "not worth attending to."[157] Christina Feldman, a contemporary Theravādin teacher, states that the teachings of no-self may evoke for women their "greatest fears of invisibility."[158] While this also may be true for men, it is often helpful to note the effect gender has on our perceptions of ourselves and of others, and on the way the teachings are encountered.

When the practitioner is enjoined, in Sōtō Zen practice, to "study the self," the self that she studies may very well influence her experience of the practice. Configurations of the self impact the way in which the teachings are heard, as well as they way they can be most effectively expressed. Gender is part of the shaping of the self, and therefore it can also influence the shape of one's subsequent experience of Buddhist practice. While it is a characteristic empty of inherent existence, it nonetheless holds a powerful sway over the experience of those for whom it is a factor—that is, for all of us. Because of this, gender must be taken into account in understanding how Sōtō Zen functions in the lives of its practitioners. Extending this examination to other categories and constructions applied to persons, such as ethnicity, race, physical ability, economic status, etc., allows us to consider the ways in which these constructions are both empty of inherent existence and relevant to the lived experience of Zen practitioners.

Conclusion

Sōtō Zen practice asks the practitioner to enter into a moment-by-moment experience where habitual attitudes and assumptions dissolve and a shift is made from a way of life centered on the perception of the self as a separate entity to one grounded in a realization of interdependent reality. The journey is not one of "carrying the self forward" toward a happier, more peaceful existence, but of allowing life itself, in all its complexity, to unfold. In doing so, the self, as it is known and clung to, opens to the possibility of identification with all of life. According to the teachings of Sōtō Zen, making the shift from basing one's life, perceptions, attitudes, emotions, and activities on and in the mistaken notion of a separate self to a subjective experince arising from interdependent reality is the action that accompanies and allows for the realization, however fleeting, that the self is not different from all beings. This is the expression of faith, a moment when "the entire body becomes faith itself."[159] Such a moment is understood as a moment of liberation.

Using the outline of Sōtō Zen presented above, we can say that this shift is the practice realization of the teachings of emptiness and no-self.

It is situated at the intersection of the two truths as well as the point at which the reality of form and emptiness is lived out. It is the expression of buddha-nature and the manifestation of thusness. It is the antidote to nihilistic tendencies and it undercuts essentialism. It is the "whole being of emptiness leaping out of itself (*konshin-choshutsu*)."[160] By making this shift, the bodhisattva vow is embodied, true compassion is present, and it becomes possible to act skillfully, in concert with others, to benefit all beings. In fact, the shift itself is understood as an expression of all beings, all being, freeing itself—expressing realization.

As we have seen in the discussion of Sōtō Zen practice, though this activity, this expression of practice realization, is rooted in zazen it is not limited to zazen. According to Sōtō Zen, all activities, from those deemed "religious" (zazen, bowing, offering incense) to those most often regarded as mundane (cleaning the floor, preparing a meal), are considered to be the Buddha Way—they are, in fact, Buddha's activity. Zazen (*shikantaza*) is the center of the practice mandala, the anchor. Without it, the human tendency to view the world as self and other, this and that, more easily reasserts itself. Zazen also expresses the teachings of emptiness and no-self directly. It is the activity, or nonactivity, that most easily allows for an experience of vital interdependency. In this way, zazen sits zazen and the practitioner realizes that she is life itself.

This spirit of practice is manifested in daily activities—at work, in relationship with others, and in engaging with the physical objects of the world. Guided by the precepts and understanding that "even one leaf of green" is Buddha, the practitioner responds, in concert with others, to skillfully meet the needs of any given situation. In ritual activities practitioners participate through forms, such as bowing, in manifesting the heart of the teachings. Each moment, each circumstance, each activity, allows the practitioner to make the shift from a self-centered experience of the world to full participation in reality, thereby expressing Buddha's Way.

The question that presents itself is: How does this shift occur? How is the practitioner able to let go of her usual notions and experience herself as the living reality of the moment? From the point of view of the deluded self, the practitioner might ask, "How do I get there from here?" But asking this question in this way repeats the pattern of "carrying the self forward" that Dōgen identifies with delusion. Instead, we can investigate the factors that support and encourage the development of a context in which the self that clings to the notion of permanence and separateness is freed from its habitual identifications, and thereby allows a subjective experience embedded in the reality of "just this" to emerge.

Again, it is crucial to note that the idea is not for the practitioner to set up an adversarial relationship between the "deluded" self and experience, much less to attempt to eradicate the creative, responsive, unique individual that arises from interdependent reality. Setting up such an opposition to the deluded self or attempting to eliminate it is simply another manifestation of dualistic thinking. This does not mean that the practitioner should not make vigorous efforts to undermine the domination of delusive thinking and identification with an imagined separate self. Rather, one's efforts, if they accord with the teachings that wisdom and compassion are inseparable, are not based in aggression and the continued hegemony of dualistic thinking.

For the Sōtō Zen practitioner, taking up the practice, living through the questions and paradoxes of a life grounded in the teachings, is the field in which the self is transformed. It requires the willingness to engage with all aspects of human experience, including some degree of physical as well as mental and/or emotional pain and suffering. The experiences that can be most challenging, as well as most liberating, are those that do exactly what the practitioner set out to do—transform the basis of his experience of the world, the self.

We return again to the question: What factors support this field of practice? How is it possible to articulate and address the factors that inhibit it? What kind of understanding can we bring to them? Using these questions and this perspective as the framework for our inquiry, in the next chapter I will introduce and outline psychoanalytic concepts that can help illuminate the experience of the individual practitioner.

Chapter 3

Including the Psychoanalytic Perspective: Self-Experience in a Sōtō Zen Context

The process of letting go of the self, as it is habitually known, and cultivating a willingness to allow life to live itself lies at the heart of Sōtō Zen practice. This process leads the practitioner to the edge of the known and beyond. It requires a willingness to allow the ground upon which one has relied to disappear beneath one's feet, and it may be experienced by the known self as a request to participate in its own demise. Yet it is grounded in and expressive of a trust not only in the self and the practice of Sōtō Zen, but in life itself.

From the perspective of Sōtō Zen Buddhism, releasing this hold on the self—a self that one has tenaciously guarded and believed in—is a necessary and radical event that is liberating, and it can also evoke all manner of responses. This is where the investigation of human experience that has occurred in what is generally termed Western psychology can be of service. Western psychology, in particular contemporary self psychology and intersubjective theory, describes the self and the human experience of subjectivity in a way that can be useful, I believe, in articulating important aspects of the personal psychological experience of a Sōtō Zen practitioner. These approaches can also give us language to describe how to best support and encourage practitioners. Specifically, they can help build an understanding of those factors that support or inhibit the shift from a belief in, and identification with, the deluded self, and those that lead to a subjectivity based in dependent co-arising. I will follow two primary and interrelated threads in my discussion of Western psychological principles and their relationship to Sōtō Zen practice: the development and experience of the self, and the development and experience of trust.

The basis of Sōtō Zen practice is the capacity to simply be present in this moment, allowing for the possibility that this is Buddha. The ability to be present, in turn, depends upon one's capacity for trust. Trust, in this context, is not trusting in a particular person or a particular outcome, but the ability to enter fully into the experience of this moment with openness, to allow oneself to *become* this moment. This capacity, this trust, is completely intertwined with, informs, and is informed by the process by which the self is developed, sustained, and transformed. With this basis of trust, the practitioner is able and willing to allow a profound shift in subjective experience that entails relinquishment of the known self. Thus, the two threads of trust and the self are deeply interrelated. In the following sections I will discuss how an exploration of these two threads, using concepts borrowed from psychoanalytic psychology, can aid us in understanding factors that support Sōtō Zen practice. In order to provide a foundation for this understanding, I will first introduce these concepts and demonstrate their applicability to a Sōtō Zen context.

Western psychology, though not as ancient or as culturally diverse a tradition as Buddhism, is nevertheless filled with complexity and contradictions. The work of Heinz Kohut and developments in the intersubjective theory that evolved from it, as well as ideas put forth by Erik Erikson on basic trust and its development and by D. W. Winnicott on early relational life, all have particular relevance to my discussion. I have focused on these theorists because the conceptualization of the self and self-experience they present is fundamentally compatible with the fluid interdependent understanding of the self found in Buddhism.

Terms

It is useful to clarify the terms I will be using with regard to the experience of the self and subjectivity as I weave psychoanalytic concepts into a discussion of the self and how it is transformed in Sōtō Zen practice. Self, no-self, subjectivity, personality, person, individual, agency, known self, deluded self, true self, authentic self—all these and other terms have been and are used in Buddhist writings in the attempt to describe individual experience as it evolves and is impacted by Buddhist practice. As I discussed above in the section on self and no-self, there can be a great deal of confusion about these terms as they appear in Zen literature. Confusion can increase exponentially when we include the entirely different vocabulary of Western psychology.

For this reason, it is essential to clearly state the Buddhist and Western psychological terms I will be using and what I mean by them. From a Buddhist perspective, the terms I have employed were not chosen because I believe that they point to some essential truth, and neither do they express perfectly the complexity, ambiguity, and paradoxical nature of human experience. I have used these terms because they help to keep reification and misunderstanding to a minimum, without losing the sense of vitality and engagement that arises when the grasp of the deluded self is relaxed or relinquished. I ask the reader to keep in mind the fact that these terms, as all others, are empty of essential nature and are merely attempts at expressing a reality not easily corralled or pointed to by words. As Anne Klein writes, "Emptiness cannot be communicated fully in language, but neither can ordinary things."[1]

I have chosen to retain the word "self" as a means of indicating the moment-by-moment reality of a subjectivity based in dependent co-arising, because the term "no-self" alone can be easily misinterpreted to mean either the absence of subjectivity or a kind of passive consciousness acted upon by a supposed separate reality. The term "self" also, I believe accurately, reflects the fact the there is a structure present in subjectivity, albeit a fluid dependently arisen one. I will qualify the term "self" in ways that will indicate what experience of subjectivity I am trying to articulate. For example, a deluded self, or as Shunryu Suzuki called it, the "small self," is one in which dualistic sensibilities prevail and form the basis of perception and action. The terms "authentic self" or "true self" used by Francis Cook and others, though susceptible to reification, convey the vitality and authenticity that occurs when these dualistic notions do not dominate.

Anne Klein uses the term "empty subject" to indicate the person whose subjectivity is "complete and at rest"[2] in the experience of emptiness. The term "subjectivity" conveys a sense of movement and process that is less apparent in the term "self." In addition, subjectivity can be used to indicate the ongoing sense of coherent awareness that is an essential aspect of each individual's life. I will also use the term "no-self." The very fact that this is a statement of negation points out an important element in the shift from a self-centered experience of the world to one based in moment-by-moment reality—that is, the absence of that very self-centeredness.

The terms that I have chosen to bring into this discussion from self psychology and intersubjective theory, such as "self," "selfobject," and "subjectivity," overlap and interact with the Buddhist terms. Even without a background in the extensive history of their place in psychoanalytic literature, the potential subtleties of each term are discernible. Because of this they will be defined as they are introduced.

Concepts in Psychoanalytic Psychology

The interplay of author and reader, and author and author, is a complex one. As Judith Guss Teicholz points out in her book on Kohut, Loewald, and postmodern psychoanalytic theory, within this interplay opportunities for misunderstanding and/or misinterpretation are endless and, perhaps to some extent, inevitable.[3] This is particularly true when an author's work is moved from its original context to another and attempts are made to extend its meaning. Great care must be taken to preserve the integrity of the author's intention, while at the same time taking the risk of making new connections. My use of the work of Heinz Kohut and the intersubjective writings of Robert D. Stolorow and others, as well as Erik Erikson and D. W. Winnicott, within the context of Sōtō Zen practice requires me to take such care and run this risk. Teicholz discusses the possibility of misunderstanding or misinterpreting living authors or those who, as she writes, "are no longer here to correct my unintentional misrepresentations." She goes on to say:

> I will inevitably be discussing my Kohut, my Loewald, and my postmoderns. I therefore apologize, in advance to readers and writers alike, for what may be the inevitable subversion of the work of others in the service of my own agenda. . . . I trust that my respect and admiration [for these authors] will be conveyed, even as I unavoidably remove their words from their own contexts and place them in mine.[4]

The spirit in which I approach and use the concepts I am introducing from psychoanalytic theory is one of respectful borrowing, as expressed by Teicholz above. Also, according to Sōtō Zen teachings, concepts are constructions, forms. I hope I have conveyed, in my discussion of Sōtō Zen practice, the fact that though they are not immutable, forms are to be treated with respect. My hope is that those who regard these forms with respect, even reverence, will not find fault in my handling of them.

The theorists and theories I am using evolved over time and contain many complex ideas. It is not my aim, and beyond the scope of this book, to discuss this rich and nuanced history in detail. Rather, my aim is to avail myself of useful terms that allow for an exploration of the experience of the Sōtō Zen practitioner. I have chosen, therefore, to bring in only those concepts that are directly relevant to the discussion at hand.

Neither is it my aim to integrate or create a synthesis of Sōtō Zen and Western psychology (nor to bring Buddhism to bear on the practice of psychotherapy). I have selected concepts and ideas that I believe will support our understanding of key elements in Sōtō Zen practice. Coming from the perspective of contemplative psychology and a basis in Sōtō Zen, my intention is to draw from these theories the concepts and articulations of human experience that can help illuminate the experience of the Zen practitioner as she encounters and grapples with the teachings and the lived experience of practice.

This brings in another important element. Like Judith Teicholz, I am placing aspects of these theories in a new context. But this context, it must be understood, is not a pattern of ideas and teachings that aim at describing reality. (This is not to suggest that psychoanalytic authors believe they are describing objective reality either.) To be sure, Buddhist conceptual and philosophical systems exist, and I have and will continue to draw on them repeatedly. But the experiential environment, the basis of Sōtō Zen practice, is not limited to delineated concepts—not even concepts held in a "postmodern" relative reality. It is a world of paradox that asks the practitioner to transform the basis on and through which he experiences the world. Conceptual schema have a respected role to play and are in no way dishonored; however, it is important to remember that Sōtō Zen is a religious system with a soteriological aim and basis, not an explanation of reality.

In building a bridge between psychoanalytic writings and theories and Buddhism, it is interesting to note that psychoanalysis itself has proven to be a mutable, evolving process. In regard to the history of psychoanalytic thought and its relationship to postmodern deconstruction, Teicholz states that psychoanalysis "always held within itself the inevitability of its own destruction."[5] That is, any attempts to freeze or codify a particular understanding of the human psyche and the human experience has inevitably been undermined by the very process of reflection that is the hallmark of psychoanalysis.

This brings up a point of contact between the work of Heinz Kohut and Sōtō Zen Buddhist teachings and practice—the question of how categorizations of reality are regarded. He writes:

> The conceptual categories of any classificatory system become a hindrance rather than a help when . . . they become concrete entities, demanding that we force the data we observe into the rubric of an unalterable scheme. My own attitude toward the classifications I have proposed has always been that they are temporary, changeable, improvable—in short, that they will cease to be useful if we are unwilling to alter them in order to accommodate new insights or facts.[6]

Kohut also cautions that all theories must remain our "helpmate[s] . . . not our masters."[7]

Ernest Wolf, perhaps the most humane interpreter of self psychology, writes:

> Generally speaking, I cannot define clearly and precisely the concepts and terms that I am using. Clarity of definition must emerge out of usage. . . . The dearth of fixed definitions of the verbal kind deters concepts from becoming fixed dogma.[8]

This understanding of the fluidity of concepts not only allows for an evolving understanding of the concepts and language within the psychoanalytic system, but is also compatible with the Buddhist attitude toward conceptual constructs: that they are empty of inherent existence. It helps considerably in describing an intersection of these two disciplines that both regard conceptual understandings as "helpmates" and not ends in themselves. In this way, to use an oft-quoted Zen analogy, if we do not mistake the finger pointing to the moon for the moon itself, we can more easily remember that this discussion is meant to point out possibilities, not describe facts.

It is possible for Wolf to make the statement that these terms "point metaphorically and evocatively to psychological experiences by use of connotation and analogy" instead of "describing" an objective reality, because both he and Kohut share an understanding of "reality" and "truth" that is complex and multidimensional.[9] Kohut writes that "[o]bjective reality is always subjective," and even goes so far as to say that "[r]eality, as I have often stressed before, is in essence unknowable."[10] Wolf echoes this:

> Because there seems to be no absolute reality, but as many realities as there are observers observing from various locations in psychic space and time, we must choose and define our "reality. . . . " Truth is not absolute but relative to the context in which it is experienced.[11]

The intersubjective theorists describe an "intersubjective reality"[12] created by the interface of two subjective realities. This intersubjective reality, they point out, has no set objective correlate; it is the dynamic experience that emerges out of a relational event.

Regarding how conceptual schemata are to be used and understood, there is clearly a useful compatibility between Buddhist and psychoanalytic teaching. It is important to point out, however, that, according to Buddhist teaching, reality is indeed "knowable." To understand this, we must examine what is meant by knowledge in this context, for this is not a type of knowledge, or realization, that falls within our usual categories of subject and object.

As described above, emptiness of inherent existence is understood to be the way things are, including the way we are. Because it is the nature of dependently co-arisen reality, not a separate phenomenon that arises and passes away, emptiness is said to be unconditioned, an absolute reality. Anne Klein writes, "The inexpressible unconditioned emptiness is not nonexistent."[13] Thinking of emptiness as a verb as opposed to a noun can be helpful in making this distinction, as long as we do not then reify it.

As Klein points out, "the possibility of experiencing the unconditioned realm of emptiness is central to Buddhist theory and practice." Describing the quality of this knowing, she continues:

> When one fully knows the absence [of inherent existence] that is emptiness, one knows it with one's full, speechless attention. . . . When emptiness is known fully and directly (these terms are synonymous in the Buddhist context), the relationship of mind to emptiness is said in Geluk texts to be like "fresh water mixed with fresh water."[14]

Thus, in Buddhist teachings, there is indeed an absolute reality, it is possible to know this reality, and this knowing is understood to be liberating. However, knowing or realizing emptiness is knowing a reality that is not separate from the subject who knows it. It is fresh water "knowing" fresh water, absolute knowledge of the empty nature of reality.

In regard to its relationship to contemporary philosophical and psychological understandings of subjective reality, Klein writes:

> By knowing emptiness, Tibetan and other Buddhist traditions maintain, the subject engages in its most quintessential quality, the one that makes all others possible. . . . The subtle knowledge of emptiness is thus the innermost and most "personal" experience possible; in another sense, however, because all emptinesses are the same, it is a universal experience. This kind of "personal" clearly cannot be conflated with the sense of particular personal and interpersonal history so important in the contemporary [W]est. . . . [T]he experience of emptiness entails a different order of interiority then the textual, content-laden localization and particularized subjectivity associated with contemporary theory and modern psychologizing.[15]

I take the time to explore the connection and difference between these two perspectives because it is important in building a basis for using psychoanalytic language and concepts in the context of Sōtō Zen. Though there are significant differences, as outlined above, there are also striking similarities in the way that these concepts may be understood as helpmates for understanding. An open attitude toward our habitual conceptual understanding of reality invites a creative and flexible use of any theories that are developed. Theories, ideas, and concepts are all important elements in the landscape of our lives. As helpmates, they can prod and guide our questioning and our practice. They can exist in a dynamic relationship with our moment-by-moment experience. However, a fundamental premise of this work is that it is in coming to fully experience—that is, trust—the ongoing process of our life, rather than our ideas about it, that allows for our full participation in and, it is hoped, realization of Zen practice.

In the remainder of this section I will address psychoanalytic perspectives on the two interconnected threads of self-experience and development, and the experience and role of trust, using concepts from the work of Heinz Kohut and other self psychology and intersubjective theorists, as well as Erik Erikson and D. W. Winnicott. To begin, I will discuss basic self-psychological and intersubjective concepts regarding the development of the self and place them in the context of Sōtō Zen practice. I will then discuss the role of trust in the development and transformation of subjective experience. My aim is to build an understanding of the self and the experience of trust that can be used to help identify the factors that support the shift in subjective experience that lies at the root of Sōtō Zen practice. I seek to illuminte the way in which a shift is made, or blocked, from identification with a self experienced as separate and in relation to an objective reality, to a subjective experience embedded in and responsive with that reality.

The Self

The self, as it is understood and described in psychoanalytic self psychology and the theories that evolved from it, can be thought to have three key aspects. First, the self is understood to be a theoretical construct, not an objectively real immutable entity. Second, this construct is thought of as a structure with enduring patterns that deeply influence our perceptions and actions. Third, the self exits as a distinct entity but it is understood as emerging from, dependent upon, and completely embedded within a relational matrix. Discussing each these three characteristics and how they relate to Sōtō Zen teaching creates a basis for the later use of self-psychoanalytic language and concepts, and weaves together a foundation that supports the introduction of these concepts into a discussion of Sōtō Zen life.

Self as Construct

Self psychologists are careful to point out that the self they are describing is a theoretical construct, a conceptual understanding of a subjective experience inferred from observation—not an objectively real entity. This is an important meeting point for Buddhism and self psychology theory. Heinz Kohut tells us that his theory "never assigns an inflexible meaning to the term self, it never explains how the essence of the self should be defined." Rather,

> The self is . . . like all reality—physical reality (the data about the world perceived by our senses) or psychological reality (the data about the world perceived via introspection and empathy)—not knowable in its essence. . . . Demands for an exact definition of the nature of the self disregard the fact that "the self" is not a concept of an abstract science, but a generalization derived from . . . inner experiences to which we later refer as "I" is gradually established and we can observe certain characteristic vicissitudes of this experience. We can describe the various cohesive forms in which the self appears. . . . We can do all that, but we will still not know the essence of the self as differentiated from its manifestations.[16]

At the same time, this construct is understood as a valid means of articulating a crucial aspect of subjective experience. The term "self," though not assumed to refer to an essence, is understood as a means of describing inner experience and as such has its uses. Wolf writes, "I of course realize the metaphorical nature of the word 'self'. . . . Yet it is extremely useful to speak in similes and analogies and probably unavoidable."[17] He later adds:

> Such definitions by usage allow one to teach and otherwise communicate what one means. But it is well to keep in mind that such definitions by usage say nothing about the essential nature of a thing.[18]

Wolf goes on to draw an interesting parallel when he states that the assumption that a self exists is "roughly on the same theoretical level as the inference, from all kinds of observations, of the existence of electrons."[19] That is, it is a conjecture based on careful observation that allows us to come to useful understandings of the nature of our world and our experience. This parallel of self and electron is an apt one. The example of the electron not only illustrates how a theoretical entity is inferred from observation but also provides us with an example of a construct that does not remain in neat, logical boundaries. The electron is said to be both wave and particle, form or structure, and process or activity. Its identity at any given moment depends on the question the observer wishes to answer through observation. Looking for location, one finds a particle; looking for behavior, one finds a wave. Neither descriptor is adequate in and of itself, and taken together they form a contradiction. In the same way, the self can be described as both a structure and as an evolving process. Keeping this in mind, we can delineate the structure of the self without falling into the belief that it can be ultimately defined.

From a Buddhist perspective, this attitude neither reifies not denies the self, and aligns with the treatment of concepts and definitions based in the idea of skillful means and the teachings of relative and absolute truths. It allows us to construct useful ideas that reflect our experience but prevents us from believing that these concepts have the status of ultimate truth. This gives us a way of grappling with what we mean by "self" as well as how it develops, is maintained, and transformed. It is a means by which we can shed light on who we experience ourselves to be and how we think we got to be that way, which can support the effort to bring greater insight to the actual experience of practicing Sōtō Zen.

Self-structure

Regarding the self as structure, Ernest Wolf writes that by attending to our everyday experience we can infer that "Apparently, the human tendency to organize experience yields psychological structures that manifest in the subjective experience of things 'making sense.'" This inferred "psychological organization that gives rise to [one's] self experience"[20] is given the label "self" and regarded as an enduring pattern of organizational principles present throughout life.

The self is regarded as a structure that organizes perception into meaningful conceptual schema. This structure is thought to have enduring patterns but also to be capable of change. In fact, change is a part of the very nature of the self because, as we will see, it is a structure that is never separate from the relational environment that shapes it. Wolf writes:

> Metaphorically we think of the self as a structure because, like a structure, the self changes only very slowly. Like all structures, we can think of the self as made of parts that either fit together, as it were, as if well glued, or can fall apart easily. Therefore . . . we speak sometimes of a self that is cohesive, which means put together well, and other times of a self that is fragile and easily fragments.[21]

This concept of self-structure is a metaphor that gives us a useful way of describing the experience of self. Using this metaphor it is possible to describe the self as cohesive, robust, and flexible, or as fragile and fragmented. Setting aside, for the moment, what constitutes a cohesive self (one that is coherent, that "sticks together") or a fragile self (one that can more easily fragment), we can see that these graphic images provide us with a means to communicate about dimensions of our human life. This language of metaphor is not a description of fact, but it is useful for an exploration of the self and self-experience.

The use of metaphor also allows us to speak directly about the existence of the self. As Wolf notes: "I am a person, an individual. I think. I feel, I experience."[22] Such a statement, by its very decisiveness, points out what, from a Sōtō Zen Buddhist perspective, could be termed the reality of "form." Just as the reminder that holding conceptual constructs lightly is essential for a balanced exploration of the experience of self, so too is a clear statement of the self's existence. Without this clear statement we can be left with only amorphous ideas about self-experience that do not reflect the actual experience of most people.

Again, from a Buddhist perspective and in the language of the *Heart Sūtra*, we are instructed to remember not only that "form is emptiness" but also that "emptiness is form." Focusing exclusively on the fluid nature of any concept of self without affirming an articulation of its existence is a misunderstanding of the teaching of emptiness that has a definite nihilistic flavor.

A vigorous affirmation of the concept of the structure of a self, in a Buddhist context, does not contradict its inherently empty nature. Notice that this concept of self does not refer to an absolute or permanent structure or agent. Using this definition, we can regard the self as a necessary structure that allows us to organize our experience and respond to/with the world. We can regard it as analogous to other forms, which are equally empty of inherent existence, that function in our lives—a chair, a road, a song. Understanding a chair as empty of inherent existence does not keep us from sitting in it. These forms are understood to be the shape of the way things are. In this way, we can say that the self has its own integrity—it is a form among other forms—and therefore, from a Sōtō Zen perspective, it can be regarded, explored, and cared for as one would any form—that is, respectfully.

Nor does the notion of the self as a structure contradict an understanding of the self, and all phenomena, as impermanent. Instead, stating that the self, as an organizing structure, exists and that it has no status as a permanent objective entity allows us to take up a conceptual formulation of the self and use it with full confidence and a balanced perspective.

Relational Self and Selfobjects

Perhaps the most distinctive aspect of the concept of the self in self psychology and later intersubjective theories, and the most important one in regard to this study, is the understanding that the self emerges from and is completely embedded in a relational matrix.[23] In exploring this third aspect, we come to a more thorough understanding of the nature of the structure of the self and its relational reality. Wolf writes:

> The most fundamental finding of self psychology is that the emergence of the self requires more than the inborn tendency to organize experience. Also required is the presence of others, technically designated objects, who provide certain types of experiences that will evoke the emergence and maintenance of the self. The perhaps awkward term for these is selfobject experiences, usually abbreviated selfobjects.[24]

This "finding" of self psychology was (and is) supported by research with infants, most notably the work of Daniel N. Stern.[25] In *The Interpersonal World of the Infant,* Stern brought a wealth of empirical research data, as well as key extrapolations from it, into the discussion of the nature of the self. Though not a self psychologist, Stern's work supports the idea of a self that emerges from relational life. He noted that infants appear to actively participate, shape, and be shaped by their environment—that the developmental progression of an infant is not a passive process but a dynamic interplay of mutually responsive participants.

According to Stern, it is through this interplay that a sense of self comes into being. He proposed that in the seventh to ninth months the infant realizes that "he or she has a mind and that other people have minds as well" and that "inner subjective experiences . . . are potentially sharable with someone else."[26] The infant's awareness and the responsive sharing with the relational environment that accompanies it—what Kohut calls the "matrix of mutual empathy"[27]—is the basis of self-formation and cannot be separated from the self itself.[28]

Self psychology authors take pains to point out that the term selfobject refers to a relational event, not a particular person. Kohut states that "the matrix of selfobjects" and the "self-selfobject relationship"[29] refer to an inner experience and a psychological reality. Wolf writes:

> Precisely defined, a selfobject is neither a self nor an object, but the subjective aspect of a self-sustaining function performed by a relationship of self to objects who by their presence or activity evoke and maintain the self and the experience of selfhood.[30]

Judith Guss Teicholz reminds us that

> the unhyphenated compound noun selfobject denotes a process of self-development in which equal weight is given to the inseparable contributions of self and object.[31]

It is in this relational milieu, what Wolf calls a "selfobject ambience consisting of a net of selfobject relationships,"[32] that the self takes shape. As selfobject needs are met and these experiences are incorporated into the growing sense of what it means to be alive, what it means to be human, and what can be expected in relationship—that is, into a (structural) means of organizing perceptions and experiences—the sense of self emerges in its own unique form. Wolf writes that "[t]he presence of the selfobject, when it is functioning appropriately, evokes and maintains the self and its concomitant sense of selfhood."[33]

Psychologists Robert D. Stolorow, Bernard Brandchaft, and George E. Atwood emphasize the relational nature of the self in their intersubjective theory.[34] They explicitly draw attention to the subjectivity of persons in relationship and endeavor to undercut any tendency to reify the self.[35] Stolorow and Atwood assert that a selfobject relationship is not a relationship between subject and object but between subject and subject in a "psychological field formed by interacting worlds of experience at whatever developmental level these worlds are organized." That is, every stage and aspect of the development of the self is dependent on the relational environment, "even the sense of distinctiveness, uniqueness and personal agency."[36] Teicholz notes that that for the intersubjective theorists, "intersubjectivity is not a developmental achievement but an unavoidable fact of human life and relationships."[37] This intersubjective field is made up of an individual's "inner experience," which is embedded "with other such worlds in a continual flow or reciprocal mutual influence,"[38] and this reciprocal influence is between two subjectivities.

This relational (selfobject) milieu is, according to self psychology, not only necessary for the formation of the self but also for its continued maintenance and health. According to this theory, the self cannot be considered outside of its relational environment. Wolf writes that a self psychological perspective assumes that "a psychological structure, my self, is a part of a psychological system or organization which gives rise to my experiences." He later posits that this assumption

> strikes deeply at our politico-religious value system in which the self-made individual is the ideal . . . [and reflects] a deeper appreciation of our inescapable embeddedness in our environment.[39]

He also notes:

> The observation that the self cannot exist for long in a psychological vacuum is a finding that is not easily accepted. The very emergence and maintenance of the self as a psychological structure depends upon the continuing presence of an evoking-sustaining-responding matrix of selfobject experiences. This discovery heralds the end of another cherished illusion of Western man, namely the illusory goal of independence, self sufficiency, and free autonomy.[40]

Stolorow and Atwood call this illusion "the myth of the isolated mind" and define it as a "central myth" in Western culture, resulting in an experience of alienation.[41] From a Sōtō Zen Buddhist perspective, this sense of alienation can be understood as a description of the subjective experience of samsara, the world of delusion—a world in which we cling to the deluded notion that we are essentially separate from life itself.[42] It is interesting to read Stolorow and Atwood on the subject of alienation from this perspective. They say that "reifications of various dimensions of subjectivity" lead to the belief that the mind is a separate entity, a "thing among things."

> Invariably associated with the image of the mind is that of an external reality or world upon which the mind-entity is presumed to look. Here we encounter a reification, in this case one involving the experience of the world as real and existing separately from the self. . . . Within the myth of the isolated mind, this world is viewed as having a definitive existence of its own; its experienced substantiality thereby becomes transformed into a metaphysical absolute. . . . This stands in contrast to the subjective sense that there is an enduring and substantial world of reality separate from the self.[43]

Again, from a Buddhist perspective, we can see this as an articulation of the way in which an inherently relational self (a self that is empty of inherent existence and is dependently co-arisen) can mistake its actual condition of embeddedness for that of having a separate existence, which in turn gives rise to a dualistic experience of the world. This dualistic experience of the world stands in contrast to an experience where rigid distinctions between subject and object no longer apply. If relationality is truly the substance of the self, then, from a Sōtō Zen perspective, the possibility exits for a person to experience subjectivity grounded in relationality instead of alienation. Relational subjectivity is not without structure or organization, it is simply an organization of relationality rather than of objectification.

I am not attempting here to equate the perspective of Stolorow and Atwood, or other self and intersubjective theorists, with that of Sōtō Zen Buddhism. Rather, I am pointing out a shared understanding of relationality as the basis of the self. From this point of view, we can hear the resonance between a Buddhist understanding of the nature of the self and, as Teicholz writes, "Kohut's conception of a self that both achieves and repeatedly dissolves its autonomy through immersion in a self-object matrix."[44]

Returning to the three elements used to describe the self in self psychology outlined above—the self is a theoretical construct, that construct is understood to have a structure, and that structure is never separate from a relational matrix—we find interesting parallels between self psychology and Buddhist teachings. First, in both approaches, the term "self" is used as a provisional means by which subjective experience can be described; it is not seen as an immutable entity with a reality of its own. Second, in self psychology the self is understood to have a structure with enduring, but not permanent, patterns that impact our perceptions and our experience. From a Buddhist perspective, our subjective experience and our actions are also understood to be deeply impacted by habitual patterns of perception and organization of experience. Third, self psychology describes a self that develops from and is dependent upon selfobject relationships. There is no self that can be conceived of as outside of relationship. This accords with the Buddhist teachings of no-self, in which subjective experience is understood to be a functional aspect of relational reality.

Self psychology and Buddhist teachings both assume a co-constituting relationship between self and object, and this dynamic responsive relationship cannot be thought of as separate from the self or its structure. There is a fundamental compatibility, then, between the self psychological understanding of the self as never separate from relationship, and the Buddhist understanding of the self as empty of inherent existence, both a part and an expression of a dependently co-arising reality.

Self-structure and Selfobject Relationships

A further understanding of human self-experience from a self psychological point of view, as well as how it can be used to articulate the experience of Sōtō Zen practice, comes with a deeper investigation of the development of selfobject relationships and self-structure. These principles and concepts are particularly relevant to developing an understanding of the way in which self-experience changes, evolves, and transforms in the context of Sōtō Zen Buddhist practice.

Selfobject relationships or functions constitute the basis of the self, contributing to the formation, maintenance, restoration, and growth of self-experience. They are the context in which the self is formed and on which it continues to rely. We can think of the self and selfobject relationships as a mutually influencing system that evolves over time.

In the early life of a child, selfobject responsiveness allows and supports the formation of self-structure. In addition, as this process develops, selfobject relationships themselves evolve. If the net of selfobject relationships meets the basic needs of the developing child, the form of adequate selfobject responsiveness will change. For example, in infancy and early childhood the actual physical presence of the caregiver is necessary in order for the child to experience the needed sense of connection. As these experiences are incorporated into the child's self and memory, the need for the physical presence of the caregiver diminishes and other kinds of supportive selfobject relationships evolve. Thus, the formation of the self is inextricably bound to the relational milieu in which it exists. The structure of the self is formed and develops in relationship, and the nature and quality of selfobject relationships also evolve.

In terms of the development of the self and selfobject relationships, Teicholz notes that once selfobject

> functioning has been adequately provided by the caretaking environment of a developing child, the child gradually takes over basic aspects of such functioning, so that earlier dependence on others for self-maintenance and enhancement is modified. As the developing individual increasingly achieves self-sustaining functions and structure in this way, she gradually gains the capacity to engage in mutually sustaining selfobject relationships with significant others. Thus, as development progresses, the need for selfobject sustenance is less absolute and less relentless (less archaic in Kohut's language) and is replaced by more mature and more reciprocal exchanges.[45]

She continues:

> In the course of normal development, the early demand for, or expectation of, immediate response and perfect attunement gives way to a tolerance for a greater degree of give and take, more mutuality in the provision of psychic sustenance, and an increased acceptance, or even embrace of, different needs, interests, and pursuits.[46]

Teicholz describes these early "archaic" selfobject relationships as ones in which "certain self-maintaining aspects of the object's psychological functioning" are experienced "as if they belonged to, or originated in, the subject not the object."[47] In other words, the other is experienced, at least in a transient way, as an extension of the self. As a consequence, if the selfobject experience does not follow according to the explicit needs of the self, it can be experienced as if a hand or a leg had a mind of its own. This is a relational experience, developmentally appropriate for an infant or a small child, who does not recognize the fact or subjectivity of the other. As Wolf notes, the term "infantile" is most often used to describe such selfobject relationships when they occur in early life. The term "archaic" is used when, due to early unmet needs, these selfobject relationships are experienced in adult life.[48]

As maturation of the self and selfobject relationships occur, through being responsively met, the way in which the so-called object is experienced changes. The need for specific and concrete selfobject relationships in which the other is experienced as an extension of the self shifts into a recognition that the other is, indeed, an other, and in the case of another being, a different subjectivity. Mutuality and reciprocity become fundamental aspects of self-experience and empathy toward others develops. In addition, there is a greater tolerance for those times in which selfobject needs are not met.

Wolf makes clear that it is not only the quality of the selfobject relationship that changes but also what can function as a selfobject.[49] The nature of what can effectively constitute a selfobject shifts and it becomes possible for selfobject needs to be met by a wider array of experiences. With maturation more symbolic selfobject relationships can come into play—for example, music or meaningful work—that also function to build, confirm, and sustain a sense of self. Thus, selfobjects are not limited to other subjective and conscious entities, as might be gathered by Stolorow and Atwood's discussion of intersubjectivity in their book *Context of Being*. In this sense, the term "selfobject" has greater applicability than the term "intersubjective," since it is inclusive of a wider array of relational experiences.

The sense of self that emerges in this process of development changes significantly. In early life, the formation of self-structure is deeply dependent on a narrow range of immediate, reliable, concrete, and effective selfobject relationships. The more mature self, though still embedded in and dependent on a relational matrix, has greater flexibility as well as inner and outer resources. This more mature self is marked not only by greater flexibility and mutuality in terms of selfobject relations but also by what, as noted above, Kohut terms "cohesion" and Teicholz terms "coherence."[50]

Cohesion can be thought of as an inner experience of continuity and reliability, a stable, consistent, and coherent sense of subjectivity. Wolf notes that "Apparently, it is a characteristic attribute of the human psyche to organize itself so that it experiences the 'I am I' as a unified and historically continuous self."[51]

Using this observation as a basis, Teicholz describes this quality of self-experience:

> The individual with a so-called sense of coherence can often bring to mind many different aspects of self, can prioritize them at a given moment or within a particular context, can feel the incompatibilities and discontinuities as well as some sense of sameness, continuity, or connection running through them all.[52]

With this cohesion of the self comes a sense of efficacy and that one's own experience has relevance. According to this understanding of self, unless one's early experience has been one of being affirmed by another, the structure of the self will be fragile and a sense of inner reliability will be absent or flawed. As Stolorow, Brandchaft, and Atwood state: "Essential to the structuralization of the self is the acquisition of a firm belief in the validity of one's own subjective experiences."[53] This "firm belief" does not imply rigid dogmatism but the ability to know one's own experience, to have a kind of faith in it, and to be able, to some extent, to express it with others.

The presence of cohesion also allows the self to be sustained under difficult circumstances. Teicholz writes:

> For Kohut, to have normal self structures meant simply to have reliable enough patterns of self experience: with such patterns, an individual would be able to experience a sense of well-being and to harness inborn potential into a richly expressive life. . . . Once established through (optimal) relational experience, these relatively stable internal phenomena or psychic structures enable individuals to weather storms of external fortune or misfortune in more intact states then might otherwise be possible.[54]

This cohesive self can be contrasted to the self that has not experienced the selfobject milieu necessary for full and healthy development. When the normal infantile/archaic selfobject needs of childhood are not adequately met, the self is unable to fully develop such psychic structures. In this case, the qualities that mark archaic selfobject relationships—concreteness, immediacy, narrowness, and an inability to recognize the other—will be retained in some form into adulthood. This is not a benign process but one that is often marked by painful and unfulfilling relationships with others.

A self that has not developed in an adequately responsive selfobject matrix is also marked by a limited and fragile sense of cohesion and continuity. If, as self psychologists suggest, we think of the self as a structure, then it is understandable that "we can speak sometimes of a self that is cohesive, which means put together well, and at other times, of a self that is fragile and easily fragments."[55] A structure that has a coherent and effective organization of experience, and therefore supports and affirms a cohesive sense of self, does not fully develop without selfobject relationships that reliably (not perfectly) meet the needs of the child. When these needs are inadequately met and a cohesive self structure has not developed, sturdiness and flexibility are absent; instead there is much greater vulnerability to distressing experiences of fragmentation.

As Wolf notes, it is important to acknowledge that everyone is subject to some degree of fragmentation under certain circumstances, and fragmentation does not necessarily imply that the self is subject to dissolution.[56] In this state,

> Aspects of one's self-experience seem no longer coordinated or fitting together. Metaphorically, one can conceptualize the structure of the self breaking up into its component fragments.[57]

These experiences include a sense of "lessened cohesion, more permeable boundaries, diminished energy and vitality." This sense of fragmentation can range from fleeting moments of discomfort to a profound sense of confusion and distress. As Wolf notes, these experiences can include a "[l]oss of . . . organization, that is, loss of the sense of selfhood, [that] can be the occasion for the greatest panic and horror." He also describes this experience as a loss of "orientation in space; instead of a meaningful and cohesive organized set of experiences, a self, it has become an incoherent and disorganized collection of experiences" often accompanied by "the terrifying certainty of imminent death."[58] Doris Brothers writes that such an experience can occasion a "nightmare world of self-fragmentation in which sanity, indeed the very continuity of existence, can no longer be taken for granted."[59]

Every human is capable of such experiences under sufficient stress, but they are more likely to arise in the absence of an adequately responsive selfobject milieu. This is particularly true for the developing child, according to Stolorow and Atwood, when there is active denial of the child's experience and needs, especially his affective experience and needs. But, as they put it, "Pain is not pathology."[60] In other words, it is not necessarily painful experiences that disrupt the maturation process but how such experiences are responded to. This is in line with Brothers' discussion of trauma. She notes that what makes an event traumatic (an event that overwhelms the capacity of a person to understand and integrate it) is tied directly to whether or not there is a selfobject milieu that responds empathetically and thereby helps to restore a sense of self-continuity and cohesion.[61] Without this selfobject responsiveness, a disruptive event cannot be integrated and the structure of the self is subsequently weakened.

Brothers puts forward the self psychological view that "the need to preserve a sense of self always assumes motivational priority in human life."[62] What is most crucial to us as human beings is the capacity to experience ourselves as competent organizational entities. The self, as Wolf notes, functions in such a way that "data are organized around a concept of the self in its imperative need to become and remain a cohesive structure that gives meaningful expression to itself."[63] This a crucial and immensely powerful aspect of self-experience tied directly to current and historical experiences of the selfobject milieu. As Wolf points out, the sense of impending death that is associated with profound experiences of fragmentation, that is, "the experience of a crumbing self is so unpleasant that people will do almost anything to escape the perceptions brought about by fragmentation."[64]

The affective qualities that accompany the sense that this organizational capacity may be compromised are fear and anxiety. This fear is what Kohut called "disintegration anxiety . . . the anticipation of the breakup of the self."[65] Kohut describes disintegration anxiety in this way:

> [These] horror experiences . . . relate to the loss of the selfobject without which the self cannot continue to exist, without which it either disintegrates or is changed so profoundly (ceasing to be a human self, we might say) that its altered state is equivalent to disintegration. It makes no difference whether we experience this fear as the permanent loss of the responses of all present and potential selfobjects . . . or whether we experience it as the irrevocable loss of the single archaic selfobject that had sustained our self before we knew of substitutes. . . . What is feared in both instances is the destruction of one's human self because of the unavailability of the psychological oxygen, the response of the empathic selfobject without which we cannot psychologically survive.[66]

Kohut posits a continuum of functioning in terms of psychological health (excluding more profound psychological disturbances, in which the structure of the self is so deeply compromised that it cannot be said to exist in functional terms). At the most painful and least functional end of the continuum, the sense of cohesion and continuity is limited and there is greater vulnerability to experiences of fragmentation, as well as ongoing attempts to contain and prevent disruptive experiences. With a more fragile self-structure the person will respond to disruptive experiences with a "temporary breakup, enfeeblement, or disharmony"[67] in the self.

Every person, under some conditions, is vulnerable to some degree of fragmentation. However, there is a greater vulnerability when the structure of the self has been compromised by traumatic events that "derive their lasting significance from the establishment of invariant and relentless principles of self organization" and reinforce a self-experience based in anxiety and fear of fragmentation. Stolorow and Atwood describe this process of reinforcement:

> Every experience of disappointment or limitation tends to confirm one or another of these principles. The impact of such experiences is not felt to be delimited and temporal, but global and eternal.[68]

They go on to say:

> Retraumatization later in life occurs when there is a close replication of the original trauma, a confirmation of the organizing principles that resulted from the original trauma, or a loss or disruption of a sustaining bond that has provided an alternative mode of organizing experience, without which the old invariant principles are brought back into the fore.[69]

If a person's early life was one in which selfobject needs were unmet or even actively denied, or if the person has sustained a traumatic blow to the self, the organizing principles of the self, the structure, is more vulnerable to fragmentation.

At the other end of the spectrum, the cohesive self, one with a coherent and effective structure, is more whole, "robust," and flexible. There is a greater openness to experience, a greater ability to grow from both positive and difficult experiences, and an increased ability to be creatively expressive in the world. This does not imply that such a person is immune to disruption or that the implied wholeness is without vulnerability, only that the vulnerability is "minimal."

Teicholz writes:

> Kohut spoke of a sense of coherence as an experience to strive for in health; an experiential quality that comes into being through relationships and that

> is furthered by the development and lived expression of talents and skills in a vitalizing selfobject milieu. This sense of coherence, argued Kohut, in turn makes possible greater mutuality in relationships, as well as the setting of goals, the pursuit of ambitions and striving toward ideals: what we might call love, work and transcendence. All these "achievements" Kohut attributed to a coherent and cohesive sense of selfhood and its structural coordinate, "the self."[70]

One important consequence of a cohesive self is that, as Teicholz notes, "the healthy individual can also surrender her sense of coherence in the pursuit of artistic creation or pleasure and reengage as needed."[71] Thus, structure does not imply immutable structure, and cohesion does not imply rigidity. When cohesion is present, the experience of inner fluidity is not greeted as a precursor to disintegration but as a means to deepen and expand self-experience. The self that has the ability to surrender its structure can be thought of as having enough experience of the reliability of an evolving self that it can allow a different kind of self-experience to emerge. This implies willingness, trust, and a sense that the continued existence of the self is not dependent on a certain set structure or experience. I will discuss how this relates to the experience of the Sōtō Zen practitioner in more detail below.

Even at the more highly functional end of the continuum, a person is never thought to outgrow his or her need for sustaining selfobject relationships. Wolf writes:

> If a person is to feel well—to feel good about himself, with a secure sense of self, enjoying good self-esteem and functioning smoothly and harmoniously without undue anxiety and depression—he must experience himself consciously or unconsciously as surrounded by responsive others.[72]

The aim of the developmental process, then, according to Kohut and those who later developed his theories, is not the elimination of selfobject relationships but rather their maturation and incorporation into a fluid structure that has available to it many ways of sustaining and supporting itself, even in times of stress and personal upheaval. Kohut writes:

> Self psychology holds that self-selfobject relationships form the essence of psychological life from birth to death, that a move from dependence (symbiosis) to independence (autonomy) in the psychological sphere is no more possible, let alone desirable, than the corresponding move from a life dependent on oxygen to a life independent of it in the biological sphere. The developments that characterize normal psychological life must, in our view,

> be seen in the changing nature of the relationship between the self and its selfobjects but not on the self's relinquishment of selfobjects.[73]

This frequently quoted statement by Kohut has important implications for the way we view a more mature self. According to him, the more mature self is aware that "the sustaining echo of empathic resonance is indeed available in the world."[74] Such a self recognizes its place in the selfobject milieu and participates fully. It organizes experience in an inclusive way and does not conceive of "objects" as merely extensions of itself. It possesses a feeling of coherence and cohesiveness and is not easily subject to experiences of fragmentation in relationships. It is also a self of complexity, uniqueness, and continuity.

Teicholz describes Kohut's mature "robust" self as entailing "affective fluidity and motion (through empathic openness to others)," "directedness (through ambitions and goals)," and "richness (through the integration and expression of the broadest and deepest self experiences from birth to death)," feelings of worth as well as a sense of growth, expansion, and enhancement. According to Teicholz, these qualities of experience were not "spelled out explicitly in Kohut's writings, but each one of them was at least strongly implied"[75] and all of them are dependent, to some extent, on the quality of the self-selfobject milieu. These are not qualities of a self that is divorced from its environment, neither are they simply passively experienced by the self. Kohut describes the mature self as one that has the capacity to experience itself, even in painful circumstances, as leading a "meaningful, joyful, and fulfilling" life[76] and marked by a real capacity for wisdom, humor, and empathy as well as playfulness and creativity. According to Wolf, ideally, it is "[s]tructurally complete, vigorous, balanced and ever-changing . . . and creatively acting in community with others."[77] It is also a self that has a unique shape and form, for maturity does not imply uniformity. As Kohut writes, "There is not one kind of healthy self."[78]

It is important to note that maturation is not thought of as a linear event, nor can it be regarded as a process without ups and downs. In fact, selfobject needs in the mature person can be highly complex[79] and will often vary with circumstances. For example, a woman giving birth may need the comforting, and in a sense more "archaic," presence of a hand to hold and/or a familiar and reassuring face. This does not imply lack of maturity. The same woman may also find her needs for comfort and reassurance met by remembering other women who have given birth, or by spiritual or religious iconography.

It is also important to note that a person may experience a deep sense of coherence and meaning in one dimension or aspect of his life, yet struggle with a sense of insecurity and fragility in another.[80] Feelings of vulnerability and fragmentation are not limited to those of us who have endured unresponsive early environments. Teicholz writes:

> To say that we need a sense of coherence and continuity denies neither the experience of multiplicity, [nor] the human capacity for fragmentation and discontinuity. . . . In Kohut's theory, our need for feelings of coherence and continuity are directly related to our very potentialities for all those opposite kinds of experiencing; small and reversible disruptions in feelings (i.e. mild and short-lived fragmentation experiences and discontinuities) are within the range of normal functioning.[81]

Again we return to one of the key points of Kohut's understanding of the structure and function of the self. Throughout life we require selfobject responsiveness in order to maintain a cohesive and vibrant self. What is transformed, in maturation, is the nature of those selfobject relationships. As maturation occurs, the self comes to experience itself as existing without the constant need for affirmation from the environment. Nor is it focused on keeping at bay experiences of fragmentation and disintegration anxiety. The sense of subjectivity itself transforms and the self, as noted by Wolf, has less need to "alter its perceptions in order to safeguard its fragile integrity."[82] This last point is especially important: if the self has less need to alter its perceptions, it is more fully able to participate in a complex and changing reality. It is also more fully able to allow experiences that can fundamentally change the way in which the world is perceived and experienced.

I would like to address two last important aspects of the development of selfobject relationships and self-structure, what Kohut has called "the developmental vicissitudes of the self."[83] They are worthy of mention because they call attention to the fact that this theory is one of great flexibility and optimism. In this way it reflects an understanding that transformation and the alleviation of suffering is possible and is not tied to a set configuration of personality characteristics.

First, as can be learned through a review of the writings of Kohut, Wolf, Stolorow, and others already discussed, the fundamental attitude of a self psychological understanding of development is that it is not irrevocably set in early development nor dependent on certain fixed relationships. Even a brief exploration of the work of these authors reveals the assumption that given a minimally functional self and a skillful, willing, and empathic other, profound healing and change can occur later in life. (Also, within the context of early development, selfobject needs can be met in a variety of ways.)

Kohut developed the idea of "compensatory structures"—the extension of structures of one aspect of the self into another aspect in order to make up for deficits. He writes:

> After prolonged attempts to obtain even minimally adequate selfobject responses for one constituent of the self have failed . . . another constituent of the self, supported by sufficiently sustaining selfobject responses, will grow with special vigor. In so doing, it is potentially able to provide the psyche with the new sectorial continuum—we speak of "compensatory structures" in this context. . . . Just as a tree will, within certain limits, be able to grow around an obstacle so that it can ultimately expose its leaves to the life-sustaining rays of the sun, so will the self in its developmental search abandon the effort to continue in one particular direction and try to move forward in another.[84]

This understanding of the development of the self takes into account the ability to incorporate obstacles. Kohut extends this understanding to include the idea that difficulties in life—the "developmental vicissitudes of the self"—can in fact enrich and deepen one's experience.

> It is my impression that the most productive and creative lives are lived by those who, despite high degrees of trauma in childhood, are able to acquire new structures by finding new routes toward completeness.[85]

Thus, in the self psychology model, self-experience (the way in which one experiences one's life and organizes that experience) is thought to be open and capable of profound and creative change and growth. Psychological growth is thought to entail the emergence of ever more elegant and responsive structures and forms of relating. The movement from infantile or archaic selfobject relationships (necessary for building the structure of the self but marked by concrete, limited, and immediate relationships which assume that to which one relates is an extension of the self) to more mature forms (marked by mutuality, flexibility, the capacity to tolerate times when needs are not met, and a wider variety of potential selfobjects) is descriptive of the development of an organization of self-experience that supports full and creative participation in life. In mature selfobject functioning, the individual is able to maintain a grounded awareness of his own subjectivity that does not exclude or deny the presence of others. In fact, the person's recognition of the presence of others is essential to subjective awareness and full functioning.

This is not meant to imply that there is a seamless perfection to the self. As Stolorow, Brandchaft, and Atwood write, careful investigation of the mature self leads to a view of the self as "multidimensional" and derived "from a multiplicity of selfobject experiences at various levels of psychological organization."[86] With the inclusion of this idea of a complex maturity, we are freed from the need to posit a uniform self-structure and also from notions that maturity in one psychological dimension implies maturity in another.

Framing human psychological life, development, and maturation in this way, within a context that assumes a complex, deeply relational, yet unique self-experience, is not only compatible with Sōtō Zen teachings but provides a language with which to describe and explore factors that support the practice of it. For example, selfobjects can be understood as a way to describe the dependently co-arisen self and its relationship with the interplay of all phenonmena.

Sōtō Zen practice takes place within the field of lived experience and is deeply impacted by the way a person organizes and understands this experience. It is, after all, an individual person, with all his complex strengths, vulnerabilities, and uniqueness, who encounters the teachings and takes up the practice. The subjective experience of that person will inevitably color the way he understands, relates to, and engages with this process. Using the language of self psychology to describe the self and the ways in which a fluid, reciprocal, and responsive (that is, mature) self-experience is developed, we can investigate the factors that support full engagement with Sōtō Zen teachings and practice as well as potential obstacles that might arise.

It is vital to note, however, that realization of the Buddha Way is not a matter of increasing maturity of the self and self-object relationships. Mistaking psychological maturity for realization and psychological development for the practice of Sōtō Zen limits the practice to a change in the structure of the self, and therefore keeps it tied to the self. The development of an increasingly fluid, responsive self-experience and a sense that one is able to engage fully with the teachings is enormously helpful to the practitioner. Realization, however, implies a fundamental shift in subjective experience that includes but is not limited to a change in the structure of the self, as we will discuss more fully below.

Nevertheless, intelligently and respectfully bringing psychological understandings into dialogue with the lived experience of the path can enhance our efforts to understand how it is best supported, as well as how to address the needs of individual persons, particularly those who find themselves in difficulty.

The concept of cohesion is a particularly relevant in this regard. Cohesion, a term used to describe a self that "experiences the 'I am I' as a unified and historically continuous self,"[87] may seem out of place or counter to the Buddhist understanding of a dependently co-arisen self that emerges moment by moment. But if we think of cohesion not as the definition of a static entity but as a description of a flowing process, difficulties with the use of the word "cohesion" to describe the self disappear. This way of understanding the concept of cohesion is analogous to the idea of "visceral coherence" put forth by Buddhist scholar Anne Klein in her description of an alternative understanding of the continuity of self that can emerge with the practice of mindfulness meditation. Based in the experience of awareness, and an observation of the content of that awareness, this is a "visceral sense of personal continuity in the midst of clearly observed flux."[88]

Visceral coherence, then, is an experience of the continuity of awareness independent of the content of awareness. It is "quite different from the narrative coherence constructed through stories." Narrative coherence creates an experience of personal continuity and stability by weaving together an understandable narrative from the content of our lived experience. Based as it is in the complex nature of a multifaceted self, "with conflicting plot lines and perspectives," it cannot, in fact, provide a personal sense of coherence with the same reliability provided by visceral coherence that "is not beholden to a story line." A coherence based on "plot lines" is vulnerable to changes in the content of the stories in a way visceral coherence is not.[89]

Viewed from this perspective, the experience of coherence in the self can be understood to include the historical perspective, the sense of an "I am I" that emerges from lived experience but it is also not dependent upon it. Cohesion of the self can be envisioned as less like a story with a beginning, middle, and end that hangs together well, and more as an ongoing process that evolves to include many dynamic aspects and many stories.

This is perhaps an extension of the meaning of the cohesion presented by the self psychologists, but it does not, I believe, violate their fundamental principles of fluidity and relationality. In fact, when we think in terms of maturity and self-structure (the way we organize our experience), we see an openess and flexibility in self-experience that blends well with this understanding of visceral coherence. In this way, narrative coherence and visceral coherence can be incorporated into a complex self-experience. A robust and flexible way of organizing reality can change, evolve, and include, in a way that does not imply the need for, an easily defined story of the self.

A self psychological perspective also posits a self that never outlives its needs for selfobject relating. I discuss below how this helps us understand the process of Zen practice, but the key point here is to understand the fundamental affinity the self psychological model of the self has for a teaching that never supposes the creation or discovery of a self outside of relational reality. The understanding and description of the mature self as fluid, open, creative, directed, and vigorous, as well as embedded in mutuality, gives us a language for discussing factors that support a person's engagement with Sōtō Zen practice without bringing in a concept of the self that is antithetical to the fundamental teachings on which the practice is based. It also proposes that the self has the capacity for a unique and creative response to the "developmental vicissitudes of the self,"[90] and includes an understanding that experiences, at least passing experiences, of fragmentation are normal for most people. Self-psychological language and its model of the self, then, are well suited to the task of shedding light on the development of the Sōtō Zen practitioner.

Types of Selfobject Relationships: Mirroring, Idealization, and Twinship

Selfobject experiences or needs take myriad forms, and have been described in many ways. The most useful descriptions for our purposes are those put forward by Kohut: mirroring, idealization, and twinship. These cover essential dimensions in the development of the self, without attempting to delineate all the possible elements of that development. They provide us with an elegant and flexible categorization, and are therefore a very usable means of articulating dimensions of self-experience in Sōtō Zen practice.

Kohut gives an overview of the meaning and function of primary modes of selfobject functioning:

> Throughout his life a person will experience himself as a cohesive harmonious firm unit in time and space, connected with his past and pointing meaningfully into a creative-productive future . . . only as long as, at each stage of his life, he experiences certain representatives of his human surroundings as joyfully responding to him [mirroring], as available to him as

> sources of idealized strength and calmness [idealization], as being silently present but in essence like him, and, at any rate, able to grasp his inner life more or less accurately so that their responses are attuned to his needs and allow him to grasp their inner life when his is in need of such sustenance [twinship].[91]

In his works *The Analysis of the Self, The Restoration of the Self,* and *How Does Analysis Cure?*, Kohut described four selfobject relationships: omnipotent merger, mirroring, idealization, and twinship. Of these four, the latter three are the most relevant to this study. Omnipotent merger was thought by Kohut to occur in the first year of life and consists of soothing and containing functions provided by the caretaker, which allow the child to develop basic self-regulation and integration, particularly of affect. This "primitive" form of relationship is based on the need to experience oneself as completely one with the other.[92] If this fundamental and primary need is unmet the developing person will have great difficulty organizing a coherent self-experience, and profound impairment results. For this reason I do not include this category in my overall discussion of selfobject relationships as they pertain to the experience of a Sōtō Zen practitioner. It is not that a person with a level of self-organization reflective of impairment in this dimension never comes to Sōtō Zen practice, but it is generally not relevant to the majority of practitioners and is best responded to in a structured psychotherapeutic relationship.

The first of the three categories of selfobject relationship, mirroring, is basically the experience of being seen, recognized, and affirmed as an existing and significant entity. Wolf writes:

> To paraphrase this mirroring experience one might say that one exists as a self because a significant someone knows and addresses us as a person, a self.[93]

Kohut includes a distinctly affective dimension in his understanding of mirroring in early development when he writes that a child needs to be seen, to be mirrored, in such a way that she is "looked upon with joy and basic approval by a delighted parental selfobject."[94] Being "seen" in this way is the essence of the mirroring experience and central to the process by which self-experiences are integrated into a rich and whole sense of self.

An understanding of the mirroring function is not complete without including what Wolf identifies as an "adversarial" selfobject, one who allows or even encourages the expression of difference or opposition. In this experience, a child, or an adult, is seen as a unique individual who is not expected to conform in order to receive affirmation. With the inclusion of this type of selfobject relationship, the range of a child's mirroring needs, the "need to feel affirmed, confirmed, recognized; to feel accepted and appreciated, especially when able to show oneself"[95] is fully (not perfectly) met.

Teicholz summarizes an understanding of mirroring as follows:

> The mirroring function affirm[s] the individual's affective experience and his sense of having a unique and valued identity consisting of the full range of developmental experiences in relation to important others.[96]

This affirmation, in turn, leads to the capacity to express self-experience and the unique talents and perspectives of the developing individual. If the mirroring selfobject need is not met in childhood, areas of experience are unable to be integrated and, subsequently, there is an increased fragility of self-structure. When this occurs, the need for recognition and approval can continue as a dominant force in adult relationships and the ability to develop and express one's unique self-experience is constricted.

Idealizing selfobject relationships, as the term implies, describe the need of the growing child to have a consistent and reliable relationship with another who they experience as strong, competent, warm, respected, and caring—someone who provides safety and is admirable. Wolf explains that, in this dimension, the child "need[s] the opportunity to be accepted by and merge into a stable calm, nonanxious, powerful, wise, protective selfobject that possesses the qualities the subject lacks."[97] Teicholz writes that development along this line depends on "the availability and suitability of the object for unquestioned admiration."[98] This is, essentially, the experience of being safely enmeshed in a selfobject milieu that communicates to the emerging self the sense that she is not alone and will not be left alone to cope with disruptive self-states. There is a consistent other with a greater capacity to contain and respond to circumstances as they arise.

When this need is adequately met, the idealized qualities form the basis for the person's values and principles:

> In addition to guiding life's choices, ideals and values become the standards against which the mature adult is able to measure her own worthiness or admirability.[99]

In its more mature form, idealization can be expressed in veneration toward and a desire to emulate respected persons, devotion to a set of values and ideals, or reverence for a religious figure. This mature form of idealizing selfobject relationship is characterized less by the desire to merge with than by a desire to emulate the idealized object.

The twinship (or alter-ego) dimension of selfobject relationships expresses the need to experience oneself as fundamentally like others, with similar and sharable desires, experiences and affective life. Wolf describes it as the "need to see and understand another who is like oneself, as well as to be seen and be understood by someone like oneself."[100] Kohut writes that early on

> The mere presence of people in the child's surroundings . . . creates a security in the child, a sense of belonging and participating . . . [a] confirmation of the feeling of being a human being among other human beings.[101]

This feeling of sameness extends as the child grows older and begins to participate in activities with others in such a way that she feels herself to be with them, like them. This leads to "the older child's sense of security as he feels himself to be a cook next to a cook or a craftsman next to a craftsman." The "vague but intense and pervasive sense of security" of the infant becomes a more concrete sense of belonging as the child grows.[102]

As with all the selfobject needs, this sense of belonging, as well as the need to feel a part of the larger group, continues into adult life. If the need has not been adequately met in early childhood, an intense need for belonging can develop, which can be concretely expressed, for example by donning a uniform or by setting up marked distinctions with those not in the group. (It is not at all a given that donning a uniform or somehow marking oneself as different from the dominant culture is an indication of immature selfobject relationships, only that it might be an expression of this.) If twinship selfobject needs mature, there is less need for obvious and concrete indications of belonging and a greater sense of commonality with a wider variety of people.

Each of these selfobject needs is present in adult life in some form. As Kohut points out in *How Does Analysis Cure?*, it is not the absence of selfobject needs that marks maturity but how they are experienced, met, and lived out. The adult continues to require the presence of affirming selfobjects but, with maturity, those selfobject needs are met with greater flexibility, less intensity, and with openness to others' needs. Affirmation can come in a variety of forms: other people or animals, a well-crafted pot, a beautiful vista, or a religious symbol. With maturation, an idealized figure does not need to embody perfection but can be complex and even flawed—that is, human. As with mirroring, mature idealization selfobject needs can also be fulfilled by symbolic means. In the realm of twinship, the maturing adult will experience a greater breadth of similarity and likeness.

Examples used by Kohut in his discussion of twinship needs in *How Does Analysis Cure?*—the girl next to her mother cooking, the boy next to his father in the workshop—illustrate that while not involved in the deepest identity of being human, gender becomes intimately tied to this sense of identity and belonging. The gendered development of the self-structure can also be discerned in the process of mirroring (which dimensions of self are seen, validated, and affirmed, and which are ignored), idealization (who is presented and experienced as embodying idealizable qualities and what happens when these qualities are expressed) and twinship (what qualities constitute similarity).

According to this formulation of development, the process of maturation is consistently characterized by an increase in flexibility and breadth in terms of selfobjects. Maturation is also marked by a decreased need for immediate satisfaction of selfobject needs, greater creativity in meeting those needs, and a greater tolerance for times when they are not met. There is great uniqueness and variety in this process. It is also important to note that a special effort must be made by those who for whatever reason—race, ethnicity, gender, physical difference, sexual identity, or any number of other characteristics—do not find images that represent their experience in the dominant culture. Experiencing oneself as different from cultural norms requires that one seek out relationships in which twinship, idealization, and mirroring can occur. It also requires a determined effort to create a sense of self that exists outside the affirmation of the dominant culture. This is a creative endeavor that, I believe, enriches us all.

The categories of selfobject functions—mirroring, idealization, and twinship—provide a fruitful way to discuss a Sōtō Zen practitioner's relationship with the animate and inanimate "objects" in his life. Again, while I will discuss this more fully below, what is important to note here is that in a tradition characterized by an emphasis on the relational quality of one's life and practice, a means to discuss such relationships is of great help. Although this schema does not include every possible relational dimension, there is an overarching inclusiveness that covers major areas.

Sex and Gender

Gender has come to be regarded as a factor that has significant impact on the experience and development of self.[103] From the perspective of self psychology, which sees the self as completely embedded in the relational surround, all aspects of the relational environment and the culture into which a child is born impact the evolution of the self. There is, perhaps, no more fundamental division we make as humans, in terms of catagorizing our human environment, than gender. Phyllis Burke, in *Gender Shock: Exploding the Myths of Male & Female,* which discusses how gender is understood, experienced, and culturally transmitted, gives an example of the primary nature of this phenomenon in her description of what often, if not usually, happens immediately after a child is born:

> The first defining moment in a human being's life occurs in the birth room, and in medical terminology it is called "the announcement." Not concerned with health, or weight, or fingers and toes, the announcement consists solely of the sex of the infant's body. From the moment of birth, the baby is handled in ways considered appropriate to the body's sex. Appropriate colors are chosen, appropriate toys are selected, appropriate religious and social ceremonies are performed.[104]

This is the moment when gender is assigned. Gender, and the experience of it, is thus an important factor in the development of selfobject relationships and consequently self-experience. Without going into all the possible, as well as important and fascinating, permutations of that experience (for example, the experience of those who do not feel that their gender identity is compatible with their physical sexual characteristics or their socially assigned gender based on those characteristics), we can understand gendered experience, which is deeply influenced by dominant cultural definitions and assumptions, as a key aspect of self-experience.

To give one example, in terms of selfobject relationships we can see how mirroring, idealization, and perhaps particularly twinship experiences can be deeply influenced by the assumed gender of the two people involved. Gender difference can present special challenges when, for example, a woman seeks to emulate or follow a male mentor or teacher. Women entering a religious lineage in which all the dominant figures are men may experience a fundamental sense of disconnection. It may be more difficult for a woman practitioner in this situation to think of herself as capable of the same realization as male predecessors. This situation, however, can also present special opportunities. For example, if a female practitioner studies with a male teacher, the chance of mistaking superficial similarities for a deep and abiding spiritual identity that is not dependent on observable categories or characteristics may be less likely to occur. Yet there are often challenges for women practitioners in a lineage made up of men, and this topic has been ably discussed by Rita M. Gross, Christina Feldman, Anne Klein, and many others.[105]

In regard to an understanding of gender in the Sōtō Zen tradition, again we find a fundamental compatibility with self psychology. Setting aside the nature vs. nurture, innate vs. socially created debate about the emergence of gender in an individual, both self psychology and Sōtō Zen Buddhism regard gender not as a characteristic that determines one's status as a creative individual but as a construct that emerges in a social milieu.

The Body

The embodied dimension of self-experience is an essential aspect of self psychology. In their discussion of the experience of alienation that results in the "central myth" of Western culture—the "myth of the isolated mind"—Stolorow and Atwood point out that the result of this myth is alienation not only from the physical or "natural" world but also from the relational world.[106] This leads to a diminished experience of "being wholly subject to the conditions and cycles of biological existence" and supports the illusory sense of being free "from the constraints of animal existence and mortality."[107]

This is an important point. According to this theory, the self and self-object relationships occur not only within a relational matrix but also within a physical one. Stern and Winnicott remind us that, developmentally, early relationships are suffused with physicality.[108] Stolorow and Atwood assert that not only is the physical dimension inherent in early life but that "[a] central constituent of cohesive selfhood is the subjective experience of embodiment."[109] Kohut called attention to the physical dimension of self-experience directly: "[T]he child needs the unqualified acceptance and admiration of his total body-mind-self." He also pointed to "body self" experiences, such as illness, that occur in adult life.[110] Simply to use the phrase "body self" undermines assumptions of a duality of the body and mind. It sets a tone for the investigation of self-experience that subverts an assumption of their inherent difference or the presumption that embodiment is uniformly experienced.

This is in line with the Sōtō Zen understanding that regarding the body and mind as separate reflects a deluded view of the nature of the self and its relationship to phenomena. In the earliest stories of the Buddha we find that it was his encounter with "old age, sickness, and death" that propelled him into a life of inquiry, practice, and realization.[111]

Turning away from our own physicality is an act that alienates us from our experience and leads, according to Buddhist teachings, to a life based in a distorted notion of our actual condition. This in turn prevents the kind of honest encounter that is the foundation of practice.

From a Sōtō Zen Buddhist perspective, one's sense of self cannot be separated from the actuality of experience; therefore, it cannot be considered to be an entity divorced from the physical world. To use the terms of self psychology, self-experience is embedded in a "matrix" of "reciprocal mutual influence" and is in no way separate from the physical reality of our lives. Dōgen says that "because the body necessarily fills the mind and the mind inevitably penetrates the body, we call this permeation body-mind."[112] According to these teachings, the point is neither identification with nor rejection of the body but the cultivation of a subjective experience grounded in the "body-mind." This attitude reflects the dependently co-arisen nature of the self and all phenomena. Without this attitude, we are not only alienated from an aspect of our being but become identified with a distorted notion of who we are.

Stolorow and Atwood write that, ultimately, alienation from the embodied dimension of our lives results in alienation from "subjectivity itself."[113] From their psychoanalytic point of view, we can understand this to mean that there is a loss of the subjective sense that one's experience is valid and is integrated into a sense of self that is physically grounded, is both whole and effective, and is in intimate relationship with others. Self psychology posits, then, an integrated body/mind that supports the emergence of a subjective experience, which in turn allows for a real encounter with life as it is.[114] In these statements by both psychoanalytic authors and Dōgen, we can hear a shared emphasis on the impossibility of separating our human subjective experience into realms of body and mind, and the understanding that the attempt to do this is not only futile but alienating.

Trust

The word "trust," if we spend time with it, can be both deeply evocative and challenging. It is tied to our bodily experience, to our emotions, and to the very ground beneath out feet. It is a word that points to a fundamental aspect of our lived experience. Like other words that point to basic human experiences, "trust" can be difficult to pin down (and, perhaps, that is not the point). Rather, we can think of it as allowing us to build a bridge between the depths of our being and our attempts to describe them.

A discussion of trust adds an affective, intuitive dimension to the concepts I have described in regard to the experience of the self. More important, I include it because it points directly to an essential dimension of Sōtō Zen practice. In fact, I would say that trust points to the heart of Sōtō Zen practice—the dimension of faith. The relationship between trust and the faith essential for full engagement in Sōtō Zen practice will be discussed in detail in the next chapter. At this point, I intend simply to build an understanding of trust as it is presented in the writings of psychoanalytic authors, show its relevance to our discussion, and introduce the two aspects of trust I will later develop.

Webster's Dictionary describes trust as "akin to the Old English *treowe,* the root of the word "true." Trust has the meaning of "assured reliance of character, ability, strength, or truth," as well as "confidence." Faith is a close relative of trust and comes from the Latin *fides,* akin to *fidere,* to trust. Confidence in turn, shares the root *fidere* and implies the "consciousness of feeling sure." Another related word is belief, defined in Webster's as "a state or habit of mind in which trust or confidence is placed in some person or thing" and a "conviction of the truth of some statement or reality of fact, especially when well grounded."

From this we can glean an understanding of the word "trust" as a sense of confidence that what is present is true and reliable. In relation to the ordinary physical world, we can say that we trust that the sun will rise each day, that the water in the kettle will boil, that gravity will keep our feet on the ground. Interpersonally, trust implies that the person one trusts is reliable, that they can be counted on to follow through on what they say, not misrepresent themselves or their intentions, and have constancy in their interactions, character, and emotional involvement. Implied in this description is a basis of respect and positive regard. This can range from a simple benign working relationship to deep lifelong intimacy. The concept of trust can also be applied to our "inner" experience. We speak of "trusting oneself" or being "sure of oneself." With such phrases we are referring, I think, to an inner sense of reliability—that one's self (so to speak) is capable of integrating and effectively responding to whatever comes in life, and that the factors that support trust will not be fundamentally absent.

From a self psychology point of view, we can say that this describes trust that one's self-structure is robust and flexible enough to sustain itself in challenging circumstances. This in turn reflects trust that the selfobject milieu will be able to provide needed supportive and restorative selfobject relationships. Doris Brothers describes what she terms "self trust" as a phenomenon that includes the tendency to view oneself as able to both elicit appropriate selfobject relationships from available selfobjects, and provide the same function for others.[115]

As we have seen in our discussion of selfobject relationships and the development of the self, for a child constancy, reliability, and positive regard, the factors that build trust, are essential. In order to make sense out of the world, in order to build a coherent universe, physical objects in the world must behave in an understandable fashion, and significant persons must behave in understandable and responsive ways. In order for a self that experiences itself as able to adequately cope with the experience of being alive to evolve, this environment and these caretakers must have continuity, coherence, and reliably warm engagement. From such a relational milieu a sense of fundamental trust develops both in others and in oneself.

Erik H. Erikson proposed a developmental schema that, while not self psychological in its outlook, is nonetheless compatible with it, and provides us with a means of understanding the relationship of trust and the formation and experience of the self.[116] Erickson put forth the idea that the first, most important task or theme of development is that of forming "basic trust." He states that an infant, cared for by a consistent caregiver with his own sense of inner trust, will come to have a basic sense that the world and her own inner states are to be trusted.

> The general state of trust . . . implies not only that one has learned to rely on the sameness and continuity of the outer providers but also that one may trust oneself.[117]

According to Erikson, when experiences of mistrust—times when the caregiver is not immediately available or perfectly responsive—are reliably followed by experiences in which the infant is carefully tended to, basic trust develops.[118] Experiences of mistrust are integrated into a sense of basic trust when they are outweighed by experiences of responsive care. In this way, a position of openness, receptivity, responsiveness, and confidence in the experience of life begins to develop and deepen. This is an interpersonal experience, what Erikson calls the "mutuality" of trust,[119] and also a physical one. It is born out of the primary experience of being held, supported (both literally and metaphorically), and loved by another. It is important to note that, according to Erikson, this other is one in whom a basic sense of trust has already been established and is communicated to the infant and child in many, often subtle, ways.

The development of basic trust, then, leads to an open and responsive relationship to another, to the ability to tolerate times in which responsiveness is not immediately available, and to a sense of personal trust that one is fully capable in relation to one's inner states. This is vital for the development of any individual, and is particularly relevant to the life of a practitioner of Sōtō Zen, because it supports a relational stance to the world and to life that is embodied, deeply engaged, and able to allow the full range of human experiences.

Erikson equates the ability to sustain an open stance, to trust, with the ability to surrender to another in the religious dimension.[120] Taken out of a theistic context, we can understand this as the capacity to allow a subjective experience to emerge that is not rigidly tied to a separate sense of self. D. W. Winnicot's discussion of development, based on his understanding of the relationship between mother and infant/caregiver, is relevant in this regard and sheds light on the capacity to trust and its emergence. Perhaps the most frequently quoted statement by Winnicott is his assertion that "[t]here is no such thing as a baby. . . a baby cannot exist alone, but is actually a part of a relationship."[121]

According to Winnicott, a baby is not understood as an entity whose subjective reality is separate from the relational context in which it lives. As Howard A. Bacal and Kenneth M. Newman point out in their book *Theories of Object Relations,* there are many overlaps, as well as significant differences, between Winnicott's discussion of human development and Kohut's theories.[122] Perhaps the most obvious kinship exists between his description of the infant-mother dyad and Kohut's discussion of selfobject relationships.

Of particular interest is the way Winnicott used his understanding of relational life to articulate what he referred to as potential or transitional space. This transitional space occurs between subject and object, or more accurately between what is perceived by the infant as "me" and what is perceived as "not-me."[123] He posits a center of gravity that is neither the mother nor the infant but the relationship they share. If in this relationship there is an atmosphere of "good enough" loving care,[124] and the child finds that those times when the presence of the supportive caregiver is lacking are reliably followed by experiences of being cared for, he will develop trust in relatedness and in his capacity to tolerate experiences when it is not concretely present.

In addition, and this is central to our discussion, the child will become comfortable in and enriched by times that can be characterized as being in transitional space, a state or experience of self that is not dependent upon the usual sense of subject and object. Winnicott describes this dimension of subjective experience in which the self's organizing capacity (to use Kohut's understanding and language) does not dominate:

> There are long stretches of time in a normal infant's life in which the baby does not mind whether he is in many bits or one whole being . . . provided that from time to time he comes together and feels something.[125]

This statement implies that "coming together to feel something," or what I would call coming together as an organized self, is an essential aspect of normal human development, but it is not the only normal aspect. Another important dimension is the experience of being "in many bits." The capacity of the self to "not mind" the experience of being "in many bits" is dependent, according to Winnicott, on the reliability and trustworthiness of the caregiving relationship—the "good-enough mothering," or, put another way, a sufficiently functional "holding" in the "relational environment." As Winnicott writes, this "happens only in relation to a feeling of confidence on the part of the baby." When confidence is present the child develops the ability to sustain herself (though, in a Kohutian sense, the word does not strictly apply, since organizing principles can be thought of as temporarily muted or suspended) in the space "between."[126] That is, she will allow a subjective experience that is not completely tied to the organizational structure of the self. She will, as Winnicott says, be

> able to unintegrate, to flounder, to be in a state in which there is no orientation, to be able to exist for a time without either being a reactor to an external impingement or an active person with a direction or movement.[127]

Winnicott writes of this space "between" subject and object as the place in which creativity and transformation occur. This is not simply a dead zone or a holding pattern to be tolerated until the next subject-object experience comes along. It is, according to Winnicott, a state of "relaxation" that depends on trust in self and other, trust that is built in a supportive, reliable, "good enough" caregiving environment.[128]

The parallels with Erikson's basic trust and Kohut's discussion of the formation of self-structure in responsive selfobject relationships are readily apparent.[129] Basic trust supports the development of a sense that one's inner and outer environments are capable of meeting basic needs, and from this basis one can maintain an open relationship to experience in general. It supports the formation of a vital and integrated self-structure and the maturation of selfobject relationships. With the addition of

Winnicott's work, we can say that with this basic trust there exists the capacity to allow periods of unintegration in which subject and object are not so neatly defined and creativity is nourished. Such periods of temporary unintegration are not experienced as substantially disruptive, contained as they are in an overarching sense that the world can be trusted to provide a supportive selfobject milieu and that the self is fully able to reconstitute itself in this milieu. This holds true not only for the developing child but also for the adult. Teicholz refers to this as the ability of a person to "surrender her sense of cohesion in the pursuit of artistic creation or pleasure and reengage when needed."[130] With this capacity, built on basic trust, an individual is able to allow, perhaps even encourage, experiences in which significant shifts in the self and selfobject experiences are possible.

It is interesting to note the similarities and differences between Winnicott's description of "between" and the self psychologists' description of fragmentation. Fragmentation, with its origin in substantially unmet selfobject needs, is an experience in which self-cohesion is painfully disrupted. The fruitful experience of transitional space, on the other hand, does not arise from unmet selfobject functions. Quite the opposite, it is engendered by a sense of their reliable presence. Reading Winnicott, we can envision an experience of "unintegration" that does not carry the emotional overtones present in fragmentation. We can say that with sufficient grounding in an experience of basic trust it is possible to experience "being in bits" not as fragmentation accompanied by disintegration anxiety but as a creative, dynamic process that does not threaten a fundamental connectedness in the world.

This is akin, I believe, to what Kohut meant when he wrote of the cohesion and fluidity of the mature self: a self process that can incorporate (a word that emphasizes the physical dimension of this experience) periods of greater and lesser coherence into a flexible, vital, and evolving sense of self. This is not to say that a person with sufficient basic trust is invulnerable to disruptive experiences. Rather it points out that "being in bits" can be associated with both positive and negative experiential qualities.

It is interesting to note that Erikson understood trust as a developmental achievement in the first phases of life, while Kohut described an infant's actions as arising from an innate confidence that her needs will be met. From the perspective of development, we can see both as applicable. A fundamental trust, or reaching out, may very well be innate; however, we can also think of the experiences of life as creating a deeper or more fragile capacity to trust.

Brothers writes that trust is

> an inborn potential that, under normal circumstances, matures and strengthens over the course of a lifetime and is disturbed only as a consequence of traumatic betrayals.[131]

From this point of view, one's experience of trust is understood not as irrevocably set in childhood but as changing throughout one's life in response to life events.

This brings in the very important topic of trauma, an aspect of human experience that has great bearing on the development and evolution of trust. Including trauma in our discussion of trust acknowledges the presence of these powerful experiences of the violation of trust, allows us to consider their impact, and deepens our understanding of the nature of trust itself.

Judith Lewis Herman, in her classic work *Trauma and Recovery,* writes that trauma—experiences of threatened or direct encounters with loss, violence, or death, such as war, rape, and natural disaster that are marked by a sense of overwhelm and helplessness—"confront[s] human beings with the extremities of helplessness and terror." She quotes the *Comprehensive Textbook of Psychiatry,* which describes the feelings of "intense fear, helplessness, loss of control and threat of annihilation" brought on by a traumatic event.[132] She evokes a sense of this dimension of experience:

> Traumatic events call into question basic human relationships. They breach the attachments of family, friendship, love and community. They shatter the construction of the self that is formed and sustained in relation to others. They undermine belief systems that give meaning to human experience. They violate the victim's faith in a natural or divine order and cast the victim into a state of existential crisis.[133]

Regarding trust and faith, she writes:

> The sense of safety in the world, or basic trust, is acquired in earliest life and in the relationship with the first caretaker. Originating with life itself, this sense of trust sustains the person throughout the life cycle. It forms the basis of all systems of relationship and faith. The original experience of care makes it possible for human beings to envisage a world in which they belong, a world hospitable to human life. Basic trust is the foundation of belief in the continuity of life, the order of nature, and the transcendent order of the divine. In situations of terror . . . [when a] cry for help is not answered, the sense of basic trust is shattered. Traumatized people feel utterly abandoned,

> utterly alone, cast out of the human and divine systems of care and protection that sustain life.[134]

This description gives us a clear and touching glimpse into what happens when basic trust is lost. It also gives us an idea of how crucial the development and maintenance of trust is for the ongoing well being of the individual. We can see in it that which is feared in Kohut's concept of disintegration anxiety (discussed in *How Does Analysis Cure?*)—the chaos that arises with the loss of self and selfobject relating.

In addition to pointing out that traumatic events result in the profoundly painful experience of loss of connection and sense of self, Herman and Brothers also state that an incomplete or flawed sense of basic trust greatly influences the way disruptive events are experienced.[135] The impact of a traumatic event is lessened to the extent that a person experiences herself as fundamentally connected to and a part of the human community, with resources available to her for coping with the aftermath of the trauma. According to these authors, a person with a fragile self-structure and a shaky sense of connection (selfobject relatedness) is more likely to experience significantly disruptive events as traumatic, thus further undermining a sense of basic trust.

Basic trust, then, can be seen as another, perhaps more viscerally connected and affectivily based, way to describe the experience of connection and viability that is part and parcel of a cohesive, vital self and selfobject world. It is also a way to discuss the experience of human vulnerability and how to support an individual in times of difficulty and transition. From this perspective, we understand that the development of basic trust is an essential correlate of the development of a functional and vital self that is fully able to engage in relational life. In addition, this self is able to allow and grow from periods of unintegration, even floundering. Winnicott writes:

> The potential space between baby and mother, between child and family, between individual and society or the world, depends on experience which leads to trust. It can be looked upon as sacred to the individual in that it is here that the individual experiences creative living.[136]

The experience of potential space, then, begins with trust built on reliable caregiving and a sustaining selfobject milieu, as described above. With this dimension of basic trust in place, the self is able to trust or rely on its capacity to weather periods of lessened cohesion as well as its ability to reach out for and obtain appropriate restorative selfobject relationships. This can be likened to trusting a very strong and resilient thread that can be relied upon not to disintegrate, or, if it does start to unravel, that one will be able to move toward that which will repair it.

With basic trust the child is able to allow the experience of being "in bits and pieces," being in a state "between" what is perceived as "me" and what is perceived as "not me," knowing that the developing self and selfobject relationships are not at risk. Extending this into adult life, we find the analogous experiences of creativity and "relaxation" described by Winnicott[137] and the surrender of coherence referred to by Teicholz. These can be thought of as experiences in which strict rules of subject and object are relaxed, a creative fluidity of experience is allowed, and an individual's sense of self and subjectivity can shift. All of this grows from a fundamental experience of trust and connectedness, as well as the vital cohesive self that emerges from and is sustained by that trust and connectedness. As I will discuss more fully below, the degree to which each of these interrelated factors are developed deeply effects an individual's experience of Sōtō Zen practice.

Discussion

The work of psychoanalytic authors provides us with relevant usable psychological concepts helpful in understanding the lived experience of Sōtō Zen practice. The psychology of self developed by Heinz Kohut[138] and extended by others, grounded as it is in relational reality, is fundamentally compatible with the teachings of emptiness and dependent co-arising, the philosophical basis of Buddhism and Sōtō Zen. In addition, both self psychology and Buddhism regard concepts as constructs and "helpmates," not definitive statements of fact. This fundamental compatibility allows for the respectful borrowing of self psychology concepts and their importation into a Sōtō Zen context. The psychology of trust that can be built from the work of Erik Erikson, D. W. Winnicott, and others also provides us with compatible and useful ways of articulating aspects of Sōtō Zen practice as it unfolds in an individual's life.

The description of self as a structure, an enduring pattern of organizing principles that is also embedded in and dependent on relational reality, is particularly useful. Such concepts as fragility, fragmentation, disintegration, cohesion, coherence, and flexibility provide metaphors and give us a means to discuss an individual's response to and growth in Sōtō Zen practice. In addition, Kohut's model of a mature self, particularly ideas of mutuality, flexibility, and creativity, can be used to shed light on aspects of self-experience relevent to Sōtō Zen practice.

The concept of selfobject relationships addresses the relational aspect of self-experience and provides a means of discussing difficulties that can arise in this dimension. Understanding how selfobject relationships mature, as well as particular kinds of selfobject relationships (mirroring, twinship, idealization), provides a conceptual basis for discussing an individual's experience of relational reality in practice. The movement from archaic selfobject relationships toward more mature relationships, in which there is an empathic recognition of the other as well as a shared relational base, accurately describes an important dimension of maturation in Sōtō Zen practice.

In addition, self psychology posits a complex multidimensional model of maturation that is compatible with Sōtō Zen. It is based on relational embeddedness as well as the inclusion of the physical dimension of our lives. It is also fundamentally optimistic about the creative potential of each individual. This model is not only compatible with a Sōtō Zen understanding but also brings a new language to the Sōtō Zen endeavor that is particularly suited for an investigation of the factors that hinder and support a person who takes up the Sōtō Zen Way.

In the same way, the language of trust can also lend concepts and ideas, as well as terminology, to an exploration of the lived experience of Sōtō Zen. Erik Erikson's concept of basic trust and D. W. Winnicott's discussion of transitional space give us a means of describing key elements in the formation of the self. They also provide a way to discuss an essential aspect of an individual's experience of the practice, particularly zazen practice: the ability to tolerate, even welcome, times in which clear distinctions between "what is me" and "what is not me" are suspended. Outside of zazen, the language of trust can be used to describe the ability to enter into relationships with both animate and inanimate objects, based on a sense of fluidity and reciprocity. In addition, as I will discuss more fully below, the language of trust can be used to describe factors that support the fundamental shift in self-experience that is central to Zen practice.

Chapter Four

Trust and the Transformation of Self-experience

In the preceding chapters I have endeavored to build a basic understanding of the practice of Sōtō Zen and introduced psychoanalytic concepts that address key elements in the human experience of the self which deeply influence and are influenced by Sōtō practice. We can now use this understanding and conceptual framework in an exploration of the fundamental question stated at the beginning: What works to support the practitioner of Sōtō Zen? How can we understand the personal experience of Sōtō Zen practice in such a way that we gain insight into making full engagement possible?

Descriptive systems attempt to capture a multifaceted living process in a net of ideas and concepts. Including aspects of a second system—in this case, psychoanalytic descriptions of self-experience in a Sōtō Zen context—may result in greater distance between the concepts presented and the lived reality. It is important to bear in mind that the point is not to arrive at an accurate description of what is, but to develop potentially helpful (and fluid) understandings that can be used to support the practice of Sōtō Zen.

It is also important to bear in mind that psychological experience of something is only a dimension of it, not the thing itself. If we assume the self is the structure that organizes experience, the psychological experience of something is the self's experience. As such, while of crucial value and relevance to us, it is only one aspect of the entirety of the circumstance. For example, when I use D. W. Winnicott's description of transitional space and "between" in regard to the practice of zazen, I am not equating the two. The experience of "between" provides us with a way of understanding the self's experience of entering zazen, it gives us a means of addressing our human experience and difficulties that may arise, but it does not describe zazen itself. With this in mind, we can use psychological language and concepts and apply them to our human experience without burdening the practice with our limited ideas about it, since a key part of the practice is the relinquishment of just such ideas.

In the practice of Sōtō Zen, the fundamental Mahāyāna teachings of emptiness and dependent co-arising bring the practitioner to a vision of reality that is radically different from our usual self-referential worldview. The practice carries these teachings into all areas of the practitioner's life. Emptiness, buddha-nature, thusness, the bodhisattva vow, and the precepts all come alive in the practice of zazen, work, sangha relationships, and ritual activity. At root, each of these dimensions of practice can be thought of as a movement from a life centered in the perception of the self as a separate, discrete, and independent entity to the subjective experience, realization, and compassionate expression of fluid interdependent reality.

If we remember that practice is not a linear process, we can think of the practitioner's engagement in Sōtō Zen as having two interdependent aspects or phases. First there is the establishment and continued evolution of a self that has developed confidence in its own existence and sustainability. This leads to a willingness to experience the self as an evolving, mutable process that rests in awareness. The second aspect involves a shift to a subjective experience that takes as its basis dependent co-arising and does not privilege self-experience. It is important to note that it also does not deny individual experience: the individual continues to express her life, as well as the bodhisattva vow and activity, in her own unique way.

Central to this process, and to the discussion in this chapter, is the experience of trust. Trust can be seen as the thread that runs through the practice life of the Sōtō Zen student. It is the basis on which the self is formed and is intimately bound to all relational life. It is also the foundation and the fundamental characteristic of the practice itself. The presence of basic trust allows for the formation of a self that is capable of full engagement in the practice. With this engagement, self-experience changes, the nature of trust evolves, and the realization of the Sōtō Zen Way emerges. By understanding the way in which trust both supports the emergence of a new subjective experience and is transformed by it, we can come to a deeper understanding of how to support the practice of Sōtō Zen.

Using the psychoanalytic concepts of basic trust and the self and selfobject relationships, I will explore these two companion aspects of practice through a discussion of three dimensions of practice life. For the sake of narrative flow, each each of these dimensions will be discussed sequentially, but they are better understood as interwoven, mutually influencing processes. This is a key point, because thinking in an exclusively linear fashion about Sōtō Zen practice, or many other forms of Buddhist practice, contradicts the complexity of its basic teaching and spirit and does not reflect its lived experience. Practice, realization, and the immediacy of buddha-nature are all central to the teachings and practice of Sōtō Zen. Presuming a strictly linear process can lead to fundamental misunderstandings.

The first dimension of practice corresponds to the first aspect or phase described above: the establishment of the self and the capacity to maintain awareness. This process takes place squarely in the realm of solid, identifiable concepts and clear-cut relationships. From the perspective of the two truths, we can say that it expresses conventional truth and linear time and process. I will present the role that the development of basic trust, self-trust, and a cohesive self-structure play in the ability of the practitioner to simply be present for and integrate his experience. This will be followed by a discussion of the key role awareness and effort play in opening up dimensions of self-experience.

The second section ventures into a realm that is more uniquely tied to Sōtō Zen and based in the Mahāyāna teachings of emptiness. In this section I will discuss the second aspect—the shift in self-experience or perspective from one centered in a separate sense of self to one grounded in dependent co-arising. Again, I bring in the language of trust to discuss the essential correlate of this shift from trust in the self and selfobject milieu to trust in life itself, what I call absolute trust.

Basic Trust, the Self, and Awareness

The fundamental stance of any Buddhist practice is one of open, calm attentiveness to whatever arises. The capacity for this nonjudgmental awareness is, therefore, vital for a full engagement in Sōtō Zen. This is most easily seen in the practice of zazen, where the practitioner carefully attends to each experience, without exception, with deep curiosity and receptivity. But it is equally important for the full functioning of other aspects of practice as well. The capacity to engage fully in work practice and sangha relationships, for example, also relies upon the ability to remain open and attentive to experience as it unfolds.

In Sōtō Zen, the practitioner attends to the basis of her experience—that is, the nature of the self and of reality—in light of the teachings of emptiness and dependent co-arising. This is not an abstract process but one that is very personal and immediate and includes every aspect of the practitioner's life. Every nook and cranny, every dimension—physical, emotional, intellectual, and spiritual—every relationship, every moment, is a part of the practice. The simple capacity to sit still (both literally in zazen and metaphorically in all activities) and remain present for the full range of experience is essential for this process to take place and mature. This capacity is established, at least in a rudimentary form, at the outset of practice, but also continues to develop over time.

The concepts of basic trust and self-cohesion provide a means for understanding factors that support this calm and open attentiveness. Sitting still implies that all areas of self and relational experience are available to one's awareness. It means that that the practitioner can maintain stability and attentiveness even when the experiences that arise are disturbing. This can be difficult, if not impossible, if basic trust in and adequate cohesion of the self are limited.

As we have seen, the formation of basic trust and self-structure are inseparable processes that occur from earliest life. The reliable and empathic responsiveness of the selfobject milieu works to create an experience of basic trust and an increasingly fluid and cohesive self-structure in the developing child. With this, she is able to integrate disruptive experiences into a resilient self-structure, tolerate periods when selfobject needs are not met, and rely on herself and others to provide for her physical and psychological needs. The coherent self that takes shape is "put together well"[1] and is able to integrate challenging experiences. In a supportive selfobject milieu, selfobject relationships develop from those in which the object is experienced purely as a means of affirming the self to those in which a reciprocal and responsive relationship is present. Trust grows in the reliability of the caretaking surround. A sense of continuity is developed, as well as the trust that the self will be sustained through periods of "unintegration."

If a responsive selfobject milieu is not present during development, a fragile self emerges, one that is prone to fragmentation. This experience of self is chaotic, disorganized, and usually frightening. Under certain circumstances, everyone is subject to experiences that challenge self-cohesion and the feeling that they are a part of an understandable and reliable universe. For a person who has developed a less cohesive self-structure, however, the capacity to stay with and integrate disruptive, difficult, or painful aspects of human experience is more limited. Experiences that threaten the self's fragile cohesiveness are avoided or denied, and there is a tendency to disavow, dissociate, or repress these intolerable experiences. This aversive stance constitutes a major barrier to the ability to be present for a full range of experiences; the realm of experience is constricted and avenues for self-transformation are limited.

Turning away from experience is particularly prevalent when the "horror"[2] of disintegration threatens. As Wolf and Brothers point out, the need to preserve a sense of self is paramount.[3] If we remember that the self referred to here is the coherent organization of perception and reality, it is easy to imagine how central this coherence is and why one's sense of self would be so vigorously defended. The fragile self, confronted with the possibility of its own disintegration and filled with anxiety, will turn away.

It is helpful to think of the cohesive and fragile self as two ends of a continuum, and every individual occupies a position on that continuum that can vary to some degree depending on circumstances. A person in a familiar, supportive environment will experience himself as more cohesive than if he were undergoing severe or prolonged stressors. Someone whose self-structure is more cohesive will be less liable to experience fragmentation under a given level of stress than someone whose self is more fragile. And a person with a more fragile sense of self will vary more along the continuum.

The person who has developed a reasonably cohesive and robust sense of self will be able to be present for a wider range of experiences. With a coherent self, experiences and affects are "seen [more] as signals of a changing self-state rather than as indicators of impending psychological disorganization and fragmentation."[4] A fundamental feeling of worth; a sense of continuity; the belief that the self will continue to be able to provide a coherent and useful organization of reality, even under stressful conditions; an "affective fluidity" and a "richness" and complexity of inner experience;[5] as well as the presence of a flexible and adaptive self-structure—all contribute to the self's ability to be present for and integrate experience.

In terms of Buddhist practice and developing the capacity to be present, we can understand this feeling of inner stability and worth as a positive valuation of self-experience and the practitioner's belief that he can fruitfully engage in the practice. There is a sense that it is possible to build a foundation of awareness and a stable relationship with a wide range of experiences. Fundamentally, it is a feeling of capability and possibility. Without this sense the obstacles that inevitably arise may be experienced as insurmountable, and a belief that the practice itself is possible may be blocked.

Limitations in the cohesion of the self are accompanied by selfobject relationships that tend toward the more archaic, less mature end of the continuum. In this case, archaic selfobject relationships, those tied to the need to affirm the fragile self, dominate. This limits reciprocity and responsiveness and their associated experiences. In a sense, we can describe the effect that immature selfobject relationships have on the capacity to simply be present by asking the question: Present for what or whom? In both self psychology and Sōtō Zen, the self is relational and its relationality is understood to be responsive and mutual, not solipsistic. The person who is caught in archaic selfobject relationships sees little outside his own limited perception of self. Perceived others (in psychoanalytic terms, "objects") are experienced as extensions of the self, with the sole purpose of affirming that self. Significant deviations from this schema evoke fear of fragmentation or disintegration anxiety. In a sense, the person who is caught in archaic selfobject relationships cannot be said to be present for anything other than her own circling around a fragile self and its needs. This does not support open attentiveness to the fullness of human experience.

In mature selfobject functioning the individual is able to maintain a grounded awareness of his own subjectivity that does not exclude or deny the presence of others. In fact, the presence of others is understood as a characteristic of reality and recognition of them as essential to full functioning. From a Buddhist perspective, a separate self that exists purely "from its own side" is not tenable. Mutuality infuses all aspects of practice life. Reciprocity, responsiveness, and co-constituting relationality, as well as the expression of one's uniqueness, are all qualities that define self-experience in the presence of mature selfobject relationships. With a firm foundation in an experience and understanding of this, the way is open for a full engagement in the practice without fear of fragmentation or disintegration.

From this, we can see that the person who has developed more mature selfobject relationships and self-cohesion has available an experience of self that is not preoccupied with filling a desperate need for affirmation and confirmation. She is able to experience herself as embodied and has developed the capacity to include a wide range of experiences and affects in her self-experience. To a great extent, she is able to meet her inner needs calmly and appropriately, and because she is able to meet her needs in this way she has a greater ability to encounter challenges with the confidence that she will not be dismantled by them. Such confidence is born from the experience of basic trust.

Of all the concepts introduced in this discussion, trust is perhaps the most helpful in describing the practice of Sōtō Zen. Understanding the development of basic trust and what Doris Brothers has called "self-trust" contribute important insights into the personal experience of the practitioner. Regarding the first dimension of practice, the capacity to be present, basic trust can be understood as the sense that one's inner and outer environments are reliable and capable. Brothers describes self-trust as the "expectation of obtaining and providing the selfobject experiences necessary for the development, maintenance, and restoration of cohesive selfhood." She continues:

> As long as self-trust binds us to others in the world of subjective reality, our selfobject fantasies remain intact and we are likely to enjoy a sense of comfort, familiarity, safety and well being in our lives. Self-trust, therefore, may be thought of as the "glue" of self-experience.[6]

In this understanding, trust is the embodied knowledge that one's self and the relational surround, the selfobject matrix in which it resides, is reliable and that one is not threatened by fragmentation and disintegration. It is the confidence that the self will be able to sustain itself through difficult or disruptive experiences and integrate them in a functional way. This is a sense that regardless of the stresses of given circumstances the self has the inner and outer resources to either maintain cohesion or reliably restore it through supportive selfobject relationships. This, in turn, supports the emergence of an open relationship to experience.

The ability to trust in this way takes on another coloration when we include the experience Winnicott describes as "being in bits."[7] In regard to this first dimension of practice, we can say that the self that has developed basic trust is able to include in its range of experiences those that temporarily loosen its organizational structure. It can knowingly enter into such an experience because it enjoys a fundamental and embodied trust that it will not lose basic connectedness and will reemerge, so to speak, as a cohesive whole, able to organize experience in a coherent and functional manner. As Winnicott writes, the ability of a person to fully experience the times "between," to "relax" in the state of being in "bits," and to be enriched by these moments is dependent on having established "confidence,"[8] a deep and abiding sense that he will come together again. In a sense we can say that the self trusts its ability to bridge the gap presented by the experience of "between." The self trusts the availability of responsive selfobjects and its own capacity to reach out for them when necessary. As Teicholz notes, this is the precondition for a "surrender" of coherence in an artistic or creative process.[9]

This has particular relevance to the practice of zazen. In transitional space, "between" clear notions of subject and object, "what is me" and "what is not me," are suspended. As mentioned above, Winnicott tells us that with sufficient trust an individual is

> able to unintegrate, to flounder, to be in a state in which there is no orientation, to be able to exist for a time without either being a reactor to an external impingement or an active person with a direction or movement.[10]

In zazen the practitioner's usual organizing schema are suspended and the effort is to simply attend to experience as it is. The practitioner neither reacts to external stimuli nor has a direction or movement other than sitting still. He will certainly unintegrate and may very well flounder or have the feeling that he has no orientation, as this is usually understood. In a sense, zazen can be thought of as the lived experience of "between." The ability to enter fully into this practice comes with the embodiment of basic trust.

We can say, then, that along with an adequately cohesive self-structure and reasonably mature selfobject relationships, basic trust supports the emergence of an ability to integrate a full range of affective and relational experiences. With basic trust an individual has the ability to attend to experience in a calm, open way. She can find some degree of ease and a sense of competence in a fluid, changeable world. This trust is expressed in an individual's confidence that she can cope with the vicissitudes of life and the challenges of Sōtō Zen practice. Experiences, particularly powerful affective experiences, are not regarded as possible precursors to a state of overwhelm, fragmentation, and disintegration.

In addition, there is an ability to trust periods of "between." In this way, trust, with regard to the self, can be thought of not so much as trust in one fixed structure (of the self) but in the flexibility and adaptability of that structure. A particular structure of the self does not need to be defended if one has confidence—in other words, trusts—that it will be able to adapt in response to a given situation or experience. In this way, self-structure is experienced as evolving. Without this basic trust and sense of self-cohesiveness, fear and anxiety, not trust and curiosity, will color the individual's engagement in practice. In this case, a feeling of confidence in one's ability to grow, through allowing the fullness of experience, is unavailable and the capacity to simply be present for moment-to-moment experience is curtailed.

Another consequence of an impairment of basic trust is the quality of awareness that the practitioner brings to his experience. If he fears that being present for his experience means running the risk of being overwhelmed and obliterated, he may set up a distanced relationship with his experience, a kind of cool, pseudo-objective observational stance, perhaps even dissociation, that can be mistaken for the equanimity spoken of and valued in Buddhist teaching. On the other hand, the practitioner can also be buffeted by thoughts and emotions and find himself unable to find purchase in a sea of tumultuous experience, with little or no sense of a stabilizing orientation. Neither of these two stances is adequate; both are hindrances. Being present does not imply a coolly distant observation of phenomena untouched by affect or concern, nor does it imply the loss of a sense of grounded subjectivity. Being present, settled in a sense of basic trust, is the ability to open to all the nuances of a given moment in every dimension of experience without being consumed by an overwhelming fear of fragmentation and without tenaciously clinging to what is known.

Lacking this fundamental openness, practice can degenerate into an activity based in aversion, not inclusion, and this can take a variety of forms. There may be a kind of sleepy inattentiveness or a tenacious clinging to opinions or set ideas about the nature of things. Of particular concern are attitudes of aggression and anger born from the need to protect the self. If his or her mind and heart are infused with judgment and a tendency toward harshness, the practitioner can easily misinterpret injunctions to "practice as if one's head is on fire" as a demand for a kind of self-punishing rigor and rigidity. The instruction to "not desire to become a buddha" may give rise to resignation based in a sense that one is excluded from enlightenment because of a flawed self. It is ironic that the very activities of practice can be turned into the "frantic lifestyles" Wolf describes,[11] which mark efforts to defend against experiences of fragmentation. Overwork, overscheduling, and assuming too many obligations are not unknown in the world of committed practitioners.

When a practitioner has established a fundamentally sound relationship to awareness, she is increasingly able to enter into the fluidity of moment-by-moment experience. There is a sense that the process of self is reliable and will continue despite upheavals and challenges. A particular configuration of the self does not need to be defended and fear of fragmentation does not preclude experiences in which the structure of the self loosens, shifts, and changes. As noted above, this shift can be experienced as the temporary suspension of self-structure in order to allow for an enriched experience.

Heinz Kohut's description of the effect that past experience and consequent assumptions have on current experience is relevent to our discussion of awareness and the capacity to be present:

> Prejudicial tendencies deeply ingrained in us will often decisively influence what part of potentially available data we perceive, which among the perceived items we consider important, and, ultimately, how we choose to explain the data we selectively perceive.[12]

Viewed from a Buddhist perspective, this can be said to accurately describe how delusion works. We view any given situation through a filter that colors our perceptions, how we explain them, and, I would add, how we then respond to them. A key element in any Buddhist practice is the ability and the willingness to become aware of one's filters, one's delusions. Extending Kohut's statement, Ernest Wolf writes that "the strengthened self will have less of a need to alter its perceptions in order to safeguard its fragile integrity."[13] From this perspective, then, we can say that by strengthening the self, and its correlate, basic trust, we can support the practitioner's ability to sit still, to remain open and calmly attentive to experience. Free from the need to alter perceptions in order to protect a fragile sense of self, the practitioner is open to a wider range of "data" as well as ways to understand and act on it. Turning Wolf's statement around, we can see sitting still as an expression of basic trust and an indication that an adequately cohesive self is present.

The idea of strengthening the self may seem to contradict, or be in opposition to, the Buddhist teaching of no-self and the aim of releasing one's attachment to the self. At first glance, it might seem more appropriate to discuss ways in which to undermine the self's cohesion. Certainly Sōtō Zen practice challenges the self as it is habitually experienced, as we will see in the next section, but this does not preclude the strengthening of the self and basic trust. Regarding this first dimension of practice in particular, if we recall that the "self" of self psychology is not a fixed immutable entity but an organizing structure and remember the qualities attributed to the cohesive self, any apparent opposition based on a misunderstanding of both the nature of the cohesive self and the teachings of no-self dissolves.

The mature self is a self that is capable of transformation and fluidity. It is not a fixed structure but one that is embedded and responsive.

Greater cohesion enhances its connectedness and allows for a more accurate and flexible organization of experience. The teaching of no-self, discussed in Chapter Two, does not imply the lack of coherent organizing principles in an individual, nor the disappearance of a creative vital subjectivity. Regarding this first aspect of practice, we can say that the achievement of a coherent and sustainable way of integrating and understanding experience is not only fully compatible with the teachings of emptiness and no-self, it actually supports their realization through increasing the practitioner's ability for calm, open awareness.

Basic trust and cohesion, then, supports the capacity to fully engage with experience without needing to alter perceptions to protect a fragile self-structure. In the practice of zazen, as well as other fields of practice, there is a greater ability to simply allow things to be as they are. At the same time, the practitioner has a sense of the validity of her experience and can engage in vigorous and fruitful dialogue with teachers and the teachings. Viewed from this perspective, using the language of trust and the self drawn from psychoanalytic theory, we can say that the formation of basic trust, an adequately cohesive self, and reasonably mature self-object relationships are all important elements in building the capacity to be simply present. The practitioner is able to attend to experience in a straightforward way, know it as valid, and integrate it. She is able to weather periods of disruption without losing a fundamental sense of connectedness and stability. This is what is possible when cohesion and basic trust are present.

It must also be pointed out, however, that such cohesion is not the aim of Sōtō Zen practice, nor does cohesion solve the fundamental question of suffering. It is also important to note that perfect cohesion, even if it were possible, is not a requirement for entering into Buddhist practice. People who take up Sōtō Zen often exhibit some degree of fragility, since vulnerability and pain are often the very impetus that leads one to explore Buddhist practice.

What cohesion does, with its companion trust, is give the practitioner an organization of experience that supports stability of awareness and a non-threatened self-identity. Cohesion functions as an essential support for the practice and allows for the transformation of difficult experiences into a deepening of practice. The ability to encounter one's human frailty directly, without blame, judgment, or avoidance, expresses and builds confidence in the capacity to see, be present for, and effectively respond to the whole range of human experience. It also allows the practitioner to view difficulties as a means for developing greater awareness about the nature of suffering and liberation.

The capacity to not turn away, to be present for one's experience of vulnerability and pain, also offers an opportunity to develop deep compassion for oneself and others. Buddhist practice is never apart from the relational world. Both psychoanalytic authors and Buddhist teachings describe self-experience as inherently embedded. The self emerges from, and is sustained by, a relational field that includes all beings, and it is usually most intimately tied to other human beings. Developing an awareness of this interconnectedness is central to Buddhist teachings and practice.

An encounter with our human frailty and suffering combined with an awareness of our interconnectedness cultivates a deep understanding of and sympathy for others' struggles and frailty. This engenders greater kindness, which in turn creates a greater capacity for inclusivity. In a sense, this is the affective side of awareness, and it is enhanced by the practitioner's encounter with her own tenderness, her sense of vulnerability and incapacity. Using Buddhist terms, we can describe this as the intimate connection between wisdom and compassion. Clear seeing (wisdom) develops an awareness of both suffering and interconnectedness and leads to a caring response to all who share this life (compassion).

With the presence of basic trust and the sense of a fundamentally cohesive self, the intention to include will not be blocked by fear and anxiety and wholesome effort can emerge. The results of this are twofold. First, there is an ever-increasing depth of stability that rests in the sense that the ability to integrate a wide range of experiences and the capacity to make the effort to fully attend are reliably present. As Francis Cook points out, we can think of this as "a process of encompassing more and more experiences as 'self.'"[14] Second, there is the dawning recognition that this inclusivity is neverending and that it is the effort, the process, not the result, that is the point. This wholehearted effort "without a gaining idea" is a radical willingness to include everything, a sitting still that includes not sitting still.

This brings us to the important topic of effort or intention. As important as the ability to sit still is in the practice of Sōtō Zen, the capacity or intention to make the effort to sit still is even more important. The practice of Sōtō Zen is not aimed at the acquisition or emergence of any particular state of mind but the realization that any state of mind is the Way. The cultivation of one's ability to calmly and kindly receive and be aware of any experience with curiosity, alertness, and nonjudgment is clearly an essential element in the life of the practitioner. But focusing solely on this aspect of practice can lead us to posit the experience of a calm mind as the end goal. This is not the case; rather, the basis of the Sōtō Zen Way is the process, the intention, the "wholehearted effort," and not any particular result that may be thereby attained. Calmness is not the point—engagement is. What is apparent is that calmness supports engagement, cohesion supports calmness, and basic trust is fundamental to both.

We can see in this a shift in focus from the development of an increased coherence of the self-structure to an emphasis on the activity of awareness, a shift from a structural metaphor to one that is centered in process. Returning to the experience of transitional space, in which the self allows itself to "be in bits," we can see that the capacity to attend to process allows for a continuity of coherence even when the self is "in bits." With this experience of coherence there is not only the sense that a reasonably familiar self will reemerge, or that restorative efforts will be successful, but that coherence itself is never absent. Such a living, mutable coherence not tied to a particular configuration of the self can become the basis on which the individual rests. As noted above, this is akin to what Anne Klein describes as "visceral coherence," in which the process of awareness rather than its content is used as the basis for a sense of self-coherence.[15] As the practitioner takes awareness itself as his point of reference, attachments to set notions of self or even to divisions between self and other are modified. This opens up the possibility of an alternate experience of subjectivity.

It also opens up the possibility of another experience of trust. This is an essential point, because the "self trust" described by Brothers is limited. From a Buddhist perspective, any sense of comfort and safety that is based on the maintenance of "selfobject fantasies" is problematic, since life itself will challenge those fantasies. This is basic to Buddhist teaching—impermanence is present in all of life and clinging to notions that we can somehow make it otherwise is the root of suffering. To take as the basis of trust reliance on any particular sense of self or other, on any single aspect of fluid reality, is false and will inevitably be shaken. Therefore, self-trust, though essential to a functional and expressive self, does not address the key source of anxiety and distress. What is needed is a different experience of trust, one that evolves and emerges as the Sōtō Zen practitioner takes up the Mahāyāna teachings of emptiness.

Trust, Emptiness, and the Practice of Sōtō Zen

"No eyes, no ears, no nose, no tongue, no body, no mind."
—*Heart Sūtra*

In discussing the first aspect of practice, I focused on the self, its aspects and its experience, as an organizational unit. Like a thread running through a variety of patterns, we have attended to its path in relation to the context. Even when the discussion turned to times when the self becomes more diffuse or momentarily disappears in a "between" state, the continuation or reemergence of the self was the focus of attention. The self, not the overall context, has remained the point of reference. This has allowed us to develop an understanding of an essential dimension of Buddhist practice: the development of the capacity to sit still, to be present. It also reflects the central position of the self in human experience and the importance of building a strong foundation for Buddhist practice. The discussion has taken place from the perspective of conventional truth and the world of form.

While important, if we limit our discussion to this dimension we will miss the essence of the Sōtō Zen Way. For it is the teachings of emptiness and the spirit of practice realization that lie at its heart. In this section, I extend the discussion to include the transformation of the basis of subjectivity itself. I stated in Chapter Two that this core dimension of practice can be thought of as the repeated shift from a perspective centered on the person as a discrete, separate entity to an orientation based in dependent co-arising, this moment, and the activity of all beings. This is a shift in subjective experience from a self that is preoccupied with its own survival to a subjective experience of the self that knows itself to be a functioning part of interdependent reality. We can liken it to shifting our perspective from the single thread and its relationship to the overall pattern to taking the pattern itself (which, of course, includes the thread) as the basis.

In light of the teachings of emptiness, the basis of Sōtō Zen practice, the idea of a self that is separate from phenomena is untenable. From a Buddhist perspective, because all phenomena are impermanent and interconnected, such a transient, though useful, organizational structure should not be mistaken for the basis on which to build one's life. According to Buddhist teachings, identification with a separate, permanent self, and being caught in a worldview that circles around and is tied to that self, is delusion, the root of suffering. Suffering is lessened by reducing one's attachment to and identification with a perception of the self as a permanent, privileged, protected focal point. Through lessening this identification, the foundation of intention, action, and perception—that is, the self—can shift and change its fundamental orientation in the world. With this shift, the self continues to function, to organize, but the nature of the self, of subjective experience, is transformed. It is now grounded in and reflective of the reality of impermanence and interconnectedness and is an expression of compassion.

In the Yogācāra system, this is referred to the "transformation at the basis" in which the seventh consciousness, *manas,* transforms into the wisdom that sees all things equally. The Vietnamese Buddhist teacher Thich Nhat Hanh, in his discussion of Yogācāra philosophy, writes:

> The bodhisattva . . . transforms the innate belief in a separate self, and *manas* becomes the Wisdom of Equality. . . . When this takes place, *manas* is transformed. Before this transformation, *manas* was the energy of grasping and discriminating. Now it becomes a kind of wisdom that can perceive the true nature of interbeing. There is no longer any discrimination between self and nonself—you are me, and I am you. . . . [T]he bodhisattva realizes his nature of interbeing and the nature of interbeing of all phenomena. The capacity to see and to live accordingly is the wisdom of equality.[16]

This interpretation of Yogācāra teachings sheds light on a dimension of practice essential to Sōtō Zen, the experience of transformation of subjective reality. It must be remembered, however, that Dōgen's teachings emphasize that even delusion is enlightenment. Therefore, it is important not to be confused about the fundamental nonsequential, paradoxical nature of Sōtō practice. The transformation at the basis occurs, but it occurs in a context where even the deluded *manas* is buddha-nature. Again, purification of consciousness is not the aim but rather the realization that all phenomena, purified or unpurified, are the manifestation of buddha-nature. All phenomena express thusness, buddha-nature, emptiness—whether or not any transformation of the self has occurred. Thusness, buddha-nature, and emptiness are not different from all phenomena.[17] At the same time, this transformative shift is understood to be liberative.

There is a relationship between basic trust, self-cohesiveness, and the capacity to make this shift in self-experience. Drawing on the discussion in the first part of this chapter, we can say that strengthening the self and the capacity to attend fully to all experiences allows for the possibility of a lessened identification with any particular structure. The cohesive self is open to a wider variety of experiences as well as new ways of interpreting them. With basic trust, this self can enter into experience fully and cultivate a stable awareness, grounded in the body and inclusive of the entire range of human experience. This ability to attend to and experience the process of awareness makes available the experience of visceral coherence. This coherence, based as it is in the process of awareness (and not the content of awareness), in effort rather than outcome, encourages the loosening of attachment to set definitions of the self and supports an experience of trust in the process itself. Particular definitions of self become less relevant as the process of awareness comes to the fore. The capacity to attend, to make awareness, not content, the principle of cohesion, means that it becomes possible for moment-to-moment experience to become the reference point. This supports the transformation of self-experience.

Awareness and self-trust set up the conditions, but it is the deep and sustained encounter with the teachings of emptiness in one's body, heart, and mind that catalyzes the profound shift which lies at the heart of Sōtō Zen practice. To hear the teachings of emptiness in a direct and personal way is to understand, at least briefly, that we are not the self we so often suppose ourselves to be; instead, we are a fluid, dependently arisen phenomenon, along with all other dependently arisen phenomena. With this understanding and the continued practice based on it, the possibility opens up for an experience in which the self is not central, is not the exclusive point of reference. From the perspective of the individual, we can say that Sōtō Zen practice challenges and ultimately transforms the basis of self. Through practice there emerges the realization of the self as none other than dependent co-arising. But again, we must recall that, according to Dōgen's teaching, practice expresses this reality from the very beginning—it is only from the perspective of the self that we can speak of transformation and emergance.

This new and different subjective experience can be related to the preceding developments but it is also, in a sense, of a different order. This profound shift in subjective experience takes place at the edge of the known, the place where maps stop and mystery is encountered. It is a realm of paradox and it is not the result of anything. While it is easy to imagine the process of practice in a linear fashion—develop the self, then transcend the self— this is not the case with Sōtō Zen practice. There can be no preparation for what is already present. The practitioner takes a leap—in a sense, she steps into not knowing, into the realization that she is already Buddha from the very beginning. Put another way, while it is the practitioner who takes the leap it is all beings who land, and that landing does not occur in a new place but in this moment.

I will take up this point again when I return to a fuller discussion of the dimension and role of trust and faith in the life of the practitioner. What is important to note at this point is that even as I propose models for practice, even as I emphasize the need for attending to the self and supporting the practitioner in identifiable and understandable ways, I am not ignoring or turning away from the immediacy and mystery that lie at the heart of the practice. Again, we return to paradox and the fundamental teaching that this moment and all phenomena already are an expression of complete and perfect enlightenment.

Whether or not the practitioner is ready to integrate the heart of Sōtō Zen teaching, she finds it in her body, heart, and mind as she practices. The recognition of this, at least to some degree, and the effort to embody it cannot be thought of as dependent on self-cohesion or any other psychological factor. Distortions and misplaced effort may be present, the inability to fully integrate the teachings is most likely present, but the intuitive response to the teachings reaches deeper than any ideas or self-conceptions. Taiken Yokoyama described this as being "pulled by the dharma."[18] Traditionally this affinity or sense of recognition is thought to be due the causes and conditions that fostered one's attraction to the teachings. It must be noted that a Buddhist understanding of karma does not posit a soul or continuous singular life-force. Rather, like the strands of a rope, it indicates merely a stream of cause and effect that is expressed in human and other life forms.

The attraction toward and deep desire to practice coexists with a wide variety of self-experiences, and it cannot be quantified or identified as the result of cultivation. Even experiences of a transformed subjectivity are not dependent on the presence of self-cohesion, though their effective integration into a viable, responsive, and integrated identity are usually the result of such self-cohesion. This implies a paradox: it is important both to support the cultivation of cohesion and basic trust and recognize the key role they play and, at the same time, to acknowledge the limitations of that perspective. Recognizing the presence of this paradox, we return to a discussion of the aspects of development that support a deep and free-flowing engagement in the practice and the central teaching of emptiness.

Encountering the Teachings of Emptiness

Much confusion can occur when an individual directly encounters the teaching of emptiness in practice. The apophatic language used in the emptiness teachings can be easily misunderstood, the identity of emptiness with dependent co-arising can be missed, and the teachings of buddha-nature and thusness misconstrued. Alternate uses of the word "empty" or "emptiness" found in psychological literature highlight sources of this potential misunderstanding. For example, Ernest Wolf equates experiences of fragmentation with an "emptiness of the self" and goes on to describe fragmentation as being associated with "loss of self esteem, or as a feeling of emptiness or depression or worthlessness or anxiety." He uses the term "empty self" and writes:

> Chronic deprivation of self organizing and selfobject experiences leave the self relatively empty of the structured complexity and energetic vitality of selfs that grew up in richly responsive environments. Clinically these people suffer from low-grade chronic depressive mood with feelings of emptiness and lack of zest.[19]

The meaning of "empty" in these quotations is clear and fits well into the overall context of the psychoanalytic writings; it denotes a painful state devoid of positive qualites. The difficulty arises when there is an attempt to translate it into a Buddhist context. For example, Anne Klein writes of an "empty subject" that is not the site of feelings of deprivation and hollowness but of vital engagement, an expression of reality, a self-experience that is "fully compatible with dynamic personal agency."[20]

Even contemporary authors writing about the integration of Buddhism, Western psychology, and psychotherapy have mixed Buddhist and Western philosophical or psychological understandings of the words "empty" and "emptiness" in a way that can be confusing to the reader, particularly someone who is new to Buddhist teachings.[21] For example, in line with Wolf's use of these terms in *Treating the Self,* Mark Epstein, in *Thoughts Without a Thinker: Psychotherapy from a Buddhist Perspective,* describes a state of severe deprivation and craving, an impossible hunger and a "desperate longing," as a "terrible emptiness." He continues by saying that these "inner feelings of emptiness and unworthiness" are paired with "compelling fantasies of reparation," and asserts that "the Western student afflicted with such feelings must make the emptiness itself the object of his or her meditation."[22]

Such a meditation has, as its object, not the dependently co-arisen nature of all phenomena but a distressing mental and emotional state, and it is clearly not the same meditation on emptiness that forms the bedrock of Tibetan Buddhist training, as discussed by Jeffrey Hopkins in his classic work, *Meditation on Emptiness.*[23] Epstein's recommendation may be intended to remove obstacles to, in this case, Buddhist mindfulness practice (commonly referred to in many Western Buddhist circles by the Pāli term *vipassana*), but it is emblematic of and contributes to a pervasive confusion about the teaching of emptiness itself (unless the author intended, for his own reasons, to blend the two meanings). In this confusion emptiness is conflated with nihilism, dependent co-arising is missed altogether, and serious obstacles to a full understanding of the teaching result.

This deep confusion can and does play itself out in the lives of practitioners. We bring our own conceptual schema to our encounter with the teachings of emptiness. That is, our own ways of organizing our perceptions and understanding the world inform how we hear and experience the teachings. This leads to inevitable distortions. According to Buddhist teachings, each of us is prone to misperceptions, delusions about the nature of the universe. We are conditioned by our previous experience, discussed in terms of the *bījas* (seeds) in consciousness posited by the Yogācārins. Who we have been colors how we perceive and act in the present. All this affects how we hear and respond to these teachings.

It is interesting to note that factors of personal experience identified by Epstein, Wolf, and others as being associated with "emptiness" are the very ones that present the most difficulties in regard to hearing the Buddhist teachings of emptiness with any clarity. In terms of understanding the teachings, the distortions that arise are particularly troublesome for those whose self-experience is marked by substantial fragility and an impaired sense of basic trust. The fragile and beleaguered self constantly defending itself from feelings of disintegration may hear in these teachings echoes of what it has known (and feared). The self that has known the painful "emptiness" described by Epstein may hear an echo of this experience in Buddhist teachings on emptiness (*śūnyatā*). For example, a person who has difficulty locating a cohesive sense of self, has been plagued by feelings of "emptiness," and has even used that word to express those feelings, may believe that they understand quite well what is meant by the statement "the self is empty (of inherent existence)." They may even experience a sense of recognition, an acknowledgement of something they have known. But this is a false recognition. It is essential, therefore, that we utilize language accurately, make a real attempt to effectively convey the teachings so as to minimize these distortions, and address misunderstandings as they arise.

In a sense, there are two layers to an encounter with the Buddhist teachings of emptiness. First, there are the distortions arising from the personal and cultural conditioning that we bring to the interchange. How we hear the teachings is impacted by all the associations we have with the language and concepts being presented. A part of the practitioner's study and practice is to uncover and work with these misunderstandings. Second, there is the engagement, on a direct and personal level, with a teaching that is fundamentally foreign to one's ordinary, habitual ways of organizing experience—that is, the belief in the self as a separate, independent entity. The challenge for the practitioner, then, is first to be able to begin to hear the teachings with reasonable accuracy and then to allow the teachings to penetrate or permeate her worldview through practice, clarifying inevitable misunderstandings and distortions as they surface. Finally, the practitioner's effort is to allow the self to actually transform in accordance with what she has experienced.

The writings of Stolorow and Atwood on "the myth of the isolated mind"[24] are relevant to this process. They propose that this myth, characterized by an enduring sense of separateness, constitutes the dominant theme of personal experience in the modern Western world. This description of self-experience is compatible with what Buddhist thinkers have described as a someone caught in samsara, the world of delusion (and while this may have particular relevance for Westerners, it is not limited to a particular cultural identity). Stolorow and Atwood write that within this myth

> [s]eparateness is seen as belonging to the mind-entity as an intrinsic feature of its being and is thus not understood to be contingent on any particular relation between the person and the surround.

They go on to say that this

> serves to disavow the exquisite vulnerability that is inherent to an unalienated awareness of the continual embeddedness of human experience in the constitutive intersubjective context.[25]

Stolorow and Atwood further point out that if a person lives in a world in which seperateness and reification are the means by which an "experienced substantiality" of the self is inferred, then any challenge to that separateness and reification can be deeply threatening. They discuss the process of shifting from a more reified, isolated experience of human life to one based in a relational (in this case, intersubjective) model: "[I]n a culture of pervasive psychological aloneness there is little to protect a person from the feeling that the solidity of things is dissolving into thin air" when he is presented with a model or experience in which "the permanence and substantiality of the world are constituted and maintained by intersubjective fields."[26]

This describes an experience not unusual in a person who encounters the teachings of emptiness. Habitually identified with a self that is experienced as a separate and independent entity, and accustomed to defending that self by disavowing its relational nature, an individual caught in this "myth" who takes up the practice of Sōtō Zen is challenging all of the ways, including the painful, self-limiting ways, he has kept himself safely defined. The "exquisite vulnerability" that emerges as he uncovers this relational nature can be disturbing and disruptive, and it can easily lead to a "feeling that the solidity of things is dissolving in thin air." Notice that it is the sense of the solidity of things that is dissolving. An understanding, or perhaps more properly a realization, of the self as a completely fluid, relational event means that there is nothing, no one, who can be threatened. But the practitioner must often come to this through the process of eliminating supports for the known self. The point at which there appears to be a self, and yet there is no ground on which to stand, can be deeply anxiety producing.

The fear that may be evoked in response to the teachings of emptiness is not unknown in Buddhist literature. Anxiety is an expected response, varying only in the degree, the effect, and the means of addressing it. Though not specifically about the practice of Sōtō Zen, Jeffrey Hopkins, in his extended discussion of a Tibetan practice of meditation on emptiness, gives us a clear view of what an emptiness-based practice entails. Describing what can be encountered with these teachings, he writes:

> You can sometimes be so stirred up . . . [that] you will rise from the meditation cushion and go and eat or turn on the t.v.—anything to avoid the anxiety that such probing of the nature of things can bring out.[27]

Hopkins later tells us that even in a preliminary intellectual reading of the teaching,

> You can be shocked to the very depth of your being that [the self] is not an analytically findable entity as you previously thought, still actual realization

> of emptiness is even more profound. The Dalai Lama described developing a correct assumption of emptiness as like being hit by lightning.[28]

He continues:

> This kind of practice is emotionally harrowing, for our mind has been convinced to remain in its place. . . . At a certain point [in our lives] we accept things as reality, no longer feeling to question. For "reality" will not bear these questions. If this is going to be reality, its very precondition is that you will not ask such questions of it. Thus when you do ask them, it is upsetting. . . . We need a willingness for a new experience even if it entails the reopening of wounds of emotions built on views of reality. This analysis involves anxiety and fear. It is necessary to build the kind of mind that will not want to sink back and be overcome by inertia, a mind willing to change, willing to see everything change.[29]

The "mind willing to change" can be thought of as a mind (and heart) that trusts the process of change. Without fundamental cohesiveness and a foundation of basic trust, basic connectedness, this is often impossible.

The Evolution of Trust

In *Trauma and Recovery*, Judith Lewis Herman writes about trust:

> Originating with life itself, this sense of [basic] trust sustains the person throughout the life cycle. It forms the basis of all systems of relationship and faith. The original experience of care makes it possible for human beings to envisage a world in which they belong, a world hospitable to human life. Basic trust is the foundation of the belief in the continuity of life, the order of nature, and the transcendent order of the divine.[30]

This extends the understanding of basic trust to include a process that sustains not just the self as it is usually known, but also the "system of relationship and faith" that contains it. From a Buddhist perspective, we can say that with a foundation of basic trust, a system where the self is not (metaphysically) privileged can be explored. This exploration will continue as long as there is a continued belief, trust, faith, or lived experience that this system is one that is "hospitable to human life." Basic trust not only allows for this exploration, it is extended by it. "Transcendent" or "divine" may not be terms that are particularly relevant in a Buddhist context, but we can say that within this context basic trust is the foundation for the belief in an order that is inclusive and reflective of the sacredness of all life, including the individual. This in turn supports a continued engagement in the teachings. From this perspective, basic trust becomes the underpinning for the evolution of practice.

From this ground another related experience of trust can emerge, one that does not rely on the structure of the self as it has been known and trusted, or on its capacity to reliably obtain needed selfobjects. Returning to our discussion of transitional space and the "between," this trust can be likened to a shift in focus from a trust that the self, as a discrete entity, can be relied upon to reappear following experiences of transitional space, to a trust in relationality and in the state of being "between." It is based in experiences in which the line between subject and object is not clearly drawn, times when what is "me" and what is "not me" are not easily distinguished. This trust does not take as its premise any particular experience of self (neither does it deny them) but requires letting go of the known self, for it reflects and expresses a different orientation. This is trust without the need to reference a self separate from all phenomena. This experience can only arise with the trust that an organization of experience, a subjectivity, that is grounded in all beings is not opposed to the deepest needs of the individual.

In reference to the work of Erik Erikson (*Childhood and Society*) and Judith Teicholz (*Kohut, Loewald, and the Postmoderns*), we can say that this trust is an expression of real surrender, a reorientation that places the entirety of life itself at the center. It is an embodied sense that one can harmoniously accord with the needs and circumstances of the situation, and that this does not threaten a perceived sense of self because the self is experienced as not different from the situation. This does not imply that a particular self-experience will be guaranteed. Instead, it is grounded in the realization that a self which sets itself apart from things as they are is the root of suffering. Freed from this delusion, harmonious accord is the self, and there is no need for opposition.

Returning to Hee-jin Kim's statement, cited in Chapter Two, about the nature of "opposites or dualities," we can say that the self, as a functioning aspect of reality, is not "obliterated," it is "realized." This self is intimately bound to moment-to-moment reality, and the experience of trust it expresses is one that "realizes itself in duality, not apart from it."[31] As Francis Cook writes, this is liberation to the world, rather than from it.[32] Trust, in this sense, has no set referent; it is trust in the expression of trust. This is a companion to the usual understanding of trust with a focus on the self. It is an aspect of trust akin to faith, which, we might say, is not generally trusted in the dominant culture of contemporary North

America. It is an alternate understanding of trust that underlies, accompanies, and expresses a fundamental shift in subjective experience. This is absolute trust.

The Japanese characters that are variously translated as "belief," "trust," and/or "faith" provide us with a way of understanding trust and its various aspects as it is experienced and evolves in Sōtō Zen practice.[33] By exploring the complex meanings of these characters we gain a deeper insight into the teachings of Sōtō Zen and how it takes shape in the lives of its practitioners. We can also explore interesting points of contact with the psychological perspective discussed above.

Faith, as Cook and others have pointed out, is an essential aspect of Dōgen's Zen.[34] The oldest Chinese character for "faith" or "trust" is *xin* (信; Jpn. *shin*). It is found in the title of the sixth-century Chinese text *Xinxin ming* (Jpn. *Shinjin mei*), or *Faith in Mind,* historically attributed to the third ancestor Sengcan.[35] The left radical of the character has the meaning of "person." The right radical of the character has the meaning of "words" or "sayings." *Shin,* then, can be understood as trusting or finding reliable the word of another. In this understanding of trust, there is the self and there is another who can be relied upon, a person who stands by his words.

We can trace the history of the term further back to the *Dasheng qixin lun* (*Awakening of Faith in the Mahāyāna*).[36] Contemporary scholars debate the actual origins of this text but agree that it was not, as was previously thought, composed by the Indian philosopher Aśvaghoṣa in the first or second century, nor translated into Chinese, at least primarily, by the great translator Paramārtha in 550 C.E. What is known is that the text spread quickly in China and was accepted as authoritative. It became a fundamental text in the Mahāyāna. The Japanese translation of this title, *Daijo kishin ron,* uses the word *shin* for faith. What is interesting is that the use of the word "Mahāyāna" in the title can be understood, in this case, not to refer to the name of a particular school of Buddhism but as an indicator of the empty nature of reality. From this perspective, "Mahāyāna" points directly to the basis of the school: the teachings of emptiness. So the title of the text can be understood to mean "arousal of faith in the empty nature of reality."

In the *Milindapañha* (*Questions of King Milinda*), part of the Burmese Pāli canon dating to 100–200 C.E., the senior monk Nāgasena is asked by the king, "What is the mark of faith?" He responds, "Faith makes serene and it leaps forward." Nāgasena compares faith to a "miraculous water-clearing gem" that clears the mind of "defilements," just as such a gem, when put into a muddy stream, would "settle the mud to the bottom [and] the stream would become clear, serene, and undisturbed." Faith inspires the practitioner to "leap forward," for when the practitioner "sees that hearts of others have been set free, he leaps forward by way of aspiration."[37] The sense in these statements is that with the presence of faith obscurations fade, the way is made clear, and the practitioner is able to continue in practice. In this way, faith can be thought of as a quality, a kind of attitude or entity, that influences a situation. Faith clarifies.

Kōshō Uchiyama deepens our understanding about the nature of faith in Zen practice by making a subtle and enlightening connection between two meanings of the word *shin.* The Japanese characters for the clarification process described above are 心澄浄, *shin chujo. Shin,* in this case, is the character for mind/heart. *Chujo* is "clear" or "clean and pure," in the sense of not obscuring what simply is. *Shin chujo,* then, can be understood as the clarification of the mind/heart but also as the clarifying activity of the mind/heart. Notice that the character *shin* (信) from the original discussion of faith in the *Xinxin ming* is not the same as the character *shin* (心) used in describing the process of clarification. Uchiyama states that faith, *shin* (信), is the process of clarifying the mind/heart, *shin* (心).[38] Thus, faith becomes not faith in something, i.e., faith in the word of another or in the teachings, but an activity in and of itself.

This exegesis has profound implications for our understanding of faith and trust in Sōtō Zen practice. Returning to the identity of the word *shin* (信) not just with faith but also with trust, if we approach it with Uchiyama's understanding, as the process of clarification rather than a state, we find that trust becomes not a quality to be sought and cultivated but the activity of the practice itself. Sitting, attending to what is as Buddha, is clarification, not in the sense of removing obscurations but in the sense of being willing to simply allow this moment as a manifestation of Buddha's Way. This is zazen, the posture and breath of faith, the expression and therefore the realization of absolute trust. Whether or not the practitioner feels what she would identify as trust in something or someone, she is living trust. In this way, she can come to trust in the Way, in trust itself. Dōgen calls this *konshin-jishin,* the "entire body becomes faith itself." The word "faith" here is a verb, and active faith is not tied to any condition. Instead it is an expression of itself as a living experience that emerges in each moment. *Shin* (faith/trust) is the activity of *shin* (heart/mind) that knows itself to be simply what is. This faith or trust is what I call absolute trust.

I wish to point out several shades of meaning of the term "absolute trust." First, absolute trust is absolute in the sense of being complete or total. Knowing that there is nothing that is not included in this moment, there is no attempt to hold back. In another sense, I draw on the way in which the word "absolute," along with its companion "relative," is used in the teachings of the two truths (correlates of the terms "ultimate" and "conventional"). "Absolute," in this case, is used to express the truth of emptiness. So we can also think of absolute trust as trust in the emptiness of all things, including the self. In this case, absolute trust is the lived expression of this truth by the practitioner. In addition, we can understand absolute trust as the trust that is expressed moment-to-moment by the absolute nature of reality. (I do not mean to suggest that there is any essence that can be identified as "the absolute," only that when we think in this way our understanding and experience of being an individual is altered and there is the implication of life itself living life.) This is akin to Dōgen's description of "the whole being of emptiness leaping out of itself."[39]

The term *jishin* (自信), "confidence," provides a means for understanding the lived personal experience of absolute trust. The great Zen master Linji (Jpn. Rinzai) taught that when we seek things outside ourselves we will never be at peace, because we cannot trust ourselves.[40] *Jishin* is comprised of the characters for "self," *ji* (自), and *shin* (信), "faith" or "trust"; literally, "self-trusting." The self to which Linji refers here, however, is not the self that believes itself to be a separate entity but one that knows itself to be an expression of dependent co-arising. According to this understanding, when we do not know such a self-experience, we seek things and people that are assumed to be outside of and separate from the self to reassure or somehow ease our distress and discomfort. Based on such a delusion, genuine, deep trust and peace are not possible. It is only when we know the true (i.e., empty) nature of the self that its inherent trustworthiness emerges. This is not mere trust in a particular outcome but deep identification with things as they are. In this way, confidence blooms and there is trust in life itself.

Confidence, *jishin,* then, is based in the realization of the dependently arisen self that expresses itself directly and personally in the activity of faith—that is, practice. This is the spirit of *shikantaza,* the spirit of Sōtō Zen. The self that so knows itself cannot be separated from trust, faith, and confidence. Knowing itself to be just this, moment after moment, how could mistrust be possible? With this realization the teaching that this moment, just as it is, is Buddha becomes real and *jishin,* confidence, emerges. In the words of Anne Klein, this confidence is expressed in the unique and individual "dynamic personal agency"[41] of a dependently arisen self.

One important dimension of this confidence occurs in the realm of a practitioner's relationship with people, texts, and situations aimed at deepening his understanding of the teachings. Such relationships require the practitioner to trust his own experience and at the same time be willing to listen deeply to another and question or "distrust" the categories he has used to understand his experience. In regard to the teaching, this requires that he is willing and able to open to the fact that the understanding he holds of his own experience may be flawed and that the teachings are worth attending to. With regard to teachers, it requires that he is willing to engage in dialogue with a reliable other, one in whom he senses an understanding and realization of the teachings and the capacity to embody wisdom and compassion.

As the practitioner listens and responds in this way, she allows herself to be challenged and threads her way to a ground of authority that allows her own personal dharma voice to emerge. The word "authority," in this context, is used in the sense of "authentic," "genuine," "trustworthy," and "honest."[42] This meaning of authority is not a matter of repeating dogma or simply parroting what one has heard but of making the teachings one's own. This occurs in the process of challenging and being challenged by the teachings, down to the bedrock of one's experience. This is the embodiment of the teachings and it is the work of a lifetime.

As the practitioner transforms the ground of her experience, an inner sense of authority emerges that is neither dependent on others' opinions nor sets itself up as eternal truth. There is an evolving sense of truth characterized not by rigidity but by deep listening and response. The practitioner shares the journey with others, expresses what is real to her, moment by moment, without attempting to find an immutable truth on which to hang her hopes and self-esteem. This confidence, based on experience, does not lead to closing down or adopting rigid opinions and positions but to a flowering of fundamental curiosity. It is both unshakable and completely fluid. Unshakable, because when the practitioner knows her own embodied and connected experience she is able to express it without fear (because she knows simply that this is the truth of her life at this moment and there is no self to defend); fluid, because it is based in and responsive to the ever-changing reality of the moment.

It is important to note here that gender can have a pronounced effect on the development of this sense of confidence and authority. As many contemporary women Buddhist teachers and authors have noted, coming to stand in and express one's own experience as valid and substantive is a process that can present special challenges to women practitioners.[43] Two of the most detailed and interesting explorations of this aspect of confidence are found not in a Buddhist text but in Caroline Walker Bynum's discussion of the nuns of Hefta, and Gerda Lerner's discussion of the topic of "self-authorization" as it developed in the lives of medieval women Christian mystics.[44] Both describe a religious authority based on direct experience. I do not intend to imply a similarity between mystical states and zazen, but rather to draw attention to an important opportunity in the lives of women (and men) who practitice Sōtō Zen in terms of coming to trust their own experience and finding a place where real dialogue with others is possible and fruitful. That opportunity lies in simply attending to the reality of experience and developing a nondefensive faith or trust in its validity.

In the career of a Zen practitioner, faith usually comes first in the shape of an affinity for or belief in the teachings, a teacher, or the practice itself. This is a kind of provisional faith that nonetheless has an important role to play. We can think of it as an expression of the first meaning of *shin,* a belief in the word of another, a respectful engagement that allows the individual to test the waters in a realistic and healthy way. It is based on the teachings making sense to the practitioner, whether rationally or intuitively. This aspect of faith is a kind of working hypothesis that is tested over time and found to be sound. The teachings and practice are found to indeed clarify the muddy water of confusion. This provisional faith is gradually replaced by the actual experience of its usefulness. Self-centered ideals are seen for what they are—notions of reality formed by and reflective of a subjective experience conditioned by the experience of separateness and duality. Doubt, in the sense of questioning and wrestling with the teachings, is an accepted part of living this faith. Trusting that what is being said is relevant, and that who is saying it is worthy of respect, wholehearted engagement that allows the teachings to permeate all aspects of life and relationships can develop.

Dōgen wrote in the fascicle *Gakudō yōjinshū:* "Those who practice the buddha way should first of all trust in the buddha way . . . should trust that they are in essence within the buddha way."[45] He is referring here to two elements of trust that together allow for the emergence of absolute trust. The second element is intimately bound to a sense of self that has developed from experiences of affirmation and support. Trusting in the Buddha Way, and trusting that one is within and of the Buddha Way regardless of circumstances, sets up the conditions for the transformation of self-experience. As the self allows itself to be transformed, ideas of what is to be gained by doing the practice begin to fade and self-centered agendas become less relevant. Through this, wholehearted engagement comes to be experienced, not as a means for the attainment or accrual of certain experiences but as an expression of the Buddha Way.

In *Shinjin gakudō* Dōgen instructs practitioners to

> Just whole-heartedly accept and trust that to study the way with mind is this mountains-rivers-and-earth mind itself thoroughly engaged in studying the way.[46]

This effort and trust, which is "neither large not small" and "beyond beginning or ending," is both the means and the expression of realization. There is a reciprocal relationship between the ability to know oneself as the "mountains-rivers-and-earth mind" and the ability to wholeheartedly accept the way. For the self to know itself as the mountains-rivers-and-earth mind/heart requires that it drop its self-referential perspective. This is an expression of trust in the Way and this entrustment is the mountains-rivers-and-earth studying the Way. This is absolute trust, a trust that is both a deeply personal experience and an expression of the nature of reality.

What is required of the individual practitioner in this process is the willingness to relinquish ordinary notions of trust as the sole means of guiding one's life. This in turn requires a thoroughgoing experience that such a leap is not suicidal. Such trust does not imply blind faith in someone or something or heedlessly extending trust when there is cause not to. This kind of trust is not defined or limited by self-centeredness, nor does it deny our humanness. Shohaku Okumura has said that we must trust even when there is no reason to trust. To understand this in a wholesome way we must investigate what trust is, what reason is, and who we are. Through this process trusting in the activity of trust—that is, practice—becomes the practitioner's home. Dōgen taught that "There is nothing in the world that is hidden."[47] Absolute trust is the enactment of this teaching. This is a trust lived out in all activities, and it is also the activity of all beings.

This is also tied to the human question of meaning, which is of great import to most practitioners and which can be deeply impacted by the teachings of emptiness and the dissolution of habitual ways of experiencing reality. Absolute trust emerges along with a new relationship to the question of meaning, one that does not reference the self as the central figure in unfolding events. In this context, the actuality of the moment itself is the meaning.[48]

Absolute trust is not tied to the perpetuation of the known self. Instead it is based on the realization that such a self is empty of inherent existence. Diving deep into the question of the nature of reality, not in an intellectual way but with his body, breath, heart, and mind, sitting in the faith that he and all beings are buddha, the practitioner evolves in his experience of trust. Knowing that the questioning itself is trustworthy, a dynamic expression of trust that is not dependent upon any particular circumstances emerges. This is trust without limit, for it is based on a nonoppositional relationship with reality itself.

It is interesting to note that, as Zen teacher Dainin Katagiri pointed out, one of the central ways a bodhisattva gives to others is by giving fearlessness.[49] Fear, which can be considered the opposite of trust, is perhaps the most potent obstacle to awareness and realization. Fear is based on notions of self and other. It pushes away the object that is feared, thereby limiting the possibility of change. It is intimately tied to the process of clinging to the known in order to protect a familiar, if limited, self-experience. The *Heart Sūtra* states that the bodhisattva relies on *prajñāpāramitā,* the teachings of emptiness, and with that reliance no fears exist. Where there is nothing to defend, there is no fear. This as another way of understanding absolute trust.

Shohaku Okumura has said that fear is the "glue" that holds the self together. It is interesting to compare this with Doris Brothers' assertion (in *Falling Backwards*) that self-trust forms the "glue" of selfhood. In a sense, we can see that both statements are true, taken in their respective contexts. The known self is held together by a (self-)trust based on the reliability of needed selfobjects. This is appropriate to the point of view of the self that experiences itself as separate and is a necessary trust that must be respected. However, this sense of trust is limited and will inevitably be shaken by Buddhist practice, if not by ordinary life. When we think in terms of a shift in self-experience and the possibility of a self-experience where these relationships do not apply, what lurks behind this sense of trust is the fear that without these selfobject relationships disintegration is inevitable. From a Buddhist perspective, we might say that old age, sickness, and death occur; suffering happens; life is uncertain. If trust means a belief that the self's needs will be met by conditional circumstances, then anxiety is inevitable and may be heightened by the teachings of emptiness.

This fear must be effectively addressed in the practice, and it is this fear that is eased by the bodhisattva. The bodhisattva gives fearlessness through her effort to practice and embody the teachings and the compassionate connectedness that arises from them. She does this not as a being somehow above the human condition but as one completely embedded in it. Katagiri Rōshi, commenting on Dōgen's fascicle "The Bodhisattva's Four Methods of Guidance," (*Bodaisatta shishōbō*) writes:

> Along with giving the Dharma, giving fearlessness is very important, particularly if we are practicing a spiritual life. . . .
>
> Through understanding the structure of human existence philosophically and psychologically, and through directly experiencing human life, we can build up perfection of character. A person's character must be perfectly beautiful, allowing us to be generous, tolerant, compassionate, kind and strong. Perfection of character is something that makes us free from human suffering, even though we are in the midst of it. Our presence is very important for all sentient beings, whoever we are. If our life wobbles and is shaky, it is very difficult to be present from moment to moment. So we must be stable when we are around people. . . . We cry, we struggle, we despair and we have many difficult experiences, but those experiences . . . inspire us and encourage us to live in peace and harmony. This is why we can practice the giving of Dharma and fearlessness.[50]

Thus, the very experiences that make for suffering and difficulty become opportunities for deepening our understanding and our relationships with others.

The practitioner's journey of trust can be seen as parallel to the evolution of the Sino-Japanese characters for trust described above. Where there is a fundamental trust in a person's word and in one's own ability, authentic engagement with the teachings and the practice is possible. From this emerges the capacity to clarify—that is, to simply be with what is, as it is. This in turn allows for the emergence of an experience of self and trust that is embedded in and responsive to moment-by-moment reality. The activity of trust, the practice of Sōtō Zen, becomes the compassionate expression of one's life and "mountains-rivers-and-earth-mind" studying the Way.

In combination with self-trust, we can think of absolute trust as forming the context for the unfolding and maturation of Sōtō Zen practice. The relationship of these two aspects of trust tells us much about the lived experience of practice. The practitioner's experience of absolute trust is determined by his experience of trust in its other manifestations.

In terms of the first aspect of practice life, we can say that basic trust supports the ability to sit still, listen, and attend, as well as the ability to trust one's own perceptions and the words and actions of another. With this ability, unintegration or "being in bits" is not associated with fragmentation or disintegration anxiety but can instead be experienced as creative and fundamentally trustworthy. In terms of the second dimension of practice life, a presentation of the teachings of emptiness, though evocative at times, does not cause a retreat into distrust. Trust can come to be trusted and increasingly relied upon in practice. A process by which awareness, not the self as a discrete entity, is the reference point becomes increasingly familiar. With this there is the possibility of a different and more thoroughgoing experience of trust. This in turn allows for the possibility of the shift in subjective experience fundamental to the practice, the realization that this self is not different from all beings.

Without basic trust, the teachings of emptiness can become an encounter with the fragmentation and fear presented by Wolf (in *Treating the Self*) and Epstein (in *Thoughts Without a Thinker*) in their discussion of "emptiness." The person who has a weakly cohesive or fragile self-structure and a more limited sense of basic trust is less able to integrate difficult experiences and is also more prone to them. Encountering the teachings of emptiness, as challenging as they are to the very existence of the self as a concrete entity in relation to identifiable others, can be one of these difficult experiences. Emptiness teachings may evoke the basic fear that lies at the root of a self that is prone to fragmentation: that it does not exist, or that it will be obliterated. The self whose primary agenda is to defend itself against these feelings will have difficulty opening to teachings or practices that function to transform the self. For the practitioner, this can mean missing the fundamental fullness present in the companion teachings of dependent co-arising. This in turn profoundly affects the ability to engage with, and ultimately embody, the teachings, since they may become associated with times in which the terror of disintegration dominated.

This can lead to an ongoing struggle between an effort to engage with the teachings and the imperative to preserve the known self and defend against the "panic and horror"[51] of disintegration anxiety. A "nightmare world of self fragmentation in which sanity, indeed the very continuity of existence, can no longer be taken for granted"[52] is not the aim of Sōtō Zen practice. Yet, particularly for the person who has a fragile basis and a weak sense of basic trust, such a nightmarish experience may be exactly what awaits in the unknowing of zazen and other Sōtō Zen practices.

This is akin to Herman's description of traumatic events that "call into question basic human relationships."[53] Brothers states that if our experience is one in which

> the bonds of self trust and connectedness are severed, we are likely to descend, like Alice down the rabbit hole, into a terrifying and surreal world in which self-experience seems to fragment or disintegrate. . . . This is precisely what happens in psychic trauma.[54]

If basic trust is not present or is compromised, teachings and practices that pose a challenge to a familiar way of experiencing relationality can be experienced as traumatic, as severing connectedness rather than realizing it. The person who has experienced the shattering overwhelm of trauma and has not sufficiently reestablished "bonds of self trust" is particularly vulnerable to this pitfall. Fluidity can be associated with passivity, openness with helpless vulnerability, and compassion with weakness and exploitation. In this case, what is familiar will be fiercely defended. No one wants to go down the rabbit hole.

The wholesale ripping apart of self-sustaining fantasies is neither compassionate nor useful. The point of practice is not to tear the practitioner away from any sense of ease and safety and thrust them into a cold and fearful darkness where all support has vanished. The purpose is to allow the emergence of an experience in which those categories do not apply. This does not mean that there will never be fear, anxiety, or trepidation; indeed, it is almost certain that such emotions will emerge. It does mean that when they do, the practitioner experiences them in the context of practice. This, in turn, implies that they are encountered in an environment where they do not threaten psychic survival nor evoke a response of withdrawal.

From a practice point of view, we can think of pushing someone, including oneself, down the rabbit hole as having (at least) three outcomes. First, it can set up a mighty resistance that only solidifies the known and entrenched self. Second, it can lead to a disruption of self-experience that creates so much fear and disturbance that the practitioner retreats from the encounter, often stopping or curtailing practice or engaging in activities that lead away from an orientation toward practice. Third, it can lead to an expansive experience that the self-centered self may use to shore up its sense of specialness or superiority, or that is viewed as aberrant and disavowed. In the latter case, the experience will be ignored as alien to the established sense of identity, and it will not be integrated into a relational responsive subjectivity that reduces suffering.

Summary

Basic trust provides the foundation on which a reliable and cohesive self is built. It is essential to the inclusion of a wide range of experiences and the welcoming of alternate ways of understanding that experience. With trust and the formation of the cohesive self there is the capacity to attend, to maintain awareness, as disintegration does not threaten. This then allows the individual to become comfortable with awareness itself as the basis for a sense of cohesion. Reciprocity and mutuality form the foundation of relational life and a full and generous engagement with others (both sentient and nonsentient), and the practice becomes possible.

With the establishment of this trust, it becomes possible to "relax" in states where subject and object are not so easily defined and open to a new experience of subjectivity. In zazen and in other dimensions of her practice life, the practitioner is able to trust not only that the self will reliably reconstitute itself and that sufficient relational support is available, she will also come to experience trust in life itself—that is, absolute trust. This evolution of trust allows the leap, so to speak, to be made from a sense of self that is bound up with a view of reality based on notions of subject and object, self and other, to one in which dependent co-arising forms the foundation of experience.

We can say that, ultimately, it is only when we realize we are not different from all phenomena, even from the rabbit hole itself, that fear can be replaced with curiosity and even wonder. Knowing the reality of dependent co-arising and thusness, the teachings of emptiness do not threaten but instead promise liberation from a bounded and limited apprehension of reality. In this way, *jishin,* self-confidence, emerges. However, this knowledge and realization is only born out of engaged practice, which in turn emerges from an experience of trust that has been nurtured in a supportive and transforming practice environment.

The topic of the next chapter is the role of the practice environment, both animate and inanimate, in facilitating the shift in trust and self-experience. I will also introduce a way of describing the role of selfobjects that includes both their transformational and supportive properties. I conclude by bringing these elements together and reflecting on their interrelationship and their implications for the teaching and practice of Sōtō Zen.

Chapter 5

The Practice Environment

The self in both Buddhism and psychoanalytic systems is a relational event, a fluid structure embedded in and emerging from the environment. The transformation of the self and self-experience takes place in this mutually influencing flow.[1] From a Sōtō Zen perspective, as Cook writes, the self is a manifestation of dependent co-arising and is not different from momentary experience.[2] From the perspective of self psychology, we understand that the structures of the self influence and organize perception, but they are also being continually affected by the milieu in which they exist. Because the self is not separate from its surrounding environment (and, in fact, according to both perspectives it cannot be), a reciprocal relationship exists and a change in the environment has the potential to deeply affect the nature and experience of the self and subjective experience. This reciprocal, ongoing mutuality between the self and the environment is a cornerstone of Sōtō Zen practice and training, found in every area of Sōtō Zen life. In this chapter I will explore some dimensions of the relationships inherent in the practice environment. From a psychoanalytic perspective, Stolorow and Atwood write about the mutual nature of the self and its surrounding environment:

> A person enters any situation with an established set of ordering principles (the subject's contribution to the intersubjective system) but it is the context that determines which among the array of these principles will be called on to determine the experience. . . . The organization of experience can therefore be seen as codetermined both by pre-existing principles and by an ongoing context that favors one or another of them over others.[3]

With reference to Sōtō Zen practice, we can say that this "ongoing context" is the practice environment made up of the people, places, and things, as well as the attitudes, history, and emotional climate, a person encounters when she comes to practice. From this perspective, we can say that the functional practice environment "favors" "preexisting principles" that are conducive to practice and thereby fulfills its intended aim of encouraging full engagement in practice.

Another equally important aspect of a functional practice environment are the "principles" and experiences that lie outside any previous frame of reference and are aimed at disrupting it. Dōgen writes in his fascicle *Yuibutsu yobutsu:*

> [R]ealization invariably differs from your expectation. Realization is not like your conception of it. Accordingly, realization can not take place as previously conceived. . . . Although realization is not like any of the thoughts preceding it, this is not because such thoughts were actually bad and could not be realization. Past thoughts in themselves were already realization. But since you were seeking elsewhere, you thought and said that thoughts cannot be realization.[4]

To understand the practice environment, then, we must take both of these dimensions into consideration. These two aspects of the practice environment, one that supports the organization of experience in a way that encourages the practitioner, and one that challenges reliance on any self-referential schema, operate effectively together when the practice milieu is functioning fully. This results in ever-increasing capacity to fully engage in and be transformed by the teachings.

The Supportive and Transforming Practice Environment

When we think of a practice environment in which an individual can deeply engage with the Sōtō Zen teachings, certain qualities emerge. First and foremost is the presence of trust. By this, I mean the presence of basic trust in the inner world of the practitioner and adequate trustworthiness in the surrounding environment. In regard to the cultivation of the ability to fruitfully enter the experience of "between," D. W. Winnicott writes:

> Account has to be taken of the reliability or unreliability of the setting in which the individual is operating . . . [that is,] the essentials that make relaxation possible.[5]

In terms of Sōtō Zen practice, this does not mean that all the needs of the self as it has been known are perfectly met, nor does it mean that there is no significant distress or disruption. It does mean that the environment has the aim of evoking a liberating subjective experience, not a disintegrating one, and it is reasonably able to fulfill that goal.

This relational milieu works in two compatible and complementary ways. First, it functions as a context in which the self is supported in its developing capacity to fully engage with the practice. I call this the supportive function. Second, it functions to transform that self-experience. With the presence of basic trust there is an opportunity for absolute trust to emerge. An effective functional practice environment, then, is comprised of qualities that provide both nourishing support and appropriate challenge.

It is important to note, again, that the attitude toward the self that informs such a functional practice environment does not regard the self as an obstacle to be overcome, a problem to be solved, or an impediment to be obliterated. Such thinking only sets up opposition that fuels a position in which the known self is defended and reinforces dualistic thinking. This in turn undermines the process by which the relationality of the self is realized.

What is required in the relational milieu of the practitioner is affirmation that a different self-experience is possible. To use Anne Klein's terminology, this is an empty subjectivity, "a self that is both contextually constructed and viable as an agent, a force to be contended with, but not the center of the world."[6] To employ a spatial metaphor suggested when thinking in terms of environment, we can refer to the self as the site or locus of the manifestation of wisdom, compassion, and the bodhisattva vow. This is in line with Dōgen's teaching that we are liberated not *from* the circumstances of the world but *to* them. We can think of the self as an embedded facet of the relational milieu, one that is intimately connected and responsive to it. As the practice environment fulfills its function to both encourage and challenge, the self-experience of those who engage with it is inevitably transformed.

Another way of discussing this paired functioning of support and challenge is in terms of two subjective experiences: a sense of coherence and cohesiveness based in a selfobject matrix that is reliably affirming, and another that rests at ease in impermanence, in emptiness, regardless of circumstance. It is clear that to create an effective practice environment both aspects must be included. If the experience of resting in impermanence is ignored practice may become nothing more than a self-improvement project, which, while understandable and progressive, remains limited. If the need for affirmation is ignored practice may become an arid spiritual athleticism lacking humility and a deepening connection to all beings that suffer and feel fear. Weaving the two aspects together, we can create a practice and a practice environment grounded in human experience, and we will be able to use that experience as a means to embody the bodhisattva vow.

The importance of the supportive aspect of the practice environment is addressed by Jeffrey Hopkins in his text on Tibetan Buddhist emptiness teachings and practices. He describes the need for the creation of a "competent mind"[7] when taking up the challenges presented by the teachings of emptiness. He notes that practices of compassion and love (or, we might say, connectedness and bonds of caring)—for example, the development of *maitrī,* or basic friendliness, toward oneself and others—are particularly helpful in creating this competency. Cultivating these qualities, the practitioner is able to establish a solid foundation of awareness and an inner stability that can meet any anxiety or fear aroused by the practice. At the same time, she is able to deepen her understanding of the nature of things—emptiness and dependent co-arising.

The creation of a competent mind and heart can be thought of as the first important task of the practice environment. A practice environment capable of doing this is comprised of elements akin to those that support the emergence of basic trust and a healthy and resilient self-structure. This is accomplished in the field of practice relationships. The teachers, sangha, ritual activities, the physical environment, and the practice schedule all combine to form this milieu. Fundamentally, such an environment provides the self with a sense that its basic needs will be adequately met and that disintegration does not threaten. (Again, it is important to note this does not imply that practice and the practice environment have the same aim as a psychotherapeutic one.) If the fear of disintegration does arise, there is a sense that the environment will provide adequate structure and support so that a functional sense of self is maintained. To paraphrase Wolf, the aim of the practice environment in this regard is to support the development of a sense of self with which the practitioner is "willing and able to actively plunge into the rough and tumble of everyday [practice]." He notes:

> If a person is to feel well—to feel good about himself, with a secure sense of self, enjoying good self esteem and functioning smoothly and harmoniously without undue anxiety and depression—he must experience himself consciously or unconsciously as surrounded by responsive others.[8]

He goes on to say:

> To maintain its cohesion, its vigor, its balance, the healthy self needs to be embedded in a milieu that is experienced as constantly supplying a self sustaining selfobject ambience.[9]

This is an interesting statement when translated into the terms of Sōtō Zen practice. It challenges us to think carefully about what actually works in the lives of practitioners. Juxtaposing Wolf's statements with the idea, stated earlier in this chapter, that a cohesive, vigorous self supports the ability to deeply engage with Zen practice, we can see that the factors that support one also support the other. In other words, taking into account and attending to the fundamental needs of the self, and including them in such a way that basic trust and cohesiveness are encouraged, is in accord with the primary aim of the practice environment in regard to the self: the transformation of its basis in line with the teachings of the tradition. Notice that Wolf does not say that there is *no* anxiety or depression, only that there is no *undue* anxiety or depression. In the course of Sōtō Zen practice, responses to the teachings and the practice often include feelings of disruption. Within in a well-functioning practice context, however, these responses do not derail the process or contribute to a state of disturbance or fragmentation that is harmful to the fundamental soundness of the practitioner's psyche.

This brings up the question of how a well-functioning practice environment includes the essential element of challenge. Stolorow and Atwood write that "a milieu in which [a person's] reality is not threatened encourages [him] to develop and expand his own capacity for self reflection."[10] This describes an environment that does not present the threat of disintegration, of fragmentation of the self, or of going down the rabbit hole. Since Sōtō Zen practice is inevitably and necessarily deeply challenging to the (perceived) reality of the practitioner, the implication is that the challenge must take place in an environment that does not overwhelm the person and evoke responses that lead to aversion. Such a practice environment thoroughly challenges the practitioner's experience and definitions of self and reality but does not threaten disintegration. Instead, it supports the growth of a different experience of self. In other words, it provides a new, though explicitly inherently empty, context for self-experience even as it dismantles the old.

Many, if not most, people enter Zen practice with some degree of impairment in basic trust, some areas of fragility and lessened cohesion of the self, and the stresses of the practice will inevitably bring existing faultlines to the surface. A supportive practice environment, however, effectively responds to these stresses in such a way that full participation in the practice can unfold.

It is important to note that, from a Buddhist perspective, faultlines can be seen as both obstacles and opportunities. They can block further engagement in the path, or they can provide an opportunity for deepening one's practice and realization. For example, if a practitioner is caught up in negatively judging her ability to sit zazen, knowing that support is available, that she is not alone, and that this difficulty is addressed within the tradition allows her to creatively engage with her experience. Viewed from this perspective, self-judgment is simply an obstacle to be overcome. Another perspective, however, can also be brought to bear on this difficulty: taking the experience of self-judgment itself as an opportunity to better understand suffering and self-clinging. The experience of self-judgment can become not simply a repetition or even a resolution of past patterns but a means to develop compassion and a sense of connection to all beings that have also suffered in this way. This cannot occur, however, in the absence of a supportive practice environment.

For this reason, it is essential that adequate attention be given to the supportive dimension of practice. Not only can the lack of adequate support lead people to withdraw or turn away from practice, it can also lead to lopsided or even harmful development. For example, unmet selfobject needs can lead a longtime practitioner or teacher to consciously or unconsciously manipulate the environment and others to meet those needs, instead of participating with others in the spirit of the bodhisattva vow. In this way, unaddressed needs can distract from the primary aim of practice: the realization and expression of Buddha's Way. Indeed, if adequate support is not given, the practice environment itself can be subverted to the dominating needs of the self and its continuance. Therefore, giving attention to these supportive selfobject relationships is not a secondary or lesser aspect of practice but the very avenue through which transformation becomes possible. We can also think of this in terms of the teachings of form and emptiness. Emptiness, if privileged, may become nothing more than the playing out of disembodied concepts unrelated to the living reality of the moment. Form, in this case the actuality of persons and their relationships, is the site of the practice and realization of the Bodhisattva Way.

An affirming practice environment is one that supports an increasing ability to rest in this moment without a sense that fragmentation and disintegration threaten. This means that the practitioner, within the context of the practice situation, does not defend against life but feels a good measure of confidence that it is possible to experience it without harm. This leads to the integration of experience that in turn supports a more solid, less fragmented sense of self and greater confidence and ability to be present in a variety of circumstances. With an increased ability to tolerate less-than-optimal selfobject relationships, the practitioner is able to use those experiences to deepen her study of the nature of the self.

This is key, because it opens up a new relationship to adverse circumstances. With this attitude a practitioner is able to regard difficult experiences as a means to join with all beings that are (also) caught in delusion. This in turn encourages a sense of connectedness and undercuts identification with the notion of an isolated self, and this results in a deeper engagement in zazen practice as well as more flexibility and compassionate responsiveness in relationship to others. Because of this connected responsiveness, the perception of an affirming environment and a greater sense of competence and confidence grows. This cycle is an important element in the continued positive development of the practitioner/environment reality. It provides the context in which both supportive and transforming relationships can fruitfully occur.

Supportive and Transforming Selfobject Relationships

Using the language and concepts of self psychology, we can say that an effective practice environment provides selfobject relationships that function in both supportive and transforming ways.[11] These selfobject relationships cannot be separated from the self and its inferred structure, and they mature with it over time. The life of a Sōtō practitioner is filled with selfobject relationships that have concurrent and overlapping supportive and transforming functions. Both of these relationships shift self-experience from that in which fear and clinging dominate to that in which a fuller participation in reality is possible. Each, however, plays a different role.

Supportive selfobject relationships maintain and restore the cohesion, continuity, and wholesome "preexisting principles" of the self. They affirm the practitioner's ability to follow the Sōtō Zen Way, to actually do the practice, and support the development of the qualities of self-experience that make this possible. Supportive selfobject relationships within the practice environment are not qualitatively different from those in other realms of life; their function is the "establishment, preservation and restoration of self-experience,"[12] in this case, a self-experience that supports engagement with Sōtō Zen practice. They provide the relational context in which the self can allow itself to fully engage with the practice without debilitating fear or anxiety.

Transforming selfobject relationships challenge and shift an individual's subjective experience. All selfobject relationships can be said to change or transform a person's experience of self in a way—after all, supporting or restoring the self is a transformation of self-experience. What distinguishes what I call transforming selfobject relationships is their function in shifting self-experience toward a subjectivity based in dependent co-arising. They express the co-constituting nature of the self and the selfobject relationship as experienced within the context of the teachings of emptiness.

For example, a practitioner's effort to regard every object, including the self and all circumstances, as Buddha can evoke a subjective experience that is not based in a separate sense of self. When this occurs, her perspective on the nature of an object, her relationship to it, and her experience of self will all be altered. The teachings that all phenomena are empty of inherent existence, and that each interaction is the expression of dependent co-arising, come alive and there is the potential to transform subjective experience in such a way that these teachings are realized.

In Dōgen's teachings in *Tenzo kyōkun* ("Instructions to the Cook") we find a description of how to relate to physical objects based in the potentially evocative and transformative nature of every interaction. When Dōgen instructs the monastic cook to "handle a leaf of green in such a way that it manifests the body of Buddha," and that by so doing she will allow "Buddha to manifest through the leaf,"[13] he is describing a selfobject relationship that transforms not only the leaf of green but also the practitioner herself. This is Buddha studying Buddha's Way.

Using the notion of selfobject relationships in this way, we can explore the practice environment from three perspectives: the nature of the object in the selfobject relationship, the ways in which the types of selfobject relationships (mirroring, idealization, and twinship) function to support and transform the practitioner's self-experience, and the process of maturation.

The Range of "Objects"

The objects that constitute the structural component of selfobject relationships have been variously described in the literature of self psychology. Although its authors are careful to point out that the selfobject relationship is an "inner experience," an "intrapsychic experience," or an "intersubjective" experience,[14] it nonetheless takes place between a subject and an object, or a subject and a subject. There is a referent in the selfobject relationship, an other that occupies a position in relation to the self.

This position can be occupied by a variety of entities, concrete or symbolic, animate or inanimate. In an effort to focus on subject/subject (intersubjective) relationships between persons and to undercut tendencies to reify the self, Stolorow, Brandchaft, and Atwood (*Psychoanalytic Treatment*) and Stolorow and Atwood (*Context of Being*) turned away from the term "selfobject" and emphasized the intersubjective nature of these relationships. In so doing, however, they created an emphasis that may imply a limitation in the potential range of these relationships: a subject/subject relationship can only exist between humans, or at least between sentient beings. But selfobject relationships can occur in a far greater range than merely between humans. Wolf writes, "Selfobject experiences can be the function not only of objects but also of symbols or ideas representing objects." He goes on to say that

> The tangible and visible things of the world have selfobject functions that make them part of our selfs and thus restore us, or sometimes give to us *de novo* our wholeness.[15]

There is a limitless array of selfobject experiences, and the "objects" that occupy the position of referent are equally unlimited. From a Sōtō Zen perspective such objects can range from a coffee cup to a sacred image, and their significance or transformative capacity is not dependent upon any conventional valuation. A statue of the Buddha carries associations that may make it a more likely recipient of and source for experiences associated with Buddhism and Zen; yet ordinary objects, such as a bowl, can also function in this way. What is key is how an individual regards an object and the context in which he encounters it. It is also important to note that even "objects" intended to lead to a transformation of limited notions of self and other and a realization of the teaching, for example a buddha image, can also be (mis)used to deepen those limited notions.

An affirming selfobject milieu can take shape in a variety of ways. A hermit living miles away from any observable contact with other people can experience herself as deeply embedded in a web of selfobject relationships that support and sustain her life. She may even have a richer selfobject life than someone in the midst of multiple social contacts. In a more ordinary context, the presence of other practitioners, the physical surroundings of the practice, as well as the teachings themselves can all function to affirm the practitioner.

Regarding the transformative potential of any object and every interaction in the Sōtō tradition, Dōgen wrote in *Bussho* ("Buddha-nature") that "there is not even a single object alien to Buddha-nature, nor is there any second existence other than this universe here and now."[16] Without constrictions imposed by ideas of a hierarchy of being, transforming relationships can come alive in ordinary circumstances as well as events that are imbued with religious or spiritual meaning. When Dōgen asserts that even a "simple green has the power to become the practice of the Buddha" and tells the cook to "never feel aversion to plain ingredients . . . [and] make the best use of whatever greens you have,"[17] he is creating a context in which all objects, no matter how mundane, can fulfill a transformative function.

To change one's relationship to the objects of the world, both inner and outer, in this way is to change the self itself. This does not mean, however, that objects are to be regarded merely as a means to transform self-experience. Such an attitude would perpetuate a dualistic and self-referential perspective that undercuts the very activity of practice. Fully participating with all aspects of reality, each occupying its own momentary uniqueness in concert with all others, forms the basis of the transformative function of relationships. This occurs in all activities and cannot be thought of as separate from the self itself.

Supportive and transformational selfobject experiences complement each other and work together. Viewed from the outside, it may be difficult to see what exactly is occuring in any given interaction. For example, a person cutting carrots could be simply doing an assigned chore, in the ordinary way of regarding such activities. Yet the simple act of cutting carrots can be a source of affirmation for the practitioner as a member of the community, and a part of a sustaining relational structure. This activity could also be the occasion of a transforming selfobject relationship between the individual, the knife, the carrot, the table, and the others present in the kitchen.

From one perspective, we can say that the activity in each case is identical, but only if one is observing the activity and defining it as the accomplishment of a task. From another perspective, that of the actual relationships between the various constituents, the activity is very different, and this difference is experienced not only by the person involved but by all aspects of the situation. The practitioner who has the intention to engage with objects as Buddha will relate to them respectfully and gratefully. This can be as simple as setting a knife down carefully and gently instead of dropping it, making sure when washing the rice that all the grains are included and nothing is wasted, or picking up a chair to move it instead of dragging it across the floor.

This respectful attentiveness to objects can extend to the careful attention given to a fellow practitioner with whom one is having difficulty—for example, listening carefully and with an open mind and heart to another's experience. This kind of selfobject relationship, when engaged with honestly, creates an atmosphere in which the practitioner can be affirmed as a part of the whole and experiences himself as a valued and deeply engaged person on and of the Way. A tone is set in such environments, a baseline of respect for all involved, sentient and nonsentient beings alike. Such an atmosphere is palpable and it is affirming.

This atmosphere also includes a transformational dimension, which in turn influences all participants. To see one leaf of green as Buddha is to transform one's relationship to it and to be transformed by it. Viewed from the outside, the activity of cutting carrots in this way evokes a simple grace and an unadulterated compassionate connection that can inspire. It is also simply cutting carrots. Regarding the fruition of this process, Katsuki Sekida writes:

> In a person mature in Zen . . . even the simplest, most trivial action, such as lighting a candle before the image of a Buddha, or the movement of his feet in white socks, stepping along the corridor like two white rabbits, takes on an indescribable beauty.[18]

Thus, an activity can be understood in an ordinary, abstract way, as the simple accomplishment of a task. Yet it can also be understood and experienced quite differently, not simply as a task to be accomplished but as an expression of the intention on which it is based.

From a Sōtō Zen perspective, then, the range of objects or referents in the selfobject relationship, as well as the type of relationship, is unlimited. A candle or buddha statue can function in either (or both) supportive or transformative ways, and there is no predicting what the nature of the relationship will be based on the object itself. In fact, there are many stories in the Zen lexicon of students being reminded, sometimes forcefully, not to confer a superior or privileged status to buddha statues or other religious objects. At the same time, the intentionally created Sōtō Zen practice environment is filled with objects that are actively intended to both support and transform the self-experience of the practitioner.

Let me offer an example from the Sōtō Zen meal practice (*ōryōki*) to illustrate this. The largest bowl used in monastic and retreat settings is referred to as the buddha bowl. (Ordained practitioners ritually receive a set of bowls, including a buddha bowl, from the sangha and teacher at the time of their ordination.) A practitioner cares for the buddha bowl in a specified manner, carrying it at the level of or above the heart, placing it respectfully when not in use, holding it in a particular way when receiving food and eating. The buddha bowl is not simply a container for food or an opportunity to practice mindful eating—it is Buddha's bowl. A practitioner may have many relationships to this ordinary, if often quite beautiful, object. It can function in a supportive sense as a reminder of his relationship to the community and his inclusion in the lineage. It can be an object of simple physical pleasure or of veneration. It can also function in a transformative manner, along with all the other aspects of the practice circumstance, as a means of waking up to the interconnected luminosity of the moment. In that moment, the ordinary object becomes, along with the self, all being.

Each object, then, can function in a variety of ways according to the situation, needs, and intention of the practitioner. In one situation, a candle can simply be a means of finding one's way to the door; in another, it can signify one's skill at the monastic job of candlemaking; and in another, it can be an offering of light to all beings and an expression of thusness. In any given circumstance there are many possibilities. The nature of the relationship is dependent not only on the circumstances but also on the practitioner's mind and maturity. In terms of the practice environment, we can say that access to such relationships fosters the transformation of self-experience and the emergence of absolute trust.

Mirroring, Idealization, and Twinship

Kohut's designation of selfobject relationships as mirroring, idealization, and twinship in *The Analysis of the Self, The Restoration of the Self,* and *How Does Analysis Cure?* provides us with another way of understanding the relationships and environment that affirm and transform the self-experience of the Sōtō Zen practitioner. In this context, mirroring can be understood, in terms of the first dimension of practice, as the affirmation of the practitioner as a person with the capacity to practice and realize Buddha's Way. It can also be understood, from the perspective of transforming selfobject relationships, as the experience of being seen (and of seeing oneself and the other) as Buddha, the moment-to-moment luminosity of all life. By enacting the teaching that every phenomenon, including the self, is Buddha, each relationship thus has the potential for reflecting back to the practitioner an experience of himself as Buddha.

In the realm of idealization, the practitioner knows himself to be in relationship to trusted others who have the wisdom and ability to serve as effective examplars and guides along the way. These can include a wide range of relationships involving elders, teachers, the lineage, and the Buddha. Enfolded in these supportive relationships, the practitioner can develop trust that difficulties are surmountable and that others have gone before. Idealized others can be relied upon for support and teaching, and as exemplars of how to effectively meet fear or anxiety when they arise.

From the perspective of twinship, we can say that an individual experiences herself to be a human practitioner among other human practitioners. She is a being among all beings, fundamentally of the same nature not only of all humans or of all living beings but of all phenomena. As an affirming process, twinship provides a sense of kinship with other practitioners, a feeling of being on the path with others. Sōtō Zen is spoken of as being transmitted "warm hand to warm hand." This way of understanding the teaching is recognition of twinship. In the transformative sense it opens up the possibility of realizing one's essential non-difference with all being, with emptiness, thusness, and buddha-nature.

We can use Kohut's description of a wholesome selfobject milieu as an outline for an affirming practice environment in terms of mirroring, idealization, and twinship. In describing the role each of these three selfobject relationships play in supporting a person's full engagement in life, he writes:

> Throughout his life a person will experience himself as a cohesive harmonious firm unit in time and space, connected with his past and pointing meaningfully into a creative-productive future . . . only as long as, at each stage in his life, he experiences certain representatives of his human surround as joyfully responding to him [mirroring], as available to him as sources of idealized strength and calmness [idealization], as being silently present but in essence like him [twinship] and, at any rate, able to grasp his inner life more or less accurately so that their responses are attuned to his needs and allow him to grasp their inner life when his is in need of such sustenance.[19]

It is important to note, again, that the experience of being a "cohesive and harmonious firm unit in time and space, connected to [one's] past and pointing meaningfully into a creative-productive future" is not antithetical to the realization that no such "unit" (self) exists as an independent permanent entity. Recalling the teachings of emptiness and the relationship of form and emptiness, we find that this self can indeed exist as a form among forms. From the practical, "human-scale" point of view, we also note that those who have limited or curtailed access to such experiences are inhibited in their ability to fully embrace the teachings of emptiness, unless this is taken into account.

In a supportive practice environment the practitioner's experience will include some sense of being deeply and meaningfully responded to by his teachers and fellow practitioners with recognition, encouragement, and even joy at his participation. This may not always take an obvious, outwardly expressed form but it is found in full inclusion in the practice and the emphasis on the teaching that all beings are buddha-nature. Such a spirit of generosity and inclusion grounds and invigorates the individual practitioner. A direct expression of this mutual recognition is the practice of bowing in greeting. In a formal Sōtō Zen practice setting each practitioner stops and bows to any other practitioner when they pass one another. This is a sign of respect and an act of seeing others beyond the realm of opinions, definitions, or likes or dislikes. It is an acknowledgement of the perceived other as Buddha. Giving and receiving this acknowledgement is an enactment of mirroring, practitioner to practitioner, Buddha to Buddha.

A supportive environment also includes a very real experience of the availability of images, stories, and persons who embody the tradition. These provide inspiration and the sense that others can be counted on to provide support and guidance. A symbolic expression of this is found in the statues and images of the Buddha present in a Sōtō temple. Traditional teaching stories also serve this function, as does the presence of senior practitioners. Perhaps the most concrete and powerful relationship for most people that occurs in the realm of idealization is the teacher-student relationship, which I discuss in more detail below.

The experience of twinship is actively lived out each time a practitioner enters the zendo. Upon entering, the practitioner experiences being surrounded by others who are, as Kohut says, "silently present but in essence like him." And it is not only one's fellow practitioners who form this silent presence, though this is the most concrete and accessible manifestation of twinship, but also the lineage and the community of all who have taken up the path. This aspect of twinship can affirm the practitioner as being one among others who are also practicing. But there is another aspect of twinship, akin to mirroring, which communicates to the practitioner her likeness to the very basis of the tradition and her inclusion in the possibility and reality of realization. By this I mean her likeness to all the teachers in the lineage.

This aspect of the twinship dimension is seen in the discussion of the relationship between Mahākāśyapa (Śākyamuni Buddha's first disciple in the Zen lineage) and a practitioner seen in the *Denkōroku* (*Record of Transmitting the Light*). The text says that if the practitioner comes to "thoroughly know" Buddha—that is, the reality of thusness, emptiness, her own true nature—"Mahākāśyapa will be able to move his toes in your sandals."[20] This very direct statement about the fundamental identity of the practitioner and the legendary figures of realization that make up the lineage serves to both affirm and challenge him. He is affirmed in the sense that he is included in the reality of buddha-nature; challenged in that he is asked to directly realize this. In this way, both a shift in self-experience and encouragement to practice are brought about.

Practice relationships take shape in a multitude of ways. Each object in the practice environment contributes to the formation of a selfobject milieu that both supports and effectively challenges the practitioner. Ordinary physical objects—from kitchen utensils to computers, rakes to toilet bowls, laundry to cars—as well as those imbued with more symbolic meanings, such as altars, statues, robes, and the whole range of relationships possible with other beings (both human and nonhuman) can all function in this way. All aspects of practice—zazen, work practice, relationships, following the precepts, participating in ritual activities, and study—are arenas in which realization can unfold. Each practitioner will find his own way but, for most, relationships within the sangha (in this case, the individuals with whom a person actively practices) and the relationship with a teacher are central. The tradition is lived out and passed on in its most immediate, vital, and intimate form in these relationships. And it is within these relationships that the dimensions of mirroring, idealization, and twinship are most concretely expressed.

Sangha and the Student-Teacher Relationship

Sangha relationships vary from practitioner to practitioner and from day to day, depending on the configuration of the relationships and the activity involved. Teaching relationships can also occur in many ways. In terms of the creation of an effective relational practice milieu, however, their essential functions can be fruitfully viewed in terms of the supportive and transforming aspects described above. Such relationships based in growing honesty, intimacy, and trust aim at the realization of the teachings. In any sangha or teaching relationship there is also the possibility (or inevitability) of misunderstandings, misperceptions, and distortions. The community and the teacher can be the object of old longings for mirroring, twinship, and idealization. Failures occur and when this happens feelings of betrayal, anger, and rejection may be evoked.

Perhaps because there is less experience in the general culture (perhaps particularly in Western culture) of small, consistently interacting communities, practitioners may bring powerful fantasies to bear on sangha life. In monastic settings this can take the shape of idealizations about the kind of life somone expects to find when he enters a practice community. For example, it is not unusual for a new member of the community or monastery to view work practice or taking responsibility for community assets as an impingement on their practice rather than an expression of it. This may reflect basic unfamiliarity with communal/monastic life, or it may be an expression of the practitioner's archaic longing for the complete caregiving of a parent. A desire to be reliably and consistently praised and affirmed, to be seamlessly met and appreciated, or to be completely cared for, if present, can and in fact most likely will result in disappointment. The practitioner must come to terms with the fact that the practice community is made up of humans and is formed not in order to sustain the self as it has been known but to transform it. As I have discussed, this does not in any way preclude support for the self but indicates that challenging relational experiences will also, necessarily, be part of the practice environment.

The teacher can reawaken or evoke childlike longings, and he or she sometimes becomes the object of a student's unmet desires for unconditional love, acceptance, support, and nurturance.[21] In addition, the teacher can be the focus of enormous idealization. This may be particularly true of Zen teachers; for many people, the notion of the "Zen master" carries mythological and romantiziced associations that "meditation teacher" simply does not. Romantic notions abound and both teacher and student can be caught up in them. This can be an opportunity for real learning as the person of the teacher is disentangled from romantic notions about her and teacher and student are able to meet intimately, eye to eye. This kind of genuine meeting, not dependent upon characteristics or conditions, fosters a trust that is also not dependent upon circumstances.

The language and concepts of self psychology give us a means of examining the process by which such distortions arise and how they can be resolved. Wolf, in discussing this eventuality, writes that when this occurs

> Some archaic selfobject need has been mobilized and requires a specific selfobject experience in order to maintain the cohesion of the self. Because it manifests in the present as a revival of an archaic need, we call this phenomenon a selfobject transference. The self of one or both of the participants has become dependent on the other for the needed selfobject support to its self. What had been an interpersonal relationship dedicated to the acquisition of skills [or the realization of Buddhist teachings] has been superseded by a selfobject experience functioning to maintain the structure and cohesion of the self.[22]

Selfobject transferences are inevitable to one degree or another in the student-teacher relationship. If handled well they can, in fact, be an important element in the maturation process. The teacher's skillful handling of this aspect of the relationship, by compassionately and firmly responding in such a way that the relationship is clarified without additional trauma, is important for the eventual and fruitful dissolution of distorted notions.

This does not mean that the teacher can or should take on the role of psychotherapist. The two roles are distinct. A teacher of Sōtō Zen is a person recognized in the community as someone who can act as a guide and a transmitter of the tradition. A psychotherapist is someone who is recognized as having the education, ability, and experience to function in that capacity. The teacher of Sōtō Zen and the psychotherapist are both highly trained individuals who perform different, though sometimes overlapping, tasks. (To borrow from a Jungian point of view, we can say that they carry or express different archetypes—the spiritual/religious teacher on one hand and the healer on the other.)

The teacher of Sōtō Zen expresses the tradition and teachings as fully as she can, motivated by the sincere desire to make the dharma as available and applicable as possible. The psychotherapist, on the other hand, attends carefully to the healing of the psyche. He too carries a tradition and a lineage, in a way, and is motivated by the desire to heal and help an individual fully engage in the life they come to envision for themselves. A psychotherapist can certainly include a spiritual dimension in his work, and a Zen teacher includes everyday interactions and experiences in her teaching relationship with the student. Both work to alleviate suffering but they set about it from different perspectives, with different aims and different training. Of course, a given individual may be qualified to occupy both roles, but even then the roles must be carefully distinguished and not confused. A person qualified to do both must make a choice as to which role she is going to take up with any given individual, and care must be taken to maintain appropriate and clear boundaries. The psychotherapy client and the Zen student are respected in this way. If this distinction between the two roles is not upheld, in my opinion, both are undercut, neither can be fully realized, and the client/student may experience potentially debilitating confusion.

What is required is that the teacher not be caught in the swirl of delusion and be able to compassionately maintain his focus and aim. For example, Sōjun Mel Weitsman Rōshi, when asked how he handled the experience of many students bowing to him in formal interviews, responded, "They are bowing to the robe, not to me." This illustrates how a teacher can be both responsive and effective, neither caught up in the student's archaic longings or idealizations nor judgmental of them. In other words, she has the ability to see delusion as delusion and to respond simply and compassionately.[23]

The primary aim of the Zen teacher is to support the student in his practice of Sōtō Zen. The practice inevitably includes the disruption of the practitioner's sense of self, the cracking apart of the patterns with which he has organized experience in order that another possibility becomes apparent. In a sense, the teacher is looking through the self in order to respond to a deeper need. The teacher mirrors the student, but she mirrors not the details of his self-experience but his innate buddha-nature, his empty, impermanent thusness. Ultimately, for the relationship to succeed, the student must experience both the teacher's devotion to the student's realization of the Way and her commitment to something "deeper" than the deluded self. The student must become familiar with and understand a fully responsive relationship with the teacher that takes into account, but is not swayed or distracted by, the needs of the deluded self. Mutual respect and caring are essential to the intimacy that develops between teacher and student. The basis of this respect and caring is found in the practice, in mutual devotion to Buddha's Way.

The nature of the student-teacher relationship makes it all the more important that trust be present, for trust is the only foundation on which this kind of relationship can be built. This trust begins with respectful mutual regard, evolves through various experiences of honest encounter, and emerges as the deep and vibrant intimacy that is present in the realm of absolute trust. Without a basic sense of mutual trust, disruptions can be experienced as retraumatizing and are not helpful. This does not mean that disturbances are to be avoided, only that there be enough trust present that they can be experienced, perhaps not completely but to some extent, as a deepening encounter with life's fullness.

If we return to the concepts of mirroring, idealization, and twinship and the selfobject relationships described above, we can say that in the realm of idealization the student finds in the teacher a living example of the Way on which he can rely for effective guidance and support.[24] In terms of mirroring, the student experiences being seen as a worthy participant in the practice, as fully capable of realization, and as an expression of that realization. Twinship is experienced in the increasing recognition that both student and teacher are followers of the Way, are fundamentally the same in that effort, and are both "flowers of emptiness," expressions of that reality. In this way, the teacher functions both to support the student but also effectively challenges him, becoming a means of transforming self-experience.

The goal of the teacher-student relationship is not the maintenance or comfort of the known self but its dissolution as a fixed entity. The teacher's allegiance is not to the known self but to realization, to Buddha, to reality, and she must not be tamed by convention. This kind of relationship allows for a certain quality of ruthlessness on the part of the teacher, what in Zen is known as "grandmotherly kindness," a ruthlessness tempered and guided by compassion, but ruthless nonetheless. For example, the teacher may directly challenge the student's perceptions of reality or simply maintain a relational stance that is not easily fixed in a conventional context. These measures, when skillfully matched with the student's readiness, will be liberating and not threatening or simply baffling. This is the art of teaching and the full expression of skillful means.

We can also think of this as the full expression of a transforming selfobject relationship, as the teacher is acting in this instance so that the student's self-experience is, at least momentarily, transformed. The teacher brings her own subjective experience to the encounter and in so doing affects the subjective experience of the student. This occurs in every aspect of the teacher-student relationship, whether or not there are direct verbal or nonverbal interactions, and can be particularly apparent in the case of the formal one-on-one meetings between teacher and student called *dokusan*. The teacher-student relationship is built on and expresses the practitioner's evolving experience of trust—in the relationship as fundamentally nonharming, in the teachings and the practice, and in his own capacity for realization. Put another way, we can say that in this relationship the practitioner expresses some level of trust in his own true nature and in the process by which he comes to experience that it is already present. Through this, absolute trust is realized.

If there is insufficient trust in the practice environment and the teacher-student relationship, or if the student's sense of self is prematurely challenged, he may retreat into a more constricted and less engaged sense of self and act to further shore up that self and defend it against any perceived threat presented by the teacher and the teachings. Alternately, if a transforming self-experience has occurred but it is insufficiently grounded in a cohesive sense of self, the practitioner may use whatever understanding or experiences that have resulted from it to weave a new and perhaps even more entrenched (and often inflated) fixed identity. What is needed is the cultivation of deeper trust and the creation of a new inner ecology in which the self knows itself to be an organizing principle functioning in the service of life.

In the ongoing dialogue between teacher and student there is a creative tension between receptivity to the teachings and a willingness to deeply listen, on the one hand, and the development of the student's unique individual understanding on the other. The student is challenged to not know, to remain open to the teachings, and at the same time to find her own authentic expression of the Way. In this creative tension the self is transformed and becomes a liberated expression of wisdom and compassion—at least for a moment. Both teacher and student must take responsibility for the creation of a dialogue in which trust flourishes and transforms and confidence and inner authority blossom. Ultimately, the student must be able to settle in her own experience and understanding and express it fully. Without this process, practice cannot mature and the student remains dependent, waiting to receive wisdom from others. When this happens, the student's unique contribution is lost, for each person expresses the dharma in his own way.

The practitioner's transition from a position of relying on outer authority to one of integrating the tradition and practice so that she is able to express her understanding clearly and honestly is central to the evolution of the practice. This occurs when trust in one's own experience, not as the truth but as a truth, becomes real and confidence is born. This requires honesty, familiarity with the feel of one's own wisdom, and the ability to stand in one's clarity (or confusion) while remaining open to others. It is the expression of *jishin,* self-trust, and is closely related to the maturity described by the self psychologists. This makes possible full engagement with all aspects of the practice environment, particularly the sangha and the teacher-student relationship. In this way, trust and the self are transformed and can be fully expressed in all dimensions of practice.

Maturity

Maturity, a term used both in Zen and in the language of self psychology, is associated with ripening. *Webster's Dictionary* defines "maturity" as "to become fully developed or ripe" or "having completed natural growth and development." In the context of Zen practice, maturity calls to mind images of a relaxed, expressive, and confident embodiment of the teachings.

The process by which maturation occurs in the Sōtō Zen practice environment is complex and is deeply influenced by the level of cohesion and basic trust present in the practitioner when he begins practice. A person who takes up the practice and must struggle with a lack of basic trust and a fragile sense of self will need to address those aspects of his experience. This does not mean that such a person should be excluded from practice—if this were so, most zendos would be sparsely populated. Effectively addressing these aspects of self-experience can include psychotherapy or other supportive activities. This requires a clear-eyed and compassionate assessment of what form of practice is best for that individual, and it may not always be Sōtō Zen.

Traditional Buddhist practices that provide support and affirmation can easily be incorporated into the life of the Sōtō Zen practitioner, for example specific loving-kindness and compassion practices borrowed from the Theravādin or Tibetan traditions. Bowing, physical work, maintaining noble silence, and regular meetings with a practice friend, as well as formal encounters with a teacher, study, chanting—all of these are options included within the Sōtō tradition. These practices can be used to address qualities such as inner aggression or negative judgment, distraction, or distressing feelings of vulnerability and isolation.

Perhaps most important in developing maturity in the practice of Sōtō Zen is the capacity of the practitioner to be honestly present with himself. As Mumon Yamada writes, "to be honest is the most important quality in the practice of zazen."[25] Honesty includes the ability to clearly and compassionately understand what one needs at a given time, as well as the ability to ask for help when, as is often the case, one cannot see clearly. This requires a compassionate and balanced regard for the self that is reasonably free from shame or judgment. In developing this capacity for inner (and outer) honesty, practices of compassion and loving-kindness can be very helpful. It is essential that the practitioner understand that she is not alone in experiencing struggle or difficulty and what may seem like hindering self-experiences. The first steps in working with difficult experiences include cultivating the capacity to admit them, the ability to be present for them, the understanding that they are shared by all humans, and, finally, using them as a means of joining with all beings. This effort engenders humility and self-honesty and supports not only full engagement in practice but also nondefensive relationships with others. With this spirit, all aspects of the practice come alive.

If the practitioner has not cultivated an open and nonjudgmental regard for self-needs, those needs will remain hidden and may emerge in ways that can be destructive for all involved. At the very least, they may be experienced as a sense of inner tension and create obstacles to full engagement with practice. Tension and a sense of obstruction can result in a painful struggle with the practice or even the (apparent) abandonment of the Way, often accompanied by a sense of failure. I say "apparent" here because it is quite possible for a person to leave a formal practice setting due to an inner struggle yet continue to be deeply engaged in practice in less specific or delineated ways. For example, a person may cease to sit zazen with a group but remain committed to the teachings and the practice of awareness and compassion in daily life. This is an important point, for Zen practice is not meant, I believe, exclusively for those who can arrange their bodies, hearts, or minds into a particular position. It is far more open than that, and far more demanding.

The self-experience that emerges as the inevitable difficulties encountered in Zen practice are resolved is deeply influenced by the teachings. The self that takes shape and matures within the context of practice is marked by that context. The experience of trust, self-cohesion, and self-structure that develops is informed by the knowledge that this self is an expression of the empty nature of reality. As Dōgen says, it is a "flower of emptiness."[26] Enveloped in the teachings of compassion and emptiness, an experience of the self emerges that, at least in some way, knows itself to be not a construct separate from and perhaps opposed to the fluidity of the moment, but an expression of it. Both the recognition and formation of basic trust and the acknowledgement and at least occasional experience of absolute trust emerge.

This has implications for our understanding of the maturation of a practitioner. A purely sequential model of development, in which the self is formed within a conventional context and then transformed by the teachings, does not apply here. The relationship of form (that is, the self) and fluidity are more complex, interdependent, and mutually influencing than a simple linear sequence of events would imply. In addition, from the perspective of deepening the capacity to embody the bodhisattva vow, an understanding of maturation that does not posit a strictly linear model means that areas of vulnerability can be understood as means of developing compassion toward others, thereby supporting the emergence of empathy and wisdom. Thus the same vulnerabilities that may be seen as indications of fragility and archaic selfobject relationships can become opportunities and invaluable avenues for a more thoroughgoing engagement with the practice. In this way, obstacles become objects of gratitude. This presumes, of course, adequate support for the challenges that occur in the process. A more complex understanding of the development in the practice also makes it possible to acknowledge that maturation may be uneven; areas of more archaic selfobject relationships may coexist with areas of deep maturity and embodiment of the teachings.

The topic of maturation also allows us to discuss the relationship between supportive and transforming selfobject relationships. Though the potential for these two functions can exist simultaneously at any given time, the ability of the self to access the transformative function is dependent on its ability to let go of the need to be affirmed and to allow full mutuality. We can understand the supportive or affirming selfobject function as setting the stage for the transformative one (while remembering that the relationship between these two functions is not strictly linear and can change from moment to moment).

The process of maturation in selfobject relationships—from archaic ones centered on supplying the self with affirmation and reassurance to those that express mutuality and serve a transformative function—can be seen in all areas of Sōtō Zen life. For example, the relationship between the practitioner and the buddha bowl discussed above may begin by being centered on the needs of the self for affirmation. Becoming familiar with the formal eating rituals in a Sōtō Zen temple can be daunting, and handling the buddha bowl efficiently and confidently represents a significant accomplishment, an affirmation to the practitioner of her ability and her belonging. This can lead to a sense of greater inclusion in the community (or it can give rise to a sense of being superior to others who are continuing to learn). The bowl may first function as reassurance to the practitioner, evidence of competence and inclusion. As (or if) the practitioner becomes increasingly settled in formal eating practice, and in himself, his relationship to the bowl may change to one of participating with the bowl in the activity of eating and opening to mutuality and transformation. A feeling of gratitude can emerge along with a sense of belonging not based on performance but on being. The bowl becomes not a means of affirming the self, not a thing that exists only in relationship to the self but a relational aspect along with the self in the entirety of the moment.

Just as the relationship to a single object can evolve with maturation, so too does the type of referent or object itself. As noted by Wolf and others, with the maturation of the self comes the ability to have substantive selfobject relationships of greater mutuality with a wider range of objects, including less concrete and more symbolic objects.[27] In the context of a spiritual or religious environment, this means that the practitioner has access to the full range of selfobject relationships available in the tradition. The referents in these relationships can range from buddha statues and altars to images found in sūtras.

In every case, the nature of the relationship is dependent on the maturity of the practitioner at that particular moment, and this can evolve over time. For example, in preparing for ordination the practitioner hand-sews a robe (*o-kesa*), which is then ritually presented to her by her teacher (a layperson sews a smaller version of the robe, called a *rakusu*, when taking the ten precepts, *jukai*). With each stitch the practitioner chants a short verse of taking refuge in the Buddha. This requires many hours of painstaking work, and with each stitch the practitioner has the opportunity to experience the process as either the accomplishment of a task, the concrete affirmation and inclusion of the self, a symbolic experience of creation, or the transforming experience of actually sewing Buddha's robe.

Maturation, in this context, is a shift toward a more participatory relationship with each stitch. It also means the ability to include the entire range of experiences in an overall sense of settledness in the various forms of self. The practitioner will most likely have all of these responses, and many more, over the course of sewing the robe. Compassionate acceptance of this variability, together with developing gratitude for the practice that makes this acceptance possible, provides the means for maturation. Maturation in the practice is not simply the evolution of a particular kind of relationship, though this is also true, but the ability to include the entirety of experience in a genuine engagement in the Way.

The "person mature in Zen" described above is one whose simplest actions are imbued with grace and "indescribable beauty." In terms of her relationships, we can say that she embodies the bodhisattva vow and Dōgen's teaching that all phenomena express Buddha's Way. She is a person who has put into action and realized the injunction to see even a leaf of green, along with herself, as Buddha. With the accomplishment of maturation, a respectful relationship exists in which the object is not experienced as merely an extension of the self or as a means of affirming its existence but as a phenomenon in its own right. Thus, relationships are not focused on the needs of the self but instead reflect all aspects of the situation.

This can be understood as another aspect of the fundamental generosity at play in the life of the bodhisattva. Dōgen tells us in *Bodaisatta shishōbō* that "To leave flowers to the wind, to leave birds to the seasons, are also acts of giving."[28] From this point of view, each phenomena is "given" to itself and to all beings, and in so doing each is able to fully express itself and thereby express all reality.[29] The person fully mature in Zen is not concerned with affirming the self, because that self is not different from all phenomena as they arise. Traditionally, this maturity is said to take the form of a "person of no rank," that is, someone who has no need of external validation and is free to respond fully in any way that is appropriate to the situation. The need to confirm a separate self is no longer relevant. In a sense, all relationships can be thought of as selfobject relationships of reality itself. Trust is complete at this point, at least for this moment, and expresses itself in complete generosity and the Bodhisattva Way.

Discussion

In his fascicle *Zazengi* Dōgen describes the balanced environment conducive for the practice of zazen and instructs that one must "Protect and maintain the place where you settle your body." There are, of course, many ways we could interpret this statement. Taken within the overall context of this essay, however, with its emphasis on the need for an environment that is neither too hot nor too cold, which is free from "drafts or smoke, rain or dew," and which includes a place to sit that is neither indulgent to the senses nor overly austere,[30] we can understand it to mean that the entire environment should be one of balanced attention to the needs of the individual aimed at the creation of an atmosphere conducive to realization of the Sōtō Way.

With this in mind, we can say that creating an affirming environment in which an individual can flourish in his effort to take up the dharma is not only an expression of the bodhisattva vow but also deeply in line with traditional Sōtō teachings. A selfobject milieu that both acknowledges the self and recognizes that it is empty of inherent existence allows for the full flowering of practice. As the practitioner matures, the availability of transforming relationships becomes more and more apparent. A loosening of self-identifications and the capacity to rest "between" takes place, and a shift in self-experience becomes possible. With this maturation, a deepening sense of authenticity, authority, and connectedness accompanies the compassionate expression of a new subjective experience. By attending to the supportive and transformational relationships that exist in the practice environment, the individual practitioner is encouraged and challenged to fully engage with the practice. In this way, trust is realized in all its forms and the individual practitioner comes to embody the tradition itself.

Chapter 6

Conclusion

The dharma, to be alive and vital, must be skillfully expressed and responsive to the needs of those who practice it. At the same time, it must not be adapted to or coopted by those needs in such a way as to perpetuate delusion. This can be a difficult task, considering the magnetic pull our habitual notions about the nature of the self and reality can exert on the way we hear, understand, and practice the dharma. This forceful pull can subvert the teachings and set up a false dichotomy between a position in which the self is experienced or thought to exist as a separate entity, and one in which it is thought of or experienced as not existing in any coherent form.

On the other hand, if we resist this magnetic pull and understand self-experience as the structure, the form, by which realization is expressed, we are free to attend to the relative self in such a way that a new experience of subjectivity can manifest, an embodied form that knows itself to be no different from the arising of moment-by-moment experience. This is the "dynamic agency" referred to by Anne Klein (in *Meeting the Great Bliss Queen*) and the "giving" spoken of by Dōgen in his many teachings. With this perspective, we can explore the nature of self-experience and relate it directly to the maturation of the practice of Sōtō Zen.

Our exploration is enriched by including the understanding of self and relational experience developed by Heinz Kohut, Erik Erikson, D. W. Winnicott, and other self psychology and intersubjective theorists. These authors not only provide valuable insights into the development and structure of self-experience, their formulations are also compatible with the fluid, relationally embedded subjectivity described in Buddhist teachings. The language and concepts about the self and the importance of trust developed by these theorists offer a means for articulating important dimensions of the experience of Sōtō Zen practitioners and the conditions that support their development.

The foundational Mahāyāna teachings of emptiness and no-self, dependent co-arising, and the bodhisattva vow, and Eihei Dōgen's understanding of the nature of realization and practice, buddha-nature, the self, and faith all build an understanding of the activities that make up the life of a practitioner—zazen, work, relational life, the precepts, ritual activity, and study—as well as the role the body and gender play in Sōtō Zen teaching.

Central to the lived experience of Sōtō Zen practice is a shift from the perception of the self as a separate entity to a subjective experience grounded in a realization and expression of interdependent reality. This shift is the practice realization of the teachings lived out in the ordinary activities of daily life as well as in the silence of zazen. It is the expression of all beings, all being, realizing itself, Buddha studying Buddha's Way.

The essential element that makes possible the shift in self-experience that lies at the heart of Sōtō Zen practice—from a self caught in the delusion of separation and permanence to one that experiences itself as in no way different from dependent co-arising—is trust. Trust allows for full participation in the practice, and it is trust that is expressed in the full embodiment of the Sōtō Zen Way. It is possible, then, to see the maturation of the practitioner of Sōtō Zen as an evolution of trust.

As we have learned from the psychoanalytic authors described above, a fundamental experience of trust, what Erikson, in *Childhood and Society*, called basic trust, supports the earliest formation of the self. The development of basic trust is inextricably bound to the emergence of a cohesive self-structure, to use the language of self psychology. This is a viable and deeply relational self, one that is capable of intimacy and full participation in life. It is important to note that this does not imply perfection or invulnerability. Rather, it is a self that can incorporate and be transformed by the whole range of life events.

The capacity to simply be aware of experience as it occurs is an essential element in any Buddhist practice. When we turn to the factors that support this ability for kindhearted and stable attentiveness, we find that the self's experience of basic trust is crucial. The cohesive self, built in a selfobject milieu where the integration of a wide range of experiences has been both possible and enriching, is able to open to moment-to-moment experience without fear of disintegration. With this capacity to attend, the ability to take awareness, rather the content of awareness, as the factor that maintains coherence develops. In addition, with the presence of this basic trust, potentially disruptive experiences of "between," in which divisions between self and other are not so clearly drawn, do not threaten. In fact, such experiences may be welcomed and regarded as sources of creativity and enrichment. Without basic trust, such experiences in which definitions of self and other are less apparent may evoke the pain and fear that accompany disintegration anxiety.

This is a particularly important consideration when the practitioner encounters the teachings of emptiness. Without a sound foundation in trust, the practitioner's ability to listen, enter into, and effectively integrate teachings of emptiness will be compromised. With the presence of basic trust and the fundamentally cohesive self that accompanies it, emptiness is not mistaken for an arid darkness, devoid of peace and comfort; rather, it can be known as the full arising of life. A willingness to step over the edge of the known, to allow the self as it has been experienced to dissolve, can only occur when a measure of trust is present. Stepping over the edge into not knowing is itself an expression of profound trust in the teachings and the practice, in the nature of life, in our own true nature. In the life of the practitioner trust transforms and grows into a vibrant expression of the practice itself. This is absolute trust, and it is accompanied by its companion, a subjective experience based not in a sense of the self as separate but in the realization of the unique particularity of dependent co-arising.

The practice environment, and the relationships that form it, is inseparable from the emergence of this experience of trust and subjectivity. These relationships function to support the development of basic trust and the emergence of a self that is capable of full and deep engagement in the practice. They also function to transform self-experience. Together, supportive and transforming relationships form a relational milieu that transmits the teachings, affirms the practitioner's ability to realize them, and moment after moment enables this transformative and liberating process to take place.

It is in the realm of supportive relationships that the greatest confusion can occur. How can supporting the self and building trust in a changeable world further the dismantling of self-attachment? The answer lies in the nature and context of that support. Support that aims at full engagement in the teachings so that they have a real and transforming impact is essential. Refraining from support of the known self undermines its very ability to engage in practice. It is counterproductive. Without this support, efforts to shift self-experience or loosen self-clinging can fall far short of the aim of the tradition—the embodied realization of the teachings.

Tending to the fundamental needs of the body, mind, and heart is a basic requisite of the practice, which aims not to indulge the self but to transform it. The creation of a selfobject milieu that intentionally supports a wholesome, cohesive self-experience and leads to the creation and deepening of basic trust is fundamentally in line with the tradition itself. It is an expression of the bodhisattva vow and the meeting of all constituent elements in moment-to-moment reality. As the practitioner is affirmed and supported, included in the community of practitioners and in relationship with trusted elders and teachers, he will come to know trust in new ways and allow it to evolve and inform his life. At the same time, he will increase his capacity to allow the structures that make up the known self to shift and loosen, thus opening to the possibility of a new subjective experience. Together with the community and the teacher, the practitioner will be able to honestly see and effectively respond to the needs of the self. This creates a context that supports deep immersion in the Way. It is an environment in which the dissolution of the known self and the emergence of a subectivity that fully expresses the compassionate nature of dependent co-arising and the bodhisattva vow may occur.

The fullness of transforming selfobject relationships, those that function to undo and transform self-experience, can emerge in such an environment. These relationships become increasingly available to the practitioner in all dimensions of her life as her capacity for full engagement in moment-by-moment reality develops. This is Buddha studying Buddha's Way and it is a full expression of absolute trust. A strictly sequential and linear process of development cannot and should not be construed from this. Maturity in Sōtō Zen practice is inclusive of all dimensions of experience and tied to none of them. Most important is the clear-eyed, compassionate acceptance and expression of a subjective reality that is not different from the whole of life as it is, moment by moment.

Buddhism is above all a pragmatic tradition. The Buddha was often likened to a physician whose aim is to relieve suffering through effective and tested means. Teachers and communities of Sōtō Zen, or any form of Buddhism, offer the medicine of the dharma and therefore are consistently engaged in the process of making that medicine useful without subverting its basic, challenging (to our ordinary understanding) message. To be real, the teachings must become real, must be evident in the moment-to-moment world of the practitioner's experience. Dōgen reminds us again and again: examine this, study this, make this real for yourselves. He offered a rigorous and compassionate practice meant to be enacted in all aspects of one's life. It is up to each of us to take up this challenge with honesty and compassion for ourselves and others and create environments and understandings that allow the teachings to take root, flourish, and transform our lives. By exploring the nature and evolution of trust, its relationship to the capacity for awareness and letting go of constricting self-experience, and pointing to a link between basic trust and the willingness to trust life itself, I hope that I have contributed to clarifying how this transformative process can occur.

Further exploration could include the application of these ideas to other traditions and the extension of them within Sōtō Zen itself. This line of inquiry could also be expanded to include other aspects of psychoanalytic theory, for example attachment theory and a discussion of object relations, with the proviso that the applicability of these or other theoretical frameworks depends on their basic compatibility with a Buddhist understanding of the nature of the self. An area of particular interest to me is the relationship of Yogācāra teachings to the evolution of the experience of trust and the self, as I have discussed in this work.

In the general field of contemplative psychology as applied to Buddhist practice, many aspects of the work of Han de Wit could be fruitful in deepening our understanding of how humans can be supported in their efforts to realize Buddha's Way. For example, de Wit points out that an important aspect of communicating the tradition is the question of how the teaching is presented in order to best meet the needs of the practitioner and avoid confusion.[1] Including a psychoanalytic perspective, we could then ask, given certain vulnerabilities and ways of organizing life experience, what are the most effective ways of presenting the teachings—perhaps most particularly the teachings of emptiness? The question of what works has many dimensions and myriad possible responses, each unique to the situation at hand.

The question of the evolution of trust and the self and how it affects the way in which teachings are heard, experienced, and lived in other Buddhist and non-Buddhist traditions would also be a fruitful exploration. Alternate formulations of trust and self-experience based in different understandings of what constitutes maturity could add depth, richness, and complexity to our understanding of this question.

A further, more detailed and nuanced discussion of what constitutes effective supportive and transforming relationships could also contribute to a fuller understanding of how to support the Sōtō Zen practitioner. This could include an exploration of all dimensions of the practice environment, for example the teacher-student relationship. It could also include the role of specific practices, such as work or bowing practices, and bring in the teachings of Dōgen and other Zen teachers, such as Keizan, with regard to each of these areas.

There are many other possible avenues of inquiry when considering practices from other Buddhist traditions that support the emergence of trust and maturation. For example, the Tibetan Buddhist text *The Great Path of Awakening: A Commentary on the Mahāyāna Teaching of the Seven Points of Mind Training*, presented by Jamgon Kongtrul,[2] gives instructions and short statements of the teachings (slogans, or *lojong*) that are used to cultivate positive mental attitudes conducive for practice. The relevance of these instructions for the development of a supportive inner (and outer) practice environment would be of great interest.

An investigation of the use of specific meditations, such as the traditional Theravādin teachings of *metta* (Skt. *maitrī;* "loving-kindness"), as a means of undercutting aggression and creating and deepening the experience of trust would also add a different and intriguing perspective. Including teachings that describe antidotes for specific mental and emotional states, for example, the cultivation of kindness as a direct response to the experience of aggression, would also be of interest. All of these possibilities could be fruitfully brought into an investigation of the factors that support the development of trust and the ability to enter into an experience of life that takes as its foundation the interconnected, empty nature of all being.

In each of these areas, the role of gender, as well as other characteristics that impact the experience of the self and trust, merit further examination, both on their own and in conjunction with other factors. By taking seriously the impact of these dimensions of experience (while at the same time realizing their empty nature) we can come to understand more fully how to meet the needs of those who seek out the teachings, and how to best support them both in flourishing in the Way and giving voice to their unique wisdom.

Notes

Chapter 1: Introduction

1 Han de Wit, *Contemplative Psychology* (Pittsburgh, PA: Duquesne University Press, 1991), p. 24.

2 de Wit, *Contemplative Psychology,* p. 73.

3 Several authors have pointed out distortions that are possible with a limited understanding of the range of practices present in Buddhism. Jan Nattier writes forcefully about the limited notions of Buddhism held by many white, middle-class Westerners in "Visible and Invisible: On the Politics of Representation in Buddhist America," *Tricycle: The Buddhist Review* (Fall 1995): 42–49. She finds that this group tends to define Buddhist practice as sitting meditation on a cushion and to dismiss other, often more relational aspects of practice life as lesser practices or not "Buddhist" at all. Nattier sees this as indicative of arrogance on the part of such practitioners who assume a knowledge of what Buddhism is and where it will lead. Robert H. Sharf, in "Buddhist Modernism and the Rhetoric of Meditative Experience," *Numen* 42/3 (1995): 228–283, discusses the overemphasis he believes Western practitioners have put on having certain experiences in meditation. He contends that it is behavior, not the attainment of particular experiences, that marks a mature practitioner, and in stating this he undercuts limited notions of practice and the nature of realization and points to an expanded notion of the nature of Buddhist practice. Feminist authors, such as Rita M. Gross in *Buddhism After Patriarchy: A Feminist History, Analysis and Reconstruction of Buddhism* (Albany, NY: State University of New York Press, 1993) and Anne Klein in *Meeting the Great Bliss Queen: Buddhists, Feminists, and the Art of the Self* (Boston: Beacon Press, 1995), have also noted an absence of emphasis on the relational quality or emotional aspect of practice that can occur.

4 Klein, *Meeting the Great Bliss Queen,* p. xv.

5 Donald Lopez, *Buddhist Hermeneutics* (Honolulu: University of Hawai'i Press, 1988), p. 1.

6 Lopez, *Buddhist Hermeneutics,* p. 66.

7 Lopez, *Buddhist Hermeneutics,* pp. 52, 67.

8 Lopez, *Buddhist Hermeneutics,* p. 9.

9 Edward Conze, *Perfect Wisdom: The Short Prajnaparamita Texts* (Totnes, UK: Buddhist Publishing Group, 1973), p. 267.

10 Gudo Nishijima and Chodo Cross, trans., *Master Dogen's Shobogenzo* (Woods Hole, MA: Windbell Publications, 1997), "Nyorai-zenshin: The Whole Body of the Tathāgata," Book 3, p. 279.

11 Shulamit Reinharz, *Feminist Methods of Social Research* (New York: Oxford University Press, 1992), pp. 6–7.

12 Reinharz, *Feminist Methods of Social Research,* p. 16.

13 de Wit, *Contemplative Psychology,* pp. 102; 105; 103; 83.

14 de Wit, *Contemplative Psychology,* pp. 106, 107.

15 Dainin Katagiri, *You Have to Say Something: Manifesting Zen Insight* (Boston: Shambhala Publications), p. 156.

Chapter 2. Fundamental Teachings of Sōtō Zen

1 Nishijima and Cross, *Master Dogen's Shobogenzo,* "Bukkyo: The Buddhist Sutras," Book 3, pp. 101–112.

2 Paul Williams, *Mahāyāna Buddhism: The Doctrinal Foundations* (New York: Routledge, 1989), p. 1.

3 Williams, *Mahāyāna Buddhism,* p. 3.

4 Peter Harvey, *An Introduction to Buddhism: Teachings, History and Practices* (New York: Cambridge University Press, 1990), p. 54.

5 Bhikkhu Bodhi, *The Connected Discourses of the Buddha: A New Translation of the Saṃyutta Nikāya* (Boston: Wisdom Publications, 2000), pp. 595–596.

6 Akira Hirakawa, *A History of Indian Buddhism from Śākyamuni to Early Mahāyāna* (Honolulu: University of Hawai'i Press, 1990); David Kalupahana, *Buddhist Philosophy: A Historical Analysis* (Honolulu: University of Hawai'i Press, 1976) and *The Principles of Buddhist Psychology* (Albany, NY: State University of New York Press, 1987).

7 Harvey, *An Introduction to Buddhism,* p. 51.

8 Walpola Rahula, *What The Buddha Taught* (New York: Grove Press, 1959), p. 62; Sue Hamilton, *Early Buddhism: A New Approach. The I of the Beholder* (Richmond, Surrey, UK: Curzon, 2000), p. 138.

9 Bhikkhu Ñāṇamoli and Bhikkhu Bodhi, trans., *The Middle Length Discourses of the Buddha: A Translation of the Majjhima Nikāya* (Boston: Wisdom Publications, 1995), pp. 91–96.

10 The relationship between the Theravāda and the Mahāyāna, both of which continue to thrive today in a variety of forms, has been a topic of heated debate for millennia. The Mahāyāna discounted the Theravāda, referring to it as the Hinayana ("Lesser Vehicle"), a derogatory term that until recently remained in

much of modern scholarship. The Theravāda has, at times, claimed a position as the keeper of the true, original teachings and viewed Mahāyāna teachings as inauthentic.

11 Jay Garfield, ed. and trans., *The Fundamental Wisdom of the Middle Way: Nāgārjuna's Mūlamadyamikakārikā* (New York: Oxford University Press, 1995).

12 Nāgārjuna's consistent use of language that undercuts any attempt at conceiving an essential nature is an example of apophatic language, what Michael Sells calls the language of "un-saying or speaking away," as opposed to the language of "affirmation, saying, speaking with," kataphasis; *The Mystical Languages of Unsaying* (Chicago: University of Chicago Press, 1994), pp. 2, 3. The language of Buddhism can be understood as dialectic between these two ways of expressing the nature of reality. In Buddhist philosophical history, the Yogācāra school (and later the Huayan school and others), which arose as a response to the Madhyamaka and which actively articulated human consciousness in more concrete, positive terms, can be seen as a katophatic balance to the apophatic emphasis of the Madhyamaka. As with the importation of any terms, we must be careful not to imply too much by their usage. For example, we are not talking about two ways of expressing the experience of an entity called "God." These two terms, however, provide a way of articulating the dynamic use of language expressed in much of Zen teaching.

13 Hamilton, *Early Buddhism: A New Approach.*

14 Garfield, *The Fundamental Wisdom of the Middle Way,* p. 89.

15 Garfield, *The Fundamental Wisdom of the Middle Way,* p. 275.

16 Garfield, *The Fundamental Wisdom of the Middle Way,* p. 91.

17 Garfield, *The Fundamental Wisdom of the Middle Way,* pp. 304, 305.

18 Klein, *Meeting the Great Bliss Queen,* p. 137.

19 For a more thorough account of Dōgen's life, see Takashi Kodera, *Dogen's Formative Years in China: An Historical Study and Annotated Translation of the 'Hōkyō-ki'* (Boulder, CO: Prajna Press, 1980); Hee-Jin Kim, *Dōgen Kigen: Mystical Realist* (Tucson: University of Arizona Press, 1987).

20 Hagiographic accounts in the Sōtō school often present this as a failing on the part of the Tendai teachings and teachers at Mt. Hiei. Jacqueline Stone points out that it is "highly unlikely that no one at Mt. Hiei was capable of addressing the relationship of practice and original enlightenment, a topic explicitly addressed in a number of medieval Tendai texts"; *Original Enlightenment and the Transformation of Medieval Japanese Buddhism* (Honolulu: University of Hawai'i Press, 1999), p. 73. Whatever the reason for his departure, Dōgen's investigation of the relationship of practice and enlightenment and the nature of reality was a lifelong endeavor.

21 Kim, *Dōgen Kigen: Mystical Realist,* p. 36.

[22] Hee-Jin Kim, "'The Reason of Words and Letters': Dōgen and Kōan Language," in William R. LaFleur, ed., *Dōgen Studies* (Honolulu: University of Hawai'i Press, 1985), p. 74.

[23] Nishijima and Cross, *Master Dogen's Shobogenzo,* "Bussho: The Buddha-nature," Book 2, pp. 1–32.

[20] Sallie B. King, *Buddha Nature* (Albany, NY: State University of New York Press, 1991), p. 56.

[25] King, *Buddha Nature,* p. 39.

[26] King, *Buddha Nature,* p. 102.

[27] Nishijima and Cross, *Master Dogen's Shobogenzo,* "Bussho: The Buddha-nature," Book 2, p. 2.

[28] Kim, *Dōgen Kigen: Mystical Realist,* p. 122.

[29] Cited in Kim, *Dōgen Kigen: Mystical Realist,* p. 122.

[30] Cited in Kim *Dōgen Kigen: Mystical Realist,* p. 89.

[31] Cited in Kim *Dōgen Kigen: Mystical Realist,* p. 126. Dōgen's work is permeated with contradiction, and these contradictions not only point out the fact that easy definitions of this and that are inaccurate but also reveal an important aspect of Dōgen's teaching—even though statements can misrepresent the teachings, still, they must be said. Dōgen, again in *Bussho,* says that any statement about the dharma can be a "vilification" or a "slanderous utterance"; cited in Kim, *Dōgen Kigen: Mystical Realist,* p. 133. The key question becomes whether or not these statements "express Buddha-nature" (p. 133). He goes on to say, "If you did, your expression is Buddha-nature."

[32] Cited in Masao Abe, "The Oneness of Practice and Attainment: Implications for the Relation between Means and Ends," in William LaFleur, ed., *Dōgen Studies* (Honolulu: University of Hawai'i Press, 1985), p. 106.

[33] Kim, *Dōgen Kigen: Mystical Realist,* p. 128. Chinese names converted to Pinyin.

[34] Cited in King, *Buddha Nature,* p. 102.

[35] Cited in Kim, *Dōgen Kigen: Mystical Realist,* p. 129.

[36] Shohaku Okumura, *Realizing Genjo Koan: The Key to Dogen's Shobogenzo* (Boston: Wisdom Publications, 2010), p. 131.

[37] Kim, *Dōgen Kigen: Mystical Realist,* p. 132.

[38] The language of buddha-nature can give rise to practitioners conceiving of it as something to which to relate. According to Buddhist teachings, this is an unavoidable consequence of perceiving of oneself as a separate entity. In fact, it can be encouraging to focus on the aspect of potentiality in the buddha-nature teachings. What must be remembered is that not only is the potential

for realization buddha-nature, but so too is the practitioner and his relationship with this perceived potential.

39 Kim, *Dōgen Kigen: Mystical Realist*, pp. 144–145.

40 Shohaku Okumura's translation of the term *nikon*, given in the Genzō-e sesshin dharma talks, unpublished lectures on Dōgen's *Sansuigyō* (*Mountain and Rivers Sūtra*), San Francisco Zen Center (SFZC), May 2002.

41 Harvey, *An Introduction to Buddhism*, pp. 102–103.

42 Cited in Kim, *Dōgen Kigen: Mystical Realist*, p. 135.

43 Kim, *Dōgen Kigen: Mystical Realist*, p. 35.

44 Shohaku Okumura and Taigen Daniel Leighton, ed. and trans., *The Wholehearted Way: A Translation of Eihei Dōgen's Bendōwa with Commentary by Kōshō Uchiyama Roshi* (Boston: Tuttle Publishing, 1997), p. 30.

45 Kim, *Dōgen Kigen: Mystical Realist*, p. 61.

46 See Hirakawa, *A History of Indian Buddhism from Śākyamuni to Early Mahāyāna;* Rahula, *What the Buddha Taught;* Hamilton, *Early Buddhism: A New Approach.*

47 Rahula, *What the Buddha Taught*, pp. 39–40.

48 Francis Cook, ed. and trans., *Sounds of Valley Streams: Enlightenment in Dōgen's Zen* (Albany, NY: State University of New York Press, 1989), p. 4.

49 Cook, *Sounds of Valley Streams*, pp. 6–7.

50 Masao Abe, "The Oneness of Practice and Attainment," in *A Study of Dōgen: His Philosophy and Religion* (Albany, NY: State University of New York Press, 1992), and others have taken the position that Dōgen questioned the teachings of *hongaku* and in the end turned away from them. Jacqueline Stone, in *Original Enlightenment*, p. 89, refutes this position and discusses how Dōgen's teachings were formed from and in response to the teachings of original enlightenment and details the antecedents to Dōgen's position of the equality of practice and realization.

51 Stone, *Original Enlightenment*, p. 3.

52 Yoshito S. Hakeda, trans., *The Awakening of Faith: Attributed to Aśvaghosha* (New York: Columbia University Press, 1967).

53 For more in-depth discussion of all aspects of the Yogācāra teachings, see Wei Tat, trans., *Ch'eng Wei-Shih Lun: Doctrine of Mere-Consciousness by Tripitaka-Master Hsüan Tsang* (Hong Kong: The Ch'eng Wei-Shih Lun Publication Committee, 1973); Kalupahana, *The Principles of Buddhist Psychology;* Thich Nhat Hanh, *Transformation at the Base: Fifty Verses on the Nature of Consciousness* (Berkeley: Parallax Press, 2001).

54 Stone, *Original Enlightenment*, p. 6.

55 Stone, *Original Enlightenment*, p. 7.

56 Stone, *Original Enlightenment*, p. 7. Again, it must be emphasized that "suchness" is not a substantive entity or essence but a description of how things are in a world that is the dynamic expression of emptiness.

57 Stone, *Original Enlightenment*, p. 7.

58 Stone, *Original Enlightenment*, p. 8.

59 Cook, *Sounds of Valley Streams*, p. 10.

60 Kim, *Dōgen Kigen: Mystical Realist*, p. 54.

61 Cook, *Sounds of Valley Streams*, p. 28.

62 Kim, *Dōgen Kigen: Mystical Realist*, pp. 52, 61–62.

63 Kim, *Dōgen Kigen: Mystical Realist*, p. 193.

64 Okumura, Genzō-e sesshin dharma talks, SFZC, 2002.

65 Okumura, Genzō-e sesshin dharma talks, SFZC, 2002.

66 Cook, *Sounds of Valley Streams*, p. 22.

67 Kōshō Uchiyama, *Refining Your Life: From the Zen Kitchen to Enlightenment* (New York: Weatherhill, 1983), p. 11.

68 Harvey, *An Introduction to Buddhism*, p. 15.

69 Egil Fronsdal, "The Dawn of the Bodhisattva Path: Studies in a Religious Ideal of Ancient Indian Buddhists with Particular Emphasis on the Earliest Extant Perfection of Wisdom Sūtra" (Ph.D. dissertation, Stanford University, 1998), p. 101. A revised version of this work has recently been published: Gil Fronsdal, *Dawn of the Bodhisattva Path: The Early Perfection of Wisdom* (Berkeley: Institute of Buddhist Studies and BDK America, Inc., 2014).

70 See Harvey, *An Introduction to Buddhism;* Williams, *Mahāyāna Buddhism.*

71 Kim, *Dōgen Kigen: Mystical Realist*, p. 195.

72 Translation by the San Francisco Zen Center (SFZC).

73 Edward Conze, trans., *The Perfection of Wisdom in Eight Thousand Lines and its Verse Summary* (San Francisco: Four Seasons Foundation, 1973), p. 238.

74 Conze, *Perfect Wisdom: The Short Prajnaparamita Texts*, p. 132.

75 Kim, *Dōgen Kigen: Mystical Realist*, p. 198.

76 Kim, *Dōgen Kigen: Mystical Realist*, p. 197.

77s Cited in Kim, *Dōgen Kigen: Mystical Realist*, pp. 199–200.

[78] Stephen Batchelor, trans., *A Guide to the Bodhisattva's Way of Life* (Dharamsala, India: Library of Tibetan Works and Archives, 1979), p. 22.

[79] Batchelor, *A Guide to the Bodhisattva's Way of Life*, pp. 23–24.

[80] Kim, *Dōgen Kigen: Mystical Realist*, p. 201.

[81] Cook, *Sounds of Valley Streams*, pp. 36; 34.

[82] Harvey, *An Introduction to Buddhism*, p. 153.

[83] Kim, *Dōgen Kigen: Mystical Realist*, p. 61.

[84] Cited in Cook, *Sounds of Valley Streams*, p. 12.

[85] Kazuaki Tanahashi, ed., *Moon in a Dewdrop: Writings of Zen Master Dōgen* (San Francisco: North Point Press, 1985), p. 155.

[86] Cited in Shohaku Okumura, *Shikantaza: An Introduction to Zazen* (Kyoto: Kyoto Sōtō-Zen Center, 1985), p. 119.

[87] Tanahashi, *Moon in a Dewdrop*, p. 147.

[88] San Franscisco Zen Center (SFZC) translation.

[89] Tanahashi, *Moon in a Dewdrop*, p. 152.

[90] Kim, *Dōgen Kigen: Mystical Realist*, p. 56.

[91] Tanahashi, *Moon in a Dewdrop*, p. 29.

[92] San Franscisco Zen Center (SFZC) translation.

[93] Tanahashi, *Moon in a Dewdrop*, pp. 71–72.

[94] Kim, *Dōgen Kigen: Mystical Realist*, pp. 59–60, 61–62.

[95] Okumura, Genzō-e sesshin dharma talks, SFZC, 2002.

[96] Tanahashi, *Moon in a Dewdrop*, p. 72; 69.

[97] Okumura, Genzō-e sesshin dharma talks, SFZC, 2002.

[98] Uchiyama, *Refining Your Life*, pp. 6; 5; 7–8.

[99] Uchiyama, *Refining Your Life*, pp. 8; 13.

[100] Kōsen Nishiyama and John Stevens, trans., *Shōbōgenzō: The Eye and Treasury of the True Law* (Tokyo: Nakayama Shobo, 1983), vol. 3, pp. 62–63.

[101] Cook, *Sounds of Valley Streams*, p. 22.

[102] Tanahashi, *Moon in a Dewdrop*, p. 72.

[103] Cited in Kim, *Dōgen Kigen: Mystical Realist*, p. 63.

[104] Tanahashi, *Moon in a Dewdrop,* pp. 135–136.

[105] Sojun Mel Weitsman, personal communication, May 2002.

[106] Taigen Daniel Leighton and Shohaku Okumura, *Dōgen's Pure Standards for the Zen Community: A Translation of Eihei Shingi* (Albany, NY: State University of New York Press, 1996), pp. 16–17.

[107] Kim, *Dōgen Kigen: Mystical Realist,* p. 224.

[108] de Wit, *Contemplative Psychology,* p. 208.

[109] Tanahashi, *Moon in a Dewdrop,* p. 34.

[110] Yvonne Rand, personal communication, 1987.

[111] Cited in Kim, *Dōgen Kigen: Mystical Realist,* p. 33.

[112] This quote and the one immediately above are from Kim, *Dōgen Kigen: Mystical Realist,* p. 222

[113] John C. H. Wu, *The Golden Age of Zen* (Taipei: United Publishing Center, 1975), p. 149.

[114] For a detailed explication of this process, see Mohan Wijayaratna, *Buddhist Monastic Life: According to the Texts of the Theravāda Tradition* (New York: Cambridge University Press, 1990); David Kalupahana, *Ethics in Early Buddhism* (Honolulu: University of Hawai'i Press, 1995); Hammalawa Saddhatissa, *Buddhist Ethics* (Boston: Wisdom Publications, 1970). For further discussion of the evolution of the Mahāyāna, see Hirakawa, *A History of Indian Buddhism;* Harvey, *An Introduction to Buddhism.*

[115] Harvey, *An Introduction to Buddhism,* p. 199.

[116] Harvey, *An Introduction to Buddhism,* p. 176.

[117] Sojun Weitsman Rōshi, Berkeley Zen Center, 2000.

[118] Okumura, *Shikantaza: An Introduction to Zazen,* p. 69.

[119] Some Sōtō Zen sanghas, such as Shasta Abbey in Mt. Shasta, California, have instituted a commitment to celibacy; most ordained women in Japan choose to live celibate lives but this commitment is not a part of the vows they receive.

[120] Nishijima and Cross, *Master Dogen's Shobogenzo,* "Shukke-kudoku: The Merit of Leaving Family Life," Book 4, pp. 133–154.

[121] Graeme McQueen, "Inspired Speech in Early Mahāyāna Buddhism I," *Religion* 11 (1981): 303–319; "Inspired Speech in Early Mahāyāna Buddhism II," *Religion* 12 (1982): 49–65.

[122] Bunno Katō and Yoshiro Tamura, trans., *The Threefold Lotus Sutra* (Tokyo: Kosei Publishing Company, 1975), p. 266.

123 Nishijima and Cross, *Master Dogen's Shobogenzo*, "Bukkyo: The Buddhist Sutras," Book 3, pp. 106, 110.

124 Tanahashi, *Moon in a Dewdrop*, p. 129.

125 Nishijima and Cross, *Master Dogen's Shobogenzo*, "Nyorai-zenshin: The Whole Body of the Tathāgata," Book 3, p. 279.

126 Okumura, Genzo-e sesshin talks, SFZC, 2002.

127 Cited in Kim, *Dōgen Kigen: Mystical Realist*, pp. 97, 98.

128 Tanahashi, *Moon in a Dewdrop*, pp. 91, 94.

129 Francis Cook, *How to Raise An Ox: Zen Practice as Taught in Zen Master Dogen's Shobogenzo* (Los Angeles: Center Publications, 1978), p. 25.

130 Cook, *How to Raise An Ox*, p. 22.

131 This quote and the one immediately above are cited in Kim, *Dōgen Kigen: Mystical Realist*, pp. 62, 63.

132 Stephen Batchelor, *The Faith to Doubt: Glimpses of Buddhist Uncertainty* (Berkeley: Parallax Press, 1990), p. 16.

133 Garma C. C. Chang, *The Buddhist Teaching of Totality: The Philosophy of Hwa Yen Buddhism* (University Park, PA: Pennsylvania State University Press, 1971), p. 75.

134 Steven Collins, *Selfless Persons: Imagery and Thought in Theravāda Buddhism* (Cambridge: Cambridge University Press, 1982), p. 73.

135 Klein, *Meeting the Great Bliss Queen*, pp. 126–127, 130.

136 Francis Cook, "Dōgen's View of Authentic Selfhood and its Socio-ethical Implications," in William R. LaFleur, ed., *Dōgen Studies* (Honolulu: University of Hawai'i Press, 1985), p. 131.

137 Cook, "Dōgen's View of Authentic Selfhood," p. 138.

138 Klein, *Meeting the Great Bliss Queen*, p. 152. It is interesting to note that in his essay "Dōgen's View of Authentic Selfhood," p. 143, Francis Cook makes the point that one implication of the realization of the "authentic self"—that is, a shift to the concrete experience of this moment as constitutive of the nature of one's existence—is that all existence holds equal value. This radically undercuts anthropomorphic identification and the consequent hierarchy of values that places human existence, experience, and history at the center of consideration and action in the world. Cook states that an inclusion of this understanding of the self would provide human beings with a sense of "continuity with the rest of nature, the essential family of things." In so doing, humans would come to a deeper appreciation for all life and be freed from the "pitiful arrogance which detracts from rather than enhances [their] humanness."

139 Cited in Kim, *Dōgen Kigen: Mystical Realist*, p. 150

140 Cited in Kim, *Dōgen Kigen: Mystical Realist*, p. 161.

141 Kim, *Dōgen Kigen: Mystical Realist*, pp. 145–146.

142 Conze, *The Perfection of Wisdom in Eight Thousand Lines*, p. 140.

143 Okumura, Genzō-e sesshin dharma talks, SFZC, 2002.

144 Cook, *Sounds of Valley Streams*, p. 66.

145 Cited in Kim, *Dōgen Kigen: Mystical Realist*, p. 63.

146 Cook, *Sounds of Valley Streams*, pp. 51–52.

147 Klein, *Meeting the Great Bliss Queen*, pp. 70; 136.

148 Klein, *Meeting the Great Bliss Queen*, p. 127.

149 It is beyond the scope of this paper to detail the historical development of Buddhism with regard to sex and gender. I refer the reader to Rita Gross, *Buddhism After Patriarchy*, and Anne Klein, *Meeting the Great Bliss Queen*, for an overview of the Mahāyāna and the interface of Buddhism and feminism. On early Indian Buddhism, see Liz Wilson, *Charming Cadavers: Horrific Figurations of the Feminine in Indian Buddhist Hagiographic Literature* (Chicago: University of Chicago Press, 1996). On the lives of nuns, see Susan Murcott, *The First Buddhist Women: Translations and Commentaries on the Therigatha* (Berkeley: Parallax Press, 1981) (Theravādin); Katherine Tsai, trans., *Lives of the Nuns: Biographies of Chinese Buddhist Nuns from the Fourth to Sixth Centuries* (Honolulu: University of Hawai'i Press, 1994) (Chinese); and Paula Arai, *Women Living Zen: Japanese Sōtō Buddhist Nuns* (New York: Oxford University Press, 1999) (Japanese). There are many contemporary women Buddhist teachers and writers. Of particular interest to the student of Sōtō Zen are the anthologies edited by Marianne Dresser, *Buddhist Women on the Edge: Contemporary Perspectives from the Western Frontier* (Berkeley: North Atlantic Books, 1996); Lenore Freidman and Susan Moon, *Being Bodies: Buddhist Women on the Paradox of Embodiment* (Boston: Shambhala Publications, 1997); and Grace Schireson, *Zen Women: Beyond Tea Ladies, Iron Maidens, and Macho Masters* (Somerville, MA: Wisdom Publications, 2009).

150 Translated in Robert A. Thurman, *The Holy Teachings of Vimilakīrti: A Mahāyāna Scripture* (University Park, PA: Pennsylvania State University Press, 1976).

151 Diana Paul, *Women in Buddhism: Images of the Feminine in Mahayana Tradition* (Berkeley: Lancaster-Miller, 1979), p. 230.

152 Nishijima and Cross, *Master Dogen's Shobogenzo*, "Raihai-tokuzui: Prostrating to Attainment of the Marrow," Book 1, pp. 75–76, 78.

153 Wilson, *Charming Cadavers*, pp. 8, 18.

154 All the quotes in this section are from Nishijima and Cross, *Master Dogen's Shobogenzo*, "Raihai-tokuzui: Prostrating to Attainment of the Marrow," Book 1, pp. 80–82.

155 Paula Arai, in *Women Living Zen,* documents the history of Sōtō Zen nuns in Japan and describes how they used the teachings to successfully gain recognition in the Sōtō Zen religious hierarchy. There is no fundamental difference between the Sōtō Zen ordination for men or women in Japan. The way these ordinations are expressed varies based on cultural differences, but it is important to note that these, too, are dependently arisen circumstances that change.

156 See Gerda Lerner, *The Creation of Feminist Consciousness: From the Middle Ages to Eighteen-seventy* (New York: Oxford University Press, 1993); Carol Gilligan, *In a Different Voice: Psychological Theory and Women's Development* (Cambridge, MA: Harvard University Press, 1982); Judith V. Jordan, Alexandra G. Kaplan, Irene P. Stiver, Janet L. Surrey, and Jean Baker Miller, eds., *Women's Growth in Connection: Writings from the Stone Center* (New York: Gilford Press, 1991); among others.

157 Klein, *Meeting the Great Bliss Queen,* p. 131.

158 Christina Feldman, *The Quest of the Woman Warrior: A Path of Healing, Empowerment, and Transformation* (London: Arkana, 1994), p. 114.

159 Cited in Kim, *Dōgen Kigen: Mystical Realist,* p. 63.

160 Cited in Kim, *Dōgen Kigen: Mystical Realist,* p. 150.

Chapter 3. Including the Psychoanalytic Perspective

1 Klein, *Meeting the Great Bliss Queen,* p. 140.

2 Klein, *Meeting the Great Bliss Queen,* p. 141.

3 Judith Guss Teicholz, *Kohut, Loewald, and the Postmoderns: A Comparative Study of Self and Relationships* (Hillsdale, NJ: The Analytic Press, 1999), p. xviii.

4 Teicholz, *Kohut, Loewald, and the Postmoderns,* p. xviii.

5 Teicholz, *Kohut, Loewald, and the Postmoderns,* p. 5. A detailed response to "postmodern" psychoanalytic ideas and theories about the self, subjectivity, meaning, the question of relative truths, and so on from the point of view of Madhyamaka and Yogācāra Buddhist philosophy would be very interesting but is also beyond the scope or intention of this work. It is interesting to note, however, that many of these questions were taken up by Nāgārjuna more than a thousand years ago. For an in-depth dialogue between Buddhism and postmodernism, see Keiji Nishitani, *Religion and Nothingness* (Berkeley: University of California Press, 1982).

6 Heinz Kohut, *How Does Analysis Cure?* (Chicago: University of Chicago Press, 1984), pp. 202–203.

7 Kohut, *How Does Analysis Cure?*, p. 67.

8 Ernest Wolf, *Treating the Self: Elements of Clinical Self Psychology* (New York: Guilford Press, 1988), pp. 9–10.

9 Wolf, *Treating the Self*, pp. 18–19.

10 Kohut, *How Does Analysis Cure?*, pp. 36; 223.

11 Wolf, *Treating the Self*, pp. 158, 160.

12 Robert D., Stolorow, Bernard Brandchaft, and George E. Atwood, *Psychoanalytic Treatment: An Intersubjective Approach* (Hillsdale: The Analytic Press, 1987), p. 7.

13 Klein, *Meeting the Great Bliss Queen*, p. 138.

14 Klein, *Meeting the Great Bliss Queen*, pp. 136; 138–139.

15 Klein, *Meeting the Great Bliss Queen*, p. 140.

16 Heinz Kohut, *The Restoration of the Self* (New York: International Universities Press, 1977), pp. 310–311.

17 Wolf, *Treating the Self*, p. 13.

18 Wolf, *Treating the Self*, p. 50.

19 Wolf, *Treating the Self*, p. 23.

20 Wolf, *Treating the Self*, pp. 11; 13.

21 Wolf, *Treating the Self*, p. 38.

22 Wolf, *Treating the Self*, p. 11.

23 There are certainly other proponents of a relational self. For a review of other psychoanalytic authors, see Teicholz, *Kohut, Loewald, and the Postmoderns.* Perhaps most notable among these are feminist authors such as Janet L. Surrey, "The 'Self-in-Relation': A Theory of Women's Development," in Judith V. Jordan, Alexandra G. Kaplan, Irene P. Stiver, Janet L. Surrey, and Jean Baker Miller, eds. *Women's Growth in Connection: Writings from the Stone Center* (New York: Gilford Press, 1991), pp. 51–66, and others from the Stone Center; Carol Gilligan, *In a Different Voice;* and the important work of Jean Baker Miller, *Toward a New Psychology of Women* (Boston: Beacon Press, 1976) and "The Development of Women's Sense of Self," in Jordan, et al., eds., *Women's Growth in Connection*, pp. 11–26. Teicholz, in *Kohut, Loewald, and the Postmoderns*, pp. 207–238, gives an excellent discussion and review of feminist theories, their relationship to Heinz Kohut, intersubjective theorists, and postmodern theories and critiques, as well as their overall influence on psychoanalysis. In the interest of brevity, and because I feel the work of Kohut and the intersubjectivists is the most relevant to this project, I have chosen to limit my research to self psychology and intersubjectivity theorists.

24 Wolf, *Treating the Self*, p. 11.

25 Daniel N. Stern, *The Interpersonal World of the Infant* (New York: Basic Books, 1985).

[26] Stern, *The Interpersonal World of the Infant*, p. 124.

[27] Kohut, *The Restoration of the Self*, p. 99.

[28] Stern, *The Interpersonal World of the Infant*, pp. 178–191.

[29] Kohut, *How Does Analysis Cure?*, pp. 61; 49.

[30] Wolf, *Treating the Self*, pp. 184–185.

[31] Teicholz, *Kohut, Loewald, and the Postmoderns*, p. 83.

[32] Wolf, *Treating the Self*, p. 15.

[33] Wolf, *Treating the Self*, p. 54.

[34] Stolorow, Brandchaft, and Atwood, *Psychoanalytic Treatment: An Intersubjective Approach;* Robert Stolorow and George Atwood, *Context of Being: The Intersubjective Foundations of Psychological Life* (Hillsdale: The Analytic Press, 1992). Stolorow and Atwood also place a great emphasis on the affective dimension of this "reciprocal mutual influence." They put forward the idea that selfobject functions are primarily focused on the "integration of affect into the organization of self experience"; Stolorow, Brandchaft, and Atwood, *Psychoanalytic Treatment*, p. 66. As a consequence, responsiveness to affective states throughout life is regarded as key. Though I appreciate their emphasis on an often underrepresented aspect of human experience (the affective dimension), I part ways with them in considering the degree to which they focus on affect. My language and emphasis is on the whole of experience, and while this certainly includes affect I do not attempt to discern the relative weight each aspect of that experience should be assigned.

[35] Though this understanding calls attention to the mutuality of human interaction, it leaves unclear the role of the inanimate or symbolic world. Taken on its face, the intersubjective perspective appears to limit selfobject relationships to those between human beings or at least between sentient beings. As I discuss below, to circumscribe selfobject relationships in this way eliminates from consideration key dimensions of relational life, particularly within the context of Sōtō Zen Buddhism. It also significantly shifts the meaning of selfobject relationships proposed by Kohut in *The Restoration of the Self.*

[36] Stolorow and Atwood, *Context of Being*, pp. 3; 23.

[37] Teicholz, *Kohut, Loewald, and the Postmoderns*, p. 177.

[38] Stolorow and Atwood, *Context of Being*, p. 18.

[39] Wolf, *Treating the Self*, pp. 12; 29.

[40] Wolf, *Treating the Self*, p. 28.

[41] Stolorow and Atwood, *Context of Being*, pp. 7–8.

[42] For an excellent further discussion of the experience of alienation and its relationship to Buddhist teachings, see Stephen Batchelor, *Alone with Others: An Existentialist Approach to Buddhism* (New York: Grove Press, 1983).

[43] Stolorow and Atwood, *Context of Being,* p. 11. From a Yogācāra perspective, we can say that this is the root action of the seventh consciousness, *manas,* that leads to delusion and suffering.

[44] Teicholz, *Kohut, Loewald, and the Postmoderns,* p. 35.

[45] Teicholz, *Kohut, Loewald, and the Postmoderns,* p. 85.

[46] Teicholz, *Kohut, Loewald, and the Postmoderns,* p. 101.

[47] Teicholz, *Kohut, Loewald, and the Postmoderns,* p. 90.

[48] Wolf, *Treating the Self,* p. 184.

[49] Wolf, *Treating the Self,* pp. 56–60.

[50] See Kohut, *The Analysis of the Self: A Systematic Approach to the Psychoanalytic Treatment of Narcissistic Personality Disorders* (New York: International Universities Press, 1971), *The Restoration of the Self,* and *How Does Analysis Cure?;* Teicholz, *Kohut, Loewald, and the Postmoderns.*

[51] Wolf, *Treating the Self,* p. 30.

[52] Teicholz, *Kohut, Loewald, and the Postmoderns,* p. 54.

[53] Stolorow, Brandchaft, and Atwood, *Psychoanalytic Treatment,* p. 133.

[54] Teicholz, *Kohut, Loewald, and the Postmoderns,* pp. 58–59.

[55] Wolf, *Treating the Self,* p. 38.

[56] Wolf, *Treating the Self,* p. 39.

[57] Wolf, *Treating the Self,* p. 13.

[58] Wolf, *Treating the Self,* pp. 39; 30; 41.

[59] Doris Brothers, *Falling Backwards: An Exploration of Trust and Self Experience* (New York: W. W. Norton, 1995), p. 56.

[60] Stolorow and Atwood, *Context of Being,* p. 54.

[61] Brothers, *Falling Backwards,* p. 56.

[62] Brothers, *Falling Backwards,* p. 56.

[63] Wolf, *Treating the Self,* p. 38.

[64] Wolf, *Treating the Self,* p. 39. The classic discussion of trauma and its impact is Judith Lewis Herman's *Trauma and Recovery: The Aftermath of Violence—From Domestic Abuse to Political Terror* (New York: Basic Books, 1992). See also

Jody M. Davies and Mary G. Frawley, *Treating the Adult Survivor of Sexual Abuse: A Psychoanalytic Perspective* (New York: Basic Books, 1994). For a further discussion of trauma from the viewpoint of self psychology, see Brothers, *Falling Backwards*, pp. 55–71.

65 Kohut, *The Restoration of the Self*, p. 104.

66 Kohut, *How Does Analysis Cure?*, p. 18.

67 Kohut, *How Does Analysis Cure?*, pp. 8–9.

68 Stolorow and Atwood, *Context of Being*, pp. 55; 97.

69 Stolorow and Atwood, *Context of Being*, p. 56.

70 Teicholz, *Kohut, Loewald, and the Postmoderns*, p. 55.

71 Teicholz, *Kohut, Loewald, and the Postmoderns*, p. 54.

72 Wolf, *Treating the Self*, p. 39.

73 Kohut, *How Does Analysis Cure?*, p. 47.

74 Kohut, *How Does Analysis Cure?*, p. 78.

75 Teicholz, *Kohut, Loewald, and the Postmoderns*, p. 45.

76 Kohut, *How Does Analysis Cure?*, p. 211.

77 Wolf, *Treating the Self*, p. 102.

78 Kohut, *How Does Analysis Cure?*, p. 44.

79 Wolf, *Treating the Self*, p. 39.

80 Wolf, *Treating the Self*, p. 40.

81 Teicholz, *Kohut, Loewald, and the Postmoderns*, pp. 53–54.

82 Wolf, *Treating the Self*, p. 161.

83 Kohut, *How Does Analysis Cure?*, p. 205.

84 Kohut, *How Does Analysis Cure?*, p. 205.

85 Kohut, *How Does Analysis Cure?*, p. 44.

86 Stolorow, Brandchaft, and Atwood, *Psychoanalytic Treatment*, p. 21.

87 Wolf, *Treating the Self*, p. 30.

88 Klein, *Meeting the Great Bliss Queen*, pp. 70; 66.

89 Klein, *Meeting the Great Bliss Queen*, p. 70.

90 Kohut, *How Does Analysis Cure?*, p. 205.

91 Kohut, *How Does Analysis Cure?*, p. 52.

92 Wolf, *Treating the Self*, p. 55.

93 Wolf, *Treating the Self*, p. 117.

94 Kohut, *How Does Analysis Cure?*, p. 143.

95 Wolf, *Treating the Self*, p. 55.

96 Teicholz, *Kohut, Loewald, and the Postmoderns*, p. 86.

97 Wolf, *Treating the Self*, p. 55.

98 Teicholz, *Kohut, Loewald, and the Postmoderns*, p. 86.

99 Teicholz, *Kohut, Loewald, and the Postmoderns*, p. 86.

100 Wolf, *Treating the Self*, p. 125.

101 Kohut, *How Does Analysis Cure?*, p. 200.

102 Kohut, *How Does Analysis Cure?*, p. 200.

103 Teicholz, *Kohut, Loewald, and the Postmoderns*, p. 208.

104 Phyllis Burke, *Gender Shock: Exploding the Myths of Male & Female* (New York: Doubleday, 1996), p. xiv.

105 Gross, *Buddhism After Patriarchy* and *Feminism & Religion: An Introduction* (Boston: Beacon Press, 1996); Feldman, *Women Awake: A Celebration of Women's Wisdom* (London: Arkana, 1990) and *The Quest of the Woman Warrior;* Klein, *Meeting the Great Bliss Queen.*

106 Again, it important to note that, at the very least, gender can play an important role in the way in which physicality is regarded and experienced. The authors mentioned in note 23 above, along with many others, have included this element in their work. In addition, see Susan Griffin, *Woman and Nature: The Roaring Inside Her* (New York: Harper & Row, 1978); Mary Daly, *Gyn/Ecology: The Metaethics of Radical Feminism* (Boston: Beacon Press, 1978); Gerda Lerner, *The Creation of Patriarchy* (New York: Oxford University Press, 1986); Burke, *Gender Shock;* Rosemarie P. Tong, *Feminist Thought: A More Comprehensive Introduction* (Boulder, CO: Westview Press, 1998). Contemporary women Buddhist authors have also addressed this question, in particular Klein, *Meeting the Great Bliss Queen;* Gross, *Buddhism After Patriarchy;* Friedman and Moon, eds., *Being Bodies;* Dresser, ed., *Buddhist Women on the Edge.*

107 Stolorow and Atwood, *Context of Being*, pp. 7–8.

108 Stern, *The Interpersonal World of the Infant;* D. W. Winnicott, *The Maturational Process and the Facilitating Environment* (New York: International Universities Press, 1965).

109 Stolorow and Atwood, *Context of Being*, p. 46.

[110] Kohut, *The Analysis of the Self,* pp. 152; 271.

[111] Bhikkhu Ñāṇamoli, *The Life of the Buddha: According to the Pāli Canon* (Kandy, Sri Lanka: Buddhist Publication Society, 1972), pp. 10–29.

[112] Cited in Kim, *Dōgen Kigen: Mystical Realist,* p. 97.

[113] Stolorow and Atwood, *Context of Being,* p. 8.

[114] Relating this to Cook's statement quoted in Chapter 2, note 138, we find that a realization of a dynamic relational "authentic" self leads to a "sense of continuity with the rest of nature" that could lead to a reduction in "anthropomorphic identification." This in turn could result in liberation from "a pitiful arrogance which detracts from, rather than enhances . . . humanness"; *Sounds of Valley Streams,* p. 143.

[115] Brothers, *Falling Backwards,* pp. 35–38.

[116] Erik H. Erikson, *Childhood and Society* (New York: W. W. Norton & Co., 1963); "Identity and the Life Cycle," in George S. Klein, ed., *Psychological Issues* (New York: International Universities Press, 1980), pp. 54–78.

[117] Erikson, *Childhood and Society,* p. 248.

[118] Erik H. Erikson, *Identity, Youth and Crisis* (New York: W. W. Norton & Co., 1968), p. 103.

[119] Erikson, *Identity, Youth and Crisis,* p. 128.

[120] Erikson, *Childhood and Society,* p. 250.

[121] D. W. Winnicott, *The Child, the Family and the Outside World* (Cambridge, MA: Perseus Publishing Group, 1987), p. 88.

[122] Howard A. Bacal and Kenneth M. Newman, *Theories of Object Relations: Bridges to Self Psychology* (New York: Colombia University Press, 1990), pp. 186–206.

[123] D. W. Winnicott, *Playing and Reality* (New York: Tavistock/Routledge, 2005), pp. 55–56; 124.

[124] Winnicott, *Playing and Reality,* pp. 13–14.

[125] Cited in Teicholz, *Kohut, Loewald, and the Postmoderns,* p. 51.

[126] Winnicott, *Playing and Reality,* pp. 14.

[127] Cited in Anne Clancier and Jeannine Kalmanovich, *Winnicott and Paradox: From Birth to Creation* (New York: Tavistock, 1987), p. 25.

[128] Winnicott, *Playing and Reality,* pp. 7; 74; 138–139.

[129] For a more in-depth discussion, see Brothers, *Falling Backwards;* Teicholz, *Kohut, Loewald, and the Postmoderns.*

[130] *Kohut, Loewald, and the Postmoderns,* p. 54.

131 Brothers, *Falling Backwards*, p. 21.

132 Judith Lewis Herman, *Trauma and Recovery: The Aftermath of Violence—From Domestic Abuse to Political Terror* (New York: Basic Books, 1992), p. 33.

133 Herman, *Trauma and Recovery*, p. 51.

134 Herman, *Trauma and Recovery*, pp. 51–52.

135 Herman, *Trauma and Recovery*, pp. 51–73; Brothers, *Falling Backwards*, pp. 55–61.

136 Cited in Brothers, *Falling Backwards*, p. 31.

137 Winnicott, *Playing and Reality*, pp. 72–76.

138 Kohut, *The Analysis of the Self, The Restoration of the Self;* "Introspection, Empathy, and the Semicircle of Mental Health"; *How Does Analysis Cure?*.

Chapter 4. Trust and the Transformation of Self-experience

1 Wolf, *Treating the Self*, p. 38.

2 Kohut, *How Does Analysis Cure?*, p. 18.

3 Wolf, *Treating the Self*, pp. 39–43; Brothers, *Falling Backwards*, p. 56.

4 Stolorow, Brandchaft, and Atwood, *Psychoanalytic Treatment*, p. 72.

5 Teicholz, *Kohut, Loewald, and the Postmoderns*, p. 45.

6 Brothers, *Falling Backwards*, pp. 33; 35.

7 Cited in Teicholz, *Kohut, Loewald, and the Postmoderns*, p. 51.

8 Winnicott, *Playing and Reality*, pp. 135; 75; 135.

9 Teicholz, *Kohut, Loewald, and the Postmoderns*, p. 54.

10 Cited in Clancier and Kalmanovich, *Winnicott and Paradox*, p. 25.

11 Wolf, *Treating the Self*, p. 43.

12 Kohut, *How Does Analysis Cure?*, p. 38.

13 Wolf, *Treating the Self*, p. 161.

14 Cook, "Dōgen's View of Authentic Selfhood," p. 131.

15 Klein, *Meeting the Great Bliss Queen*, p. 70.

16 Nhat Hanh, *Transformation at the Base*, p. 117.

17 For a detailed discussion of the transformation of *manas* to equality wisdom, see Wei Tat, *Ch'eng Wei-Shih Lun*, p. 777.

18 Taiken Yokoyama, lectures on the teachings of Eihei Dōgen given at San Francisco Zen Center, 2002.

19 Wolf, *Treating the Self,* pp. 11; 39; 52.

20 Klein, *Meeting the Great Bliss Queen,* pp. 141; 127.

21 The synthesis or integration of Buddhism and psychotherapy is not the focus of this paper. A thorough exploration and critique of the literature currently available on this topic, though very interesting, is therefore not included. These writings, however, are widely read and may contribute both to understanding and misunderstandings of the nature of Sōtō Zen practice. Misunderstandings may occur because some authors do not sufficiently articulate the differences that exist between various traditions and their presentations of the dharma, or because they do not understand them. Regarding the teachings of emptiness, it is also possible that some authors are not sufficiently grounded in the nuances of the teachings and therefore cannot accurately discuss them.

22 Quoted words/phrases are from Mark Epstein, *Thoughts Without a Thinker: Psychotherapy from a Buddhist Perspective* (New York: Basic Books, 1995), pp. 28, 30, 31.

23 Jeffrey Hopkins, *Meditation on Emptiness* (London: Wisdom Publications, 1983).

24 Stolorow and Atwood, *Context of Being,* p. 7.

25 Stolorow and Atwood, *Context of Being,* pp. 10; 22.

26 Stolorow and Atwood, *Context of Being,* p. 11.

27 Jeffrey Hopkins, *Emptiness Yoga: The Middle Way Consequence School* (Ithaca, NY: Snow Lion Publications, 1987), p. 134.

28 Hopkins, *Emptiness Yoga,* p. 251.

29 Hopkins, *Emptiness Yoga,* pp. 259–260.

30 Herman, *Trauma and Recovery,* pp. 51–52.

31 Kim, *Dōgen Kigen: Mystical Realist,* p. 53.

32 Cook, *Sounds of Valley Streams,* p. 28.

33 This explication of the meaning and transformation of the Chinese characters for "faith" was given to me by Shohaku Okumura (Genzō-e sesshin dharma talks, SFZC, 2002) based on his study and practice as well as the teachings of his teacher, Kōshō Uchiyama Rōshi.

34 Cook, *How to Raise An Ox,* pp. 19–33.

35 Translated in Master Sheng-Yen, *Faith in Mind: A Guide to Ch'an Practice* (Elmhurst, NY: Dharma Drum Publications, 1987).

36 Translated in Hakeda, *The Awakening of Faith.*

37 Cited in Edward Conze, *Buddhist Scriptures* (London: Penguin Books, 1959), pp. 151–152.

[38] Kōshō Uchiyama, cited by Shohaku Okumura, Genzō-e sesshin dharma talks, SFZC, 2002.

[39] Cited in Kim, *Dōgen Kigen: Mystical Realist,* p. 150.

[40] Okumura, Genzō-e sesshin dharma talks, SFZC, 2002.

[41] Klein, *Meeting the Great Bliss Queen,* p. 127.

[42] *Merriam Webster's New Collegiate Dictionary* (Springfield: G. C. Merriam Company, 1976).

[43] See Marilyn Senf, "Unlearning Silence: A Further Feminist Revaluation of Buddhist Practice," in Marianne Dresser, ed., *Buddhist Women on the Edge: Contemporary Perspectives from the Western Frontier* (Berkeley: North Atlantic Books, 1996), pp. 69–81; Klein, *Meeting the Great Bliss Queen;* Feldman, *Woman Awake* and *The Quest of the Woman Warrior.*

[44] Caroline Walker Bynum, *Jesus as Mother: Studies in the Spirituality of the High Middle Ages* (Berkeley and Los Angeles: University of California Press, 1982), pp. 170–262; Lerner, *The Creation of Feminist Consciousness,* pp. 46–87.

[45] Tanahashi, *Moon in a Dewdrop,* p. 42.

[46] Tanahashi, *Moon in a Dewdrop,* p. 89.

[47] Uchiyama, *Refining Your Life,* p. 11.

[48] Nishitani, in *Religion and Nothingness,* pp. 178, 179, writes that "In Japanese the 'meaning' of a given *koto* (a term signifying either "matter" or "affair" as well as "word") can also be called its 'mind,' or *kokoro.*" The "mind" of a given circumstance is shared by the participants and is fully present in those circumstances. Meaning, from this perspective, is not created or found in a situation but is, in a sense, the situation itself. Nishitani describes the embeddedness, mutuality, and fluidity of this understanding of meaning and writes that meaning is not something that exists separate from our experience, something that we "grasp." Instead, the relationship is in a sense reversed. Understanding or realization arises when mind and *koto* move in mutuality. Nishitani describes this as a process wherein a *koto* "transfers" to us and we "transfer" into it. Any meaning created from this is, by its very nature, separate from it. He says that this meaning is "merely a mirror image of reality projected onto the dimension of the intellect." The relationship to meaning described by Nishitani is one that is free from false abstractions and is therefore, in a sense, a kind of meaninglessness. To use Hee-Jin Kim's description in *Dōgen Kigen: Mystical Realist,* p. 35, it is "Buddha-nature . . . unfold[ing] through human activities and expressions."

[49] Dainin Katagiri, *Returning to Silence: Zen Practice in Daily Life* (Boston: Shambhala Publications, 1988), p. 145.

[50] Katagiri, *Returning to Silence,* pp. 145–147.

51 Wolf, *Treating the Self,* p. 30.

52 Brothers, *Falling Backwards,* p. 56.

53 Herman, *Trauma and Recovery,* p. 51.

54 Brothers, *Falling Backwards,* p. 35.

Chapter 5. The Practice Environment

1 It is important to note that the environment I describe here is not meant to be one whose aim is a psychotherapeutic outcome. I am not confusing Sōtō Zen practice and psychotherapy. The practice environment is not intended to serve the primary aim of healing the psyche, but neither does it deny that healing may be necessary and can occur in the context of practice. The practice environment should be regarded as a means to meet the needs of a practitioner in order that she may fully engage in the practice. The judicious inclusion by the practitioner of psychotherapy as well as involvement in organizations, groups, activities, or relationships specifically aimed at supporting psychological healing can be helpful, sometimes essential, to the development and deepening of practice. Likewise, the inclusion of relationships and groups that specifically address alcoholism and addiction, for example Alcoholics Anonymous and other twelve-step programs, can also make essential contributions.

2 Cook, *Sounds of Valley Streams,* p. 52.

3 Stolorow and Atwood, *Context of Being,* p. 24.

4 Tanahashi, *Moon in a Dewdrop,* p. 161.

5 Winnicott, *Playing and Reality,* p. 74.

6 Klein, *Meeting the Great Bliss Queen,* p. 136.

7 Hopkins, *Emptiness Yoga,* p. 260.

8 Wolf, *Treating the Self,* pp. 102; 39.

9 Wolf, *Treating the Self,* p. 55.

10 Stolorow and Atwood, *Context of Being,* p. 96.

11 I have chosen to introduce the notion of selfobject relationships and describe them in terms of their supportive and transformative functions not to indicate that these designations have any absolute validity, nor to propose that they actually describe the events that occur. This is particularly true of the transformative dimension. My intention is to provide a means for describing an environment that meets the needs of the practitioner as she endeavors to follow the Sōtō Way.

12 Brothers, *Falling Backwards,* p. 33.

13 Uchiyama, *Refining Your Life,* pp. 7–8.

14 Kohut, *How Does Analysis Cure?*, p. 50; Wolf, *Treating the Self*, p. 53; Stolorow and Atwood, *Context of Being*, p. 2.

15 Wolf, *Treating the Self*, p. 53; 164–165.

16 Cited in Kim, *Dōgen Kigen: Mystical Realist*, p. 122.

17 Uchiyama, *Refining Your Life*, p. 13.

18 Katsuki Sekida, *Zen Training: Methods and Philosophy* (New York: Weatherhill, 1975), pp. 244–245.

19 Kohut, *How Does Analysis Cure?*, p. 52.

20 Francis Cook, trans., *The Record of Transmitting the Light: Zen Master Keizan's Denkoroku* (Los Angeles: Center Publications, 1991), p. 31.

21 This process can be deeply influenced by gender, as well as the student's past history with people in positions of authority. Some students more easily identify a male teacher with the Zen masters in the ancient lineage, and it may often be assumed that a female teacher will be more conventionally compassionate. This can add to potential misunderstandings and veils between student and teacher.

22 Wolf, *Treating the Self*, pp. 63–64.

23 It is important to note that this process occurs not only in the student but also in the teacher. Learning in this way means that the teacher must bring the same clear-eyed appraisal of her own foibles and self-clinging that she does to the student's. In particular, exploitive behavior, the opposite of the compassionate engagement of a mature teacher, violating a student's trust, or betraying the dharma by breaking the precepts are never acceptable. Responsibility, a commitment to utter honesty with oneself and others, and a complete devotion to expressing the dharma as clearly and compassionately as possible are essential to the formation of an effective teacher. Combined with the presence of clear feedback from the community, as well as the presence of a trusted elder teacher, either one's own or another, these factors create an environment in which the teacher can develop and ripen in order to most effectively serve others.

24 It is important to note that by using these concepts I am not attempting to reduce the student-teacher relationship to the terms of self psychology. We could just as easily speak of this relationship in terms of karmic connections formed in past lives, the working through of Oedipal issues, intuitive affinity based on similar or complementary lifestyles, cultural factors, and so on. None of these conceptual schema expresses the profound link that can exist between a teacher and a student who have taken up the practice together. However, shedding light on this relationship from a particular perspective can help to illuminate the factors that support its growth and maturation.

25 Mumon Yamada, *How to Practice Zazen* (Kyoto: Institute for Zen Studies, n.d.), p. 22.

[26] Cited in Kim, *Dōgen Kigen: Mystical Realist,* p. 87.

[27] Wolf, *Treating the Self,* p. 53.

[28] Tanahashi, *Moon in a Dewdrop,* p. 45.

[29] It is also not different from the Yogācāra teaching describing a transformation of the basis of self-experience, in which the seventh consciousness, *manas,* is not obliterated but undergoes a transformation into equality wisdom.

[30] Tanahashi, *Moon in a Dewdrop,* p. 29.

Chapter 6. Conclusion

[1] de Wit, *Contemplative Psychology,* p. 130.

[2] Jamgon Kongtrul, *The Great Path of Awakening: A Commentary on the Mahāyāna Teaching of the Seven Points of Mind Training* (Boston: Shambhala Publications, 1987).

References

Works by Eihei Dōgen

Bendōwa (1231)

"On the Endeavor of the Way: Bendō-wa," in Kazuaki Tanahashi, ed. *Moon in a Dewdrop: Writings of Zen Master Dōgen,* pp. 143–161. San Francisco: North Point Press, 1985.

"Talk on Wholehearted Practice of the Way: A Translation of Eihei Dōgen's Bendōwa," in Shohaku Okumura and Taigen Daniel Leighton, ed. and trans., *The Wholehearted Way: A Translation of Eihei Dōgen's Bendōwa with Commentary by Kōshō Uchiyama Roshi,* pp. 19–41. Boston: Tuttle, 1997.

Bodaisatta shishōbō (1243)

"Bodaisatta-shishobo: Four Elements of a Bodhisattva's Social Relations," in Gudo Nishijima and Chodo Cross, trans., *Master Dogen's Shobogenzo,* Book 3, pp. 29–34. Woods Hole, MA: Windbell Publications, 1997.

"Bodhisattva's Four Methods of Guidance: Bodaisatta Shishō-hō," in Kazuaki Tanahashi, ed., *Moon in a Dewdrop: Writings of Zen Master Dōgen,* pp. 44–48. San Francisco: North Point Press, 1985.

Bukkyō (1243)

"Bukkyo: The Buddhist Sutras," in Gudo Nishijima and Chodo Cross, trans., *Master Dogen's Shobogenzo,* Book 3, pp. 101–112. Woods Hole, MA: Windbell Publications, 1997.

Busshō (1241)

"Bussho: The Buddha-nature," in Gudo Nishijima and Chodo Cross, trans., *Master Dogen's Shobogenzo,* Book 2, pp. 1–32. Woods Hole, MA: Windbell Publications, 1996.

Busso (1241)

"Buddha Ancestors: Busso," in Kazuaki Tanahashi, ed., *Moon in a Dewdrop: Writings of Zen Master Dōgen,* pp. 184–185. San Francisco: North Point Books, 1985.

Eihei shingi (1237, 1244, 1246)

Taigen Daniel Leighton and Shohaku Okumura, trans., *Dōgen's Pure Standards for the Zen Community: A Translation of the 'Eihei Shingi,'* pp. 33–204. Albany, NY: State University of New York Press, 1996.

Fukanzazengi (1227)

"Fukanzazengi: 'General Recommendations for Doing Zazen,'" in Francis H. Cook, ed. and trans., *How to Raise An Ox: Zen Practice as Taught in Zen Master Dōgen's Shōbōgenzō,* pp. 95–100. Los Angeles: Zen Center of Los Angeles, 1978.

"Fukanzazengi: "The Way of Zen Recommended to Everyone," in Shohaku

Okumura, trans., *Shikantaza: An Introduction to Zazen*, pp. 39–44. Kyoto, Japan: Kyoto Sōtō-Zen Center, 1985.

Gabyō (1242)

"Gabyō: A Painting of a Rice Cake," in Francis H. Cook, ed. and trans., *Sounds of Valley Streams: Enlightenment in Dōgen's Zen*, pp. 77–82. Albany, NY: State University of New York Press, 1989.

"Painting of a Rice-cake: Gabyō," in Kazuaki Tanahashi, ed., *Moon in a Dewdrop: Writings of Zen Master Dōgen*, pp. 134–142. San Francisco: North Point Press, 1985.

Gakudō yōjinshū (thirteenth century)

Gakudō-Yōjinshū: "Points to Watch in Practicing the Way," in Shohaku Okumura, trans., *Dōgen's Zen*, pp. 1–42. Kyoto, Japan: Kyoto Sōtō-Zen Center, 1988.

"Guidelines for Studying the Way: Gakudō Yōjin-shū," in Kazuaki Tanahashi, ed., *Moon in a Dewdrop: Writings of Zen Master Dōgen*, pp. 31–43. San Francisco: North Point Press, 1985.

Genjō kōan (1233, 1252)

"Actualizing the Fundamental Point: Genjō Kōan," in Kazuaki Tanahashi, ed., *Moon in a Dewdrop: Writings of Zen Master Dōgen*, pp. 69–73. San Francisco: North Point Press, 1985.

"Genjō Kōan: Manifesting Absolute Reality," in Francis H. Cook, ed. and trans., *Sounds of Valley Streams: Enlightenment in Dōgen's Zen*, pp. 65–71. Albany, NY: State University of New York Press, 1989.

Jintsū (1241)

"Jintsū—Miraculous powers," in Kōsen Nishiyama and John Stevens, trans., *Shōbōgenzō: The Eye and Treasury of the True Law*, vol. 3, pp. 60–67. Tokyo: Nakayama Shobo, 1983.

"Jinzu: Mystical Power," in Gudo Nishijima and Chodo Cross, trans., *Master Dogen's Shobogenzo*, Book 2, pp. 59–68. Woods Hole, MA: Windbell Publications, 1996.

Nyorai zenshin (1244)

"Nyorai-zenshin: The Whole Body of the Tathagata," in Gudo Nishijima and Chodo Cross, trans., *Master Dogen's Shobogenzo*, Book 3, pp. 277–280. Woods Hole, MA: Windbell Publications, 1997.

Raihai tokuzui (1240)

"Raihai tokuzui: Paying Homage and Acquiring the Essence," in Francis H. Cook, ed. and trans., *How to Raise An Ox: Zen Practice as Taught in Zen Master Dōgen's Shōbōgenzō*, pp. 133–150. Los Angeles: Center Publications, 1978.

"Raihai-tokuzui: Prostrating to Attainment of the Marrow," in Gudo Nishijima and Chodo Cross, trans., *Master Dogen's Shobogenzo*, Book 1, pp. 69–84. Woods Hole, MA: Windbell Publications, 1994.

Sansuigyō (1240)

"Mountains and Waters Sūtra: Sansui-kyō," in Kazuaki Tanahashi, ed., *Moon in a Dewdrop: Writings of Zen Master Dōgen*, pp. 97–107. San Francisco: North Point Press, 1985

"Sansuigyō: The Sutra of Mountains and Water," in Gudo Nishijima and Chodo Cross, trans., *Master Dogen's Shobogenzo,* Book 1, pp. 167–180. Woods Hole, MA: Windbell Publications, 1994.

Shinjin gakudō (1242)

"Body-and-Mind Study of the Way: Shinjin-gakudō," in Kazuaki Tanahashi, ed., *Moon in a Dewdrop: Writings of Zen Master Dōgen,* pp. 87–96. San Francisco: North Point Press, 1985.

Shōbōgenzō zuimonki (thirteenth century)

Shobogenzō Zuimonki: "The Recorded Sayings of Dogen Zenji," in Shohaku Okumura, trans., *Shikantaza: An Introduction to Zazen,* pp. 69–77. Kyoto, Japan: Kyoto Sōtō-Zen Center, 1985.

Shukke kudoku (thirteenth century)

"Shukke-kudoku: The Merit of Leaving Family Life," in Gudo Nishijima and Chodo Cross, trans., *Master Dogen's Shobogenzo,* Book 4, pp. 133–154. Woods Hole, MA: Windbell Publications, 1999.

Tenzo kyōkun (1237)

"Instruction for the Tenzo: Tenzo Kyōkun," in Kazuaki Tanahashi, ed., *Moon in a Dewdrop: Writings of Zen Master Dōgen,* pp. 53–68. San Francisco: North Point Press, 1985.

"Instructions for the Zen Cook: Tenzo Kyōkun," in Eihei Dogen and Kosho Uchiyama, *Refining Your Life: From the Zen Kitchen to Enlightenment,* pp. 3–22. New York: Weatherhill, 1983.

Tenzokyokun: "Instructions for the Tenzo," in Taigen Daniel Leighton and Shohaku Okumura, trans., *Dōgen's Pure Standards for the Zen Community: A Translation of the 'Eihei Shingi,'* pp. 33–62. Albany, NY: State University of New York Press, 1996.

Tenzokyokun: "Instructions for the Cook," Griffith Foulk, trans., in Jisho Warner, Shohaku Okumura, John McRae, and Taigen Daniel Leighton, eds., *Nothing is Hidden: Essays on Zen Master Dōgen's Instructions for the Cook,* pp. 21–41. New York: Weatherhill, 2001.

Tsuki (1243)

"The Moon: Tsuki," in Kazuaki Tanahashi, ed., *Moon in a Dewdrop: Writings of Zen Master Dōgen,* pp. 129–133. San Francisco: North Point Press, 1985.

Uji (1240)

"The Time-Being: Uji," in Kazuaki Tanahashi, ed., *Moon in a Dewdrop: Writings of Zen Master Dōgen,* pp. 76–83. San Francisco: North Point Press, 1985.

"Uji: Existence-time," in Gudo Nishijima and Chodo Cross, trans., *Master Dogen's Shobogenzo,* Book 1, pp. 109–118. Woods Hole, MA: Windbell Publications, 1994.

Yuibutsu yobutsu (thirteenth century)

"Only Buddha and Buddha: Yuibutsu Yobutsu," in Kazuaki Tanahashi, ed., *Moon in a Dewdrop: Writings of Zen Master Dōgen,* pp. 161–167. San Francisco: North Point Press, 1985.

Zazengi (1243)

"Rules for Zazen: Zazen-gi," in Kazuaki Tanahashi, ed., *Moon in a Dewdrop: Writings of Zen Master Dōgen,* pp. 29–30. San Francisco: North Point Press, 1985.

Zenki (1242)

"Undivided Activity: Zenki," in Kazuaki Tanahashi, ed., *Moon in a Dewdrop: Writings of Zen Master Dōgen,* pp. 84–86. San Francisco: North Point Press, 1985.

"Zenki: All Functions," in Gudo Nishijima and Chodo Cross, trans., *Master Dogen's Shobogenzo,* Book 2, pp. 243–245. Woods Hole, MA: Windbell Publications, 1996.

General References

Abe, Masao. *A Study of Dōgen: His Philosophy and Religion.* Albany, NY: State University of New York Press, 1992.

—."The Oneness of Practice and Attainment: Implications for the Relation between Means and Ends," in William LaFleur, ed., *Dogen Studies,* pp. 99–112. Honolulu: University of Hawai'i Press, 1985.

Arai, Paula. *Women Living Zen: Japanese Sōtō Buddhist Nuns.* New York: Oxford University Press, 1999.

Bacal, Howard A., and Kenneth M. Newman. *Theories of Object Relations: Bridges to Self Psychology.* New York: Colombia University Press, 1990.

Batchelor, Stephen, trans. *A Guide to the Bodhisattva's Way of Life.* Dharamsala, India: Library of Tibetan Works and Archives, 1979. Translation of Śāntideva's *Bodhisattvacaryāvatāra* (seventh century).

—.*Alone with Others: An Existentialist Approach to Buddhism.* New York: Grove Press, 1983.

—.*The Faith to Doubt: Glimpses of Buddhist Uncertainty.* Berkeley: Parallax Press, 1990.

Bodhi, Bhikkhu. *The Connected Discourses of the Buddha: A New Translation of the Saṃyutta Nikāya,* 2 vols. Boston: Wisdom Publications, 2000.

Brothers, Doris. *Falling Backwards: An Exploration of Trust and Self Experience.* New York: W. W. Norton, 1995.

Burke, Phyllis. *Gender Shock: Exploding the Myths of Male & Female.* New York: Doubleday, 1996.

Chang, Garma C. C. *The Buddhist Teaching of Totality: The Philosophy of Hwa Yen Buddhism.* University Park, PA: Pennsylvania State University Press, 1971.

Clancier, Anne, and Jeannine Kalmanovich. *Winnicott and Paradox: From Birth to Creation.* Alan Sheridan, trans. New York: Tavistock, 1987.

Coates, Susan W., and Sabrina M. Wolfe. "Gender Identity in Boys: The Interface of Constitution and Early Experience," *Psychoanalytic Inquiry* 15 (1995): 6–38.

Collins, Steven. *Selfless Persons: Imagery and Thought in Theravāda Buddhism.* Cambridge: Cambridge University Press, 1982.

Conze, Edward. *Buddhist Scriptures.* London: Penguin Books, 1959.

—.*Buddhist Wisdom Books.* London: George Allen & Unwin, 1958.

—,trans. *Perfect Wisdom: The Short Prajnaparamita Texts.* Totnes, UK: Buddhist Publishing Group, 1973.

—, trans. *The Perfection of Wisdom in Eight Thousand Lines and its Verse Summary.* San Francisco: Four Seasons Foundation, 1973.

Cook, Francis. "Dōgen's View of Authentic Selfhood and its Socio-ethical Implications," in William R. LaFleur, ed., *Dōgen Studies,* pp. 131–149. Honolulu: University of Hawai'i Press, 1985.

—, ed. and trans. *How to Raise An Ox: Zen Practice as Taught in Zen Master Dogen's Shobogenzo.* Los Angeles: Center Publications, 1978.

—, ed. and trans. *Sounds of Valley Streams: Enlightenment in Dōgen's Zen.* Albany, NY: State University of New York Press, 1989.

—, trans. *The Record of Transmitting the Light: Zen Master Keizan's Denkoroku.* Los Angeles: Center Publications, 1991.

Daly, Mary. *Gyn/Ecology: The Metaethics of Radical Feminism.* Boston: Beacon Press, 1978.

Davies, Jody M., and Mary G. Frawley. *Treating the Adult Survivor of Sexual Abuse: A Psychoanalytic Perspective.* New York: Basic Books, 1994.

de Wit, Han F. *Contemplative Psychology.* Marie L. Baird, trans. Pittsburgh, PA: Duquesne University Press, 1991.

Dresser, Marianne, ed. *Buddhist Women on the Edge: Contemporary Perspectives from the Western Frontier.* Berkeley: North Atlantic Books, 1996.

Epstein, Mark. *Thoughts Without a Thinker: Psychotherapy from a Buddhist Perspective.* New York: Basic Books, 1995.

Erikson, Erik H. *Childhood and Society.* New York: W. W. Norton & Co., 1963.

—. "Identity and the Life Cycle," in George S. Klein, ed., *Psychological Issues,* pp. 54–78. New York: International Universities Press, 1980.

—. *Identity, Youth and Crisis.* New York: W. W. Norton & Co., 1968.

Feldman, Christina. *The Quest of the Woman Warrior: A Path of Healing, Empowerment, and Transformation.* London: Arkana, 1994.

—. *Woman Awake: A Celebration of Women's Wisdom.* London: Arkana, 1990.

Flax, Jane. *Thinking Fragments: Psychoanalysis, Feminism, and Postmodernism in the Contemporary West.* Berkeley: University of California Press, 1990.

Friedman, Leonore, and Susan Moon, eds. *Being Bodies: Buddhist Women on the Paradox of Embodiment.* Boston: Shambhala Publications, 1997.

Fronsdal, Gil (Egil). *Dawn of the Bodhisattva Path: The Early Perfection of Wisdom.* Berkeley: Institute of Buddhist Studies and BDK America, Inc., 2014.

—. "The Dawn of the Bodhisattva Path: Studies in a Religious Ideal of Ancient Indian Buddhists with Particular Emphasis on the Earliest Extant Perfection of Wisdom Sutra." Ph.D. dissertation, Stanford University, 1998. Dissertation Abstracts International 59 (8), 3038. Accession no. AAT9901501.

Garfield, Jay L., ed. and trans. *The Fundamental Wisdom of the Middle Way: Nāgārjuna's Mūlamadyamikakārikā.* New York: Oxford University Press, 1995.

Gilligan, Carol. *In a Different Voice: Psychological Theory and Women's Development.* Cambridge, MA: Harvard University Press, 1982.

Gilligan, Carol, Nona P. Lyons, and Trudy J. Hanmer, eds. *Making Connections: The Relational World of Adolescent Girls at Emma Willard School.* Cambridge, MA: Harvard University Press, 1990.

Griffin, Susan. *Woman and Nature: The Roaring Inside Her.* New York: Harper & Row, 1978.

Gross, Rita M. *Buddhism After Patriarchy: A Feminist History, Analysis and Reconstruction of Buddhism.* Albany, NY: State University of New York Press, 1993.

—. *Feminism & Religion: An Introduction.* Boston: Beacon Press, 1996.

Hakeda, Yoshito S., trans. *The Awakening of Faith: Attributed to Aśvaghosha.* New York: Columbia University Press, 1967.

Hamilton, Sue. *Early Buddhism: A New Approach. The I of the Beholder.* Richmond, Surrey, UK: Curzon, 2000.

Harvey, Peter. *An Introduction to Buddhism: Teachings, History and Practices.* New York: Cambridge University Press, 1990.

Herman, Judith L. *Trauma and Recovery: The Aftermath of Violence—From Domestic Abuse to Political Terror.* New York: Basic Books, 1992.

Hirakawa, Akira. *A History of Indian Buddhism from Śākyamuni to Early Mahāyāna.* Honolulu: University of Hawai'i Press, 1990.

Hopkins, Jeffrey. *Emptiness Yoga: The Middle Way Consequence School.* Ithaca, NY: Snow Lion Publications, 1987.

—. *Meditation on Emptiness.* London: Wisdom Publications, 1983.

Jordan, Judith V., Alexandra G. Kaplan, Irene P. Stiver, Janet L. Surrey, and Jean Baker Miller, eds. *Women's Growth in Connection: Writings from the Stone Center.* New York: Gilford Press, 1991.

Kalupahana, David. *Buddhist Philosophy: A Historical Analysis.* Honolulu: University of Hawai'i Press, 1976.

—. *Ethics in Early Buddhism.* Honolulu: University of Hawai'i Press, 1995.

—, trans. *Nāgārjuna: The Philosophy of the Middle Way.* Albany, NY: State University of New York Press, 1986.

—. *The Principles of Buddhist Psychology.* Albany, NY: State University of New York Press, 1987.

Katagiri, Dainin. *Returning to Silence: Zen Practice in Daily Life.* Boston: Shambhala Publications, 1988.

—. *You Have to Say Something: Manifesting Zen Insight.* Boston: Shambhala Publications, 1998.

Katō, Bunno, and Yoshiro Tamura, trans. *The Threefold Lotus Sutra.* Tokyo: Kosei Publishing Company, 1975.

Kim, Hee-Jin. *Dōgen Kigen: Mystical Realist.* Tucson: University of Arizona Press, 1987.

—, trans. *Flowers of Emptiness: Selections from Dōgen's Shōbōgenzō.* Lewiston: Edwin Mellen Press, 1985.

—. "'The Reason of Words and Letters': Dōgen and Kōan Language," in William R. LaFleur, ed., *Dōgen Studies,* pp. 54–82. Honolulu: University of Hawai'i Press, 1985.

King, Sallie B. *Buddha Nature.* Albany, NY: State University of New York Press, 1991.

Klein, Anne C. *Meeting the Great Bliss Queen: Buddhists, Feminists, and the Art of the Self.* Boston: Beacon Press, 1995.

Kodera, Takashi. *Dogen's Formative Years in China: An Historical Study and Annotated Translation of the 'Hōkyō-ki.'* Boulder, CO: Prajna Press, 1980.

Kohut, Heinz. *How Does Analysis Cure?* Arnold Goldberg and Paul E. Stepansky, eds. Chicago: University of Chicago Press, 1984.

—. "Introspection, Empathy, and the Semicircle of Mental Health," in Paul H. Ornstein, ed., *The Search for the Self: Selected Writings of Heinz Kohut: 1978–1981,* vol. 4, pp. 537–568. New York: International Universities Press, 1981.

—. *The Analysis of the Self: A Systematic Approach to the Psychoanalytic Treatment of Narcissistic Personality Disorders.* New York: International Universities Press, 1971.

—. *The Restoration of the Self.* New York: International Universities Press, 1977.

Kongtrul, Jamgon. *The Great Path of Awakening: A Commentary on the Mahayana Teaching of the Seven Points of Mind Training.* Ken McLeod, trans. Boston: Shambhala Publications, 1987. Original teaching attributed to Atiśa (eleventh century); original text and commentary published in the nineteenth century.

Leighton, Taigen Daniel, and Shohaku Okumura, ed. and trans. *Dōgen's Pure Standards for the Zen Community: A Translation of Eihei Shingi.* Albany, NY: State University of New York Press, 1996.

Lerner, Gerda. *The Creation of Feminist Consciousness: From the Middle Ages to Eighteen-seventy.* New York: Oxford University Press, 1993.

—. *The Creation of Patriarchy.* New York: Oxford University Press, 1986.

Lopez, Donald S., ed. *Buddhist Hermeneutics.* Honolulu: University of Hawai'i Press, 1988.

McQueen, Graeme. "Inspired Speech in Early Mahāyāna Buddhism I," *Religion* 11 (1981): 303–319.

—. "Inspired Speech in Early Mahāyāna Buddhism II," *Religion* 12 (1982): 49–65.

Merriam Webster's New Collegiate Dictionary. Springfield: G. C. Merriam Company, 1976.

Miller, Jean Baker. "The Development of Women's Sense of Self," in Judith V. Jordan, Alexandra G. Kaplan, Jean Baker Miller, Irene P. Stiver, and Janet L Surrey, eds., *Women's Growth in Connection: Writings from the Stone Center,* pp. 11–26. New York: Gilford Press, 1991.

—. *Toward a New Psychology of Women.* Boston: Beacon Press, 1976.

Murcott, Susan. *The First Buddhist Women: Translations and Commentaries on the Therigatha.* Berkeley: Parallax Press, 1981.

Ñāṇamoli, Bhikkhu. *The Life of the Buddha: According to the Pāli Canon.* Kandy, Sri Lanka: Buddhist Publication Society, 1972.

—, trans. *The Path of Purification, Visuddhi Magga: The Classic Manual of Buddhist Doctrine and Meditation.* Kandy, Sri Lanka: Buddhist Publication Society, 1979.

Ñāṇamoli, Bhikkhu, and Bhikkhu Bodhi, trans. *The Middle Length Discourses of the Buddha: A Translation of the Majjhima Nikāya.* Boston: Wisdom, Publications, 1995.

Nattier, Jan. "Visible and Invisible: On the Politics of Representation in Buddhist America," *Tricycle: The Buddhist Review* (Fall 1995): 42–49.

Nhat Hanh, Thich. *Transformation at the Base: Fifty Verses on the Nature of Consciousness.* Berkeley: Parallax Press, 2001.

Nishijima, Gudo, and Chodo Cross, trans. *Master Dogen's Shobogenzo,* 4 vols. Woods Hole, MA: Windbell Publications, 1994–1999.

Nishitani, Keiji. *Religion and Nothingness.* Jan van Bragt, trans. and introduction. Berkeley: University of California Press, 1982.

Nishiyama, Kōsen, and John Stevens, trans. *Shōbōgenzō: The Eye and Treasury of the True Law,* 4 vols. Tokyo: Nakayama Shobo, 1975–1983.

Okumura, Shohaku, trans. *Dōgen Zen.* Kyoto: Kyoto Sōtō-Zen Center, 1988.

—. Genzō-e sesshin Dharma talks. Unpublished lectures on Dōgen's teachings, the *Sansuigyō* (*Mountain and Rivers Sūtra*), San Francisco Zen Center, May 2002.

—. *Realizing Genjo Koan: The Key to Dogen's Shobogenzo.* Boston: Wisdom Publications, 2010.

—. *Shikantaza: An Introduction to Zazen.* Kyoto: Kyoto Sōtō-Zen Center, 1985.

Okumura, Shohaku, and Taigen Daniel Leighton, ed. and trans. *The Wholehearted Way: A Translation of Eihei Dōgen's Bendōwa with Commentary by Kōshō Uchiyama Roshi.* Boston: Tuttle Publishing, 1997.

Paul, Diana. *Women in Buddhism: Images of the Feminine in Mahayana Tradition.* Berkeley: Lancaster-Miller, 1979.

Rahula, Walpola. *What the Buddha Taught.* New York: Grove Press, 1959.

Reinharz, Shulamit. *Feminist Methods of Social Research.* New York: Oxford University Press, 1992.

Saddhatissa, Hammalawa. *Buddhist Ethics.* Boston: Wisdom Publications, 1970.

Schireson, Grace. *Zen Women: Beyond Tea Ladies, Iron Maidens, and Macho Masters.* Somerville, MA: Wisdom Publications, 2009.

Sekida, Katsuki. *Zen Training: Methods and Philosophy.* New York: Weatherhill, 1975.

Sells, Michael A. *The Mystical Languages of Unsaying.* Chicago: University of Chicago Press, 1994.

Senf, Marilyn. "Unlearning Silence: A Further Feminist Revaluation of Buddhist Practice," in Marianne Dresser, ed., *Buddhist Women on the Edge: Contemporary Perspectives from the Western Frontier,* pp. 69–81. Berkeley: North Atlantic Books, 1996.

Sharf, Robert H. "Buddhist Modernism and the Rhetoric of Meditative Experience," *Numen* 42/3 (1995): 228–283.

Sheng-Yen, Master. *Faith in Mind: A Guide to Ch'an Practice.* Elmhurst, NY: Dharma Drum Publications, 1987.

Stambaugh, Joan. *Impermanence is Buddha Nature: Dōgen's Understanding of Temporality.* Honolulu: University of Hawai'i Press, 1990.

—. *The Formless Self.* Albany, NY: State University of New York Press, 1999.

Stern, Daniel N. *The Interpersonal World of the Infant: A View from Psychoanalysis and Developmental Psychology.* New York: Basic Books, 1985.

Stolorow, Robert D., and George E. Atwood. *Context of Being: The Intersubjective Foundations of Psychological Life.* Hillsdale: The Analytic Press, 1992.

Stolorow, Robert D., Bernard Brandchaft, and George E. Atwood. *Psychoanalytic Treatment: An Intersubjective Approach.* Hillsdale: The Analytic Press, 1987.

Stone, Jacqueline I. *Original Enlightenment and the Transformation of Medieval Japanese Buddhism.* Honolulu: University of Hawai'i Press, 1999.

Surrey, Janet L. "The 'Self-in-Relation': A Theory of Women's Development," in Judith V. Jordan, Alexandra G. Kaplan, Irene P. Stiver, Janet L. Surrey, and Jean Baker Miller, eds., *Women's Growth in Connection: Writings from the Stone Center,* pp. 51–66. New York: Gilford Press, 1991.

Suzuki, Shunryu. *Zen Mind, Beginner's Mind.* Trudy Dixon, ed. New York: Weatherhill, 1970.

Tanahashi, Kazuaki, ed. *Moon in a Dewdrop: Writings of Zen Master Dōgen.* San Francisco: North Point Press, 1985.

Teicholz, Judith G. *Kohut, Loewald, and the Postmoderns: A Comparative Study of Self and Relationships.* Hillsdale, NJ: The Analytic Press, 1999.

Thurman, Robert A., trans. *The Holy Teachings of Vimalakīrti: A Mahāyāna Scripture.* University Park, PA: Pennsylvania State University Press, 1976.

Tong, Rosemarie P. *Feminist Thought: A More Comprehensive Introduction.* Boulder, CO: Westview Press, 1998.

Tsai, Kathryn A., trans. *Lives of the Nuns: Biographies of Chinese Buddhist Nuns from the Fourth to Sixth Centuries.* Honolulu: University of Hawai'i Press, 1994.

Uchiyama, Kōshō. "How to Cook Your Life: Jinsei Ryōri no Hon," in Eihei Dōgen and Kōshō Uchiyama, *Refining Your Life: From the Zen Kitchen to Enlightenment,* pp. 23–98. New York: Weatherhill, 1983.

—,trans. *Refining Your Life: From the Zen Kitchen to Enlightenment.* New York: Weatherhill, 1983.

Walker, Carolyn Bynum. *Jesus as Mother: Studies in the Spirituality of the High Middle Ages.* Berkeley and Los Angeles: University of California Press, 1982.

Warner, Jisho, Shohaku Okumura, John McRae, and Taigen Daniel Leighton, eds. *Nothing is Hidden: Essays on Zen Master Dōgen's Instructions for the Cook.* New York: Weatherhill, 2001.

Wei Tat, trans. *Ch'eng Wei-Shih Lun: Doctrine of Mere-Consciousness by Tripitaka-Master Hsüan Tsang.* Hong Kong: The Ch'eng Wei-Shih Lun Publication Committee, 1973. Original work published in the seventh century.

Wijayaratna, Mohan. *Buddhist Monastic Life: According to the Texts of the Theravāda Tradition.* Claude Grangier and Steven Collins, trans. New York: Cambridge University Press, 1990.

Williams, Paul. *Mahāyāna Buddhism: The Doctrinal Foundations.* New York: Routledge, 1989.

Wilson, Liz. *Charming Cadavers: Horrific Figurations of the Feminine in Indian Buddhist Hagiographic Literature.* Chicago: University of Chicago Press, 1996.

Winnicott, Donald W. *Collected Papers: Through Paediatrics to Psycho-analysis.* New York: Basic Books, 1975.

—. *Playing and Reality.* New York: Tavistock/Routledge, 2005.

—. *The Child, the Family and the Outside World.* Cambridge: Perseus Publishing Group, 1987.

—. *The Maturational Process and the Facilitating Environment.* New York: International Universities Press, 1965.

Wolf, Ernest S. *Treating the Self: Elements of Clinical Self Psychology.* New York: Guilford Press, 1988.

Wu, John C. H. *The Golden Age of Zen.* Taipei: United Publishing Center, 1975.

Yamada, Mumon. *How to Practice Zazen.* Kyoto: Institute for Zen Studies, n.d.

Yokoyama, Taiken. Unpublished lectures on the teachings of Eihei Dōgen, San Francisco Zen Center, April 2002.

Index

C

T